Cultivating

"Reading this new edition of *Cultivating the Strategic Mind* resurfaces so many wonderful memories of Blake's earning trust and respect from corporate leaders, managers, and employees by bringing them effective solutions to irksome problems. His creative ideas, fresh approaches, and bountiful lessons spring from a deep source of practical experiences. As one of his former colleagues, I know that Blake's framework has been battle-tested — because I witnessed it firsthand from within the same foxhole for a decade. Positive results and personal integrity are his hallmark."

Lou Romero (retired)
Internal Facilitator & Change Consultant
and one of only three USDA Forest Service
Organizational Leadership Award recipients since 1905

"For many Human Resources professionals, hearing the word 'strategic' (yet again) provokes a negative reflexive response. We hear it all day every day, in countless talent reviews, and most often associated with descriptions of high-potential employees skyrocketing to the top. And we know all too well that to earn a seat at the table, Human Resources must be a 'strategic' internal partner. But how many of us *truly* understand what it means — in the very fibers of our being — or can objectively evaluate it, much less develop it purposefully, methodically, systematically, at scale, and across cultures around the globe? Very few, I would submit. By weaving the complex with the simple, the extraordinary with the prosaic, the theoretical with the practical, and the expansive with the granular, Blake illuminates what is often there yet rarely seen and, from where I sit, that is nothing less than magical."

Greg Holden
Director, Human Resources, Raytheon

"Blake is a masterful teacher and behaviorist, and *Cultivating the Strategic Mind* is a wonderful playbook that wins every time. The U.S. national defense acquisition process is among the most complicated bureaucracies in the world, and Blake's methodology helped our teams become greater than the sum of their parts. His work improved our culture, delivered results, and led to greater employee fulfillment, and his writing is proof positive that strategy can be both engaging and fun."

Colonel Darren L. Cochran (retired)
U.S. Air Force

"Dr. Leath has captured with courage and brilliance the essence of LEADERSHIP. This book is table stakes for everyone in a position of influence."

Joe Brouillette
Chairman, Delta Energy & Communications

"*Cultivating the Strategic Mind* is essential for any serious leader's toolkit. Dr. Leath crystallizes his key messages through a compelling, engaging, and relatable author's pen and storyboard. His authentic, unique perspective is a gift and treasure as the pages unfold. Importantly, Blake's lessons and insights have become an integral part of my repertoire for leadership…and life."

Susan Engebrecht Thoma
Performance Consultant & Executive Coach

"*Cultivating the Strategic Mind* is a brilliant melding of theoretical concepts and practical applications. Dr. Leath is dynamite; he is a wealth of information. His passion for the topic makes it easy for me to engage."

Jim Maggio
Technical Team Lead, Exadel

"Business today is about gathering data, discerning patterns, and applying those patterns to the larger questions of strategy. We call it *reasoned intelligence* and it seldom works. Blake, however, reaches beyond the pattern. He puts the algorithm in context, drawing on his rich experience and witty, insightful mind. The result is a masterpiece of, 'Hmm, that makes a lot of sense!'"

Gary Moreau
Author of *Understanding Business: The Logic of Balance*
(a Kirkus Reviews "Best Indie Book of 2017" selection)

"Blake Leath is terrifically successful at delivering insightful messages through compelling stories, vivid analogies, and pithy historical perspectives. His engaging personal spirit carries through in his writing, which grips the reader from the outset. Wherever and whatever you are in your life, *Cultivating the Strategic Mind* provides tremendously useful life lessons."

Timothy T. Paige
Vice President, Human Resources, Bryant University

"Everything Blake produces has tremendous utility in the real world, and *Cultivating the Strategic Mind* exemplifies the fact. His knowledge and wisdom have proven instrumental in my career for 20 years."

Samuel Street
Human Resources Business Partner, Newmont Mining Corporation

"Understanding and effectively acting on strategic issues in today's turbulent world is increasingly difficult. Through stories and metaphors that make critical concepts easy, entertaining, and insightful, *Cultivating the Strategic Mind* has reshaped my thinking and, for that, I say, 'Thank you.'"

Dr. Knute Sorenson
Adjunct Professor, Wayland Baptist University and Embry-Riddle Aeronautical University

"Countless organizations cannot go where they want or need to because their executives' and leaders' thinking is too shallow. Strategic thinking is hard work; it requires a level of mindfulness to do the type of thinking that today's complex businesses and organizations require. In the midst of our hyper-speed culture, Dr. Leath unveils a simple, clear, pragmatic approach for developing the *Strategic Mind* that will change how you think about and run your business or organization — forever."

Jim Horan
President, The One Page Business Plan Company

"*Cultivating the Strategic Mind* was a dazzling head trip. I had a blast! Leath breezes along and lifts you higher until you forget we're talking about *strategy* here. I lost myself in his stories, arriving 30 pages further and filled to the gills with tools I can use tomorrow."

Robin Blakeley
Marketing & Business Development, HKS Sports & Entertainment

"Blake Leath proves once again that he is among the brightest people around. He is unafraid to take strong stands, oftentimes shaking you by your shirt collar. The *Ideas and Tools* chapter is especially useful, chock-full of resources you can share with family and friends, and altogether invaluable to your own strategic development. Blake's unbelievably broad source materials leave you amazed at how much things change, and uniquely encouraged by how much they stay the same. In a word, timeless."

Allen L. West
Chief Analytics Officer, Lockton Dunning Benefits Company

"Here's the apparent recipe for writing the definitive, contemporary book on strategy: Take one part Mark Twain, two parts Will Rogers, a dash of Greek philosophy, a teaspoon of surprising perspectives about perennial truths, a tablespoon of three unique contributions to scholarly thought, and a generous helping of tools. Add wit, fold in some mind-bending and unexpected observations regarding leadership and culture, bake for one week, and voilà, *Cultivating the Strategic Mind!* You hold in your hands meal enough to feed an army of strategists."

Phil G. Davis II
Senior Vice President, PSCU Financial Services

"*Cultivating the Strategic Mind* is a must-read for any leader who expects to develop *a thinking and strategy-based culture* that can execute and achieve sustainable results."

Tony Jeary
Founder, High Performance Resources

"Dr. Leath has taken an arcane subject and made it entirely concrete, ushering us into a new era of strategy. Were it not for the apparent choice to make strategy feel so palpable, I fear he might have otherwise written an academically oriented book that would have been read by about three people. I consider it a gift that he wrote a book anyone can sink his teeth into and benefit from immediately. *Cultivating the Strategic Mind* is fun and successfully decodes what many leaders struggle to implement on a daily basis. I strongly recommend *Cultivating the Strategic Mind* to anyone needing to think and execute at a higher level. Leath has so swiftly and gracefully demystified strategy that this could very well have been *Strategy for Dummies.*"

Jeffery D. Price, CFM
Sales Manager & Wealth Management Advisor
Merrill Lynch Wealth Management
Bank of America Corporation

"*Cultivating the Strategic Mind* pulls the rabbit from the hat by seamlessly integrating theory and practice, which is inspiring, because it demonstrates time and again that nothing is as practical as a good theory. This is the rare leadership tome that transcends hype, ultimately proving practical and altogether pleasurable from start to finish. Though unusual to laugh or cry while reading about strategy, Blake's personal stories may just get you to do both, and what a wonderful guide his creation will be for your career."

Eric van Arendonk
Senior Adviseur, Florpartners BV

"As leadership development professionals, *Cultivating the Strategic Mind* has been required reading for hundreds of our clients. The insights that Blake captures and the tools he shares are invaluable for moving individuals and organizations from operational to strategic thinking and implementation. And, it's a fun read! Blake's wisdom, sense of humor, and charismatic energy dance and bound from page to page."

Raquel Romero, Principal Consultant
and
Dr. Michael Wood, President
High Ridge Leadership, LLC

"In short, *Cultivating the Strategic Mind* is awesome. What a great tool. I can't believe how much of it has stuck with me. I'm using *Cultivating the Strategic Mind* with our staff, and the *Omniscience Octagon* has proven to be an invaluable resource for our strategic thinking and planning. Dr. Leath's models improve upon many of the strategic concepts I learned as a fighter pilot and tactics officer in the Air Force. I was able to apply them to our business and a sister company almost instantly. The best part is that these principles have helped my wife and I develop a strategy to deal with some very complicated issues for our family."

John Moore
Principal, John Moore Associates, Inc.

"I met Blake in the 25th of my 43-year-long career. At the time, I called his work (some of which is distilled here) revelatory. His insights enhanced my personal and professional leadership, career, contributions, and our corporate culture extensively, and they can do the same for you and yours. Today, however, I do not call him revelatory — I call him Friend."

Richard Reynolds (retired)
COO, CFO, and EVP—Strategy Program Management
Libbey Inc.

cultivating the
STRATEGIC
MIND

growing from **leader** to **visionary**, **creator**, and **architect** of **strategy**

blake leath, phd

Published in the United States by Blake Leath.

>In association with:
>IBJ Book Publishing, LLC
>Indianapolis, IN
>www.ibjbp.com

Copyright © 2017 by Blake Leath.

ALL RIGHTS RESERVED. No part of this book may be reproduced in any manner without the express written consent of the publisher. All inquiries should be made to Blake Leath.

Cover art by Mark Boardman.

Interior art by William David Rigdon and Keith Crabtree.

Layout and design by Ashley Day.

Editing by Sharon Anderson.

Printed in the United States of America on acid-free paper.

ISBN 978-1-939550-37-8
Cultivating the Strategic Mind, Second Edition

Library of Congress Control Number: 2017958417

www.leathgroup.com

Other Publications by Blake Leath

Dynamic Leadership for Turbulent Times

Organizational Design Elements

Out of Dodge: A Transformational Journey from Heroic to Post-Heroic Leadership

The Drill vs. The Hole

The Family-Owned Business: A Case in Point

The Heart of Change is Employee Engagement

The Triune for Attraction & Retention: Creating a Culture of Good Leaders, a Great Workplace, and Sustaining Employer of Choice Designation

Workplace Involvement—Common Forces, Attributes, and Outcomes Within a Maximum Heterogeneous Sample of Highly-Involved Employees

Dedication

To all my teachers, coaches, council sponsors, friends' parents and parents' friends, professors, advisors, great and lousy bosses, mentors, and faithful clients who, in equal measure, have encouraged and harangued me at key inflection points along the way — I'm the better for it.

It's true what they say, "Failure is a greater teacher," though I'm especially indebted to Mrs. Yeats, who — in 3rd grade — demonstrated how learning could be fun. To Mrs. McCauley, who — in 4th grade — introduced SRA Reading Materials and taught me the power of incremental, progressive, aspirational learning (and made purple beautiful). To mid-school and high school faculty and persons of influence who made me want to be a better person: Barbara Harris, Bobby Davidson, Brant Buck, Charles Dixon, Danny Henson, Dennie Allie, Dr. Clayton Downing, Dr. Vic Rucker, Jackie Dulan, James Odoms, James Sweat, Jeanne Pearson, Jeff King, Jerry Pemberton, Martha Moore, Mike Burt, Pat Shovlin, Rocky Brookmole, Ron Greinke, Rory Durham, and Tom Laughlin. To Buck Henderson, whose yellow bus (#65) carried me to and from school for many years. Your smile in the morning put a spring in my step and taught me a courtesy that reaps dividends to this day. To John Smith, my Industrial Arts teacher, who taught me to measure twice and cut once. (And that digits don't grow on trees.) To Billie Earle, who taught me to type so that my fingers might accompany my thoughts. To Gary Stalcup, who taught me that tough is love. To Gloria Swearingen, who introduced me to Cheez Whiz, tortilla chips, and the transformative power of microwave technology. To Nancy Jones, who taught me God is always Him, forgave me when I broke the van window just as we were departing, forgave me again when I sneaked upstairs to visit with Daryl Hall and John Oates, and who inspired legions of students to reach for what John Cheever described as, "a page of good prose [that] remains invincible." To Principal Sigler, for treating me like an adult long before I was one and, not coincidentally, making me a man. What I know of the Pygmalion Effect, I attribute to you. To Que Brittain, who demonstrated grace under fire, and taught wee lads how gentlemen handle disappointment, failure, and anger in the public sphere. To Steve Telaneus, who said, "Run through the pain; winning is on the other side." To Tom Delgado — forever in blue jeans, sport coat, and tie — who believed in me and said so. To Tom Everest, who shouted and flailed his arms every time he corrected me, always concluding with, "You're smart, Leath; you'll figure it out." To Winford Groves, who made an acetate transparency of my 8th grade algebra homework, placed it gingerly on the overhead projector, cast the image brightly on the wall for all to see, and began, "Let's review how to *not* do algebra," and to Mrs. St. Pierre, who remarked, "This is how one should *never* diagram sentences." Together, you taught me perseverance, and overcoming embarrassment and shame. I treasure your fire; it humbled and refined me, and taught me empathy before my 14th birthday. To Ellen Tillotson, my high school Speech & Communications teacher. In our drills on improvisational speaking, you stuffed tiny, crumpled pieces of paper with random words scrawled on them (like "chlorophyll") in a fishbowl, placed the bowl upon a stool, blew a whistle and started a stopwatch — and gave me the confidence to speak extemporaneously before my peers on topics about which I know very little. To Fred McBride, my imposing and fierce taekwondo, hapkido, and kumdo instructor, who consistently punched me about the head and face and kicked me in the ribs and solar plexus for 10 agonizing years. Fifteen years later, I flew home to attend your funeral — which was standing-room only — and understood for the first time the notion of legacy, which is clearly the consequence of *Impact*, which I understand now to be *Force* × *Heat* × *Time*. (You also taught me, "Watch the belly," which is as applicable in business, relationships, and life as it is in a street-fight.) To Dr. Richard Chewning, who taught me, unequivocally, that success in business without ethics is abject failure. To Dr. Edward Wingard, who — in my 29th year — taught me to think more critically than I ever had before, and who said the words, "You'll need to learn rejection," then led me through the postgraduate process that rewired my brain forever and afforded me the vocation of a lifetime. To Thomas Abbatiello for getting me in, Paul Argenti for letting me stay, and Garth McGee (an Irishman, no less) for making me feel at home in my own country. To Dr. Marshall Goldsmith, who reminded me of the priority of receiving over transmitting, and how personal stories can soften the heart which, in turn, flings open the mind. To Dr. Pino Audia, who made me feel more than enough when I doubted I was. To Dr. Ron Adner, whose work encouraged me and broadened my aperture. To Dr. Sydney Finkelstein, whose life displays three sparkling exhibits that I pursue with renewed vigor: strategy + leadership + professionalism.

And to Mom and Dad, who — now in the winter of their lives — cheer me on as if it were spring and I stood a chance to win. Though there are no words, let's try, "I love you and I thank you." To Tracy, equal parts critic and fan, who — in exchange for my listening just a little bit more — laughs at my every joke. To Mrs. Judy Carruthers, my 7th grade English teacher who knowingly launched this ship after reading my Thanksgiving story aloud in class and pronouncing, "You are a writer; go write." To inimitable Lauren and indomitable Dawn, who love so mightily and so beautifully, beyond measure, and find in everyone the person we absolutely dream to become. And to our beloved Will, in whose spirit we write the very best we can, every day, in word and deed.

Together, you are the roots and wings of a man in progress.

Commemorating Ten Years with a Second Edition

In 1850, upon publishing the second edition of *The Scarlet Letter,* Nathaniel Hawthorne documented, "[I have] carefully read over the introductory pages, with a purpose to alter or expunge whatever might be found amiss, and to make the best reparation in my power for the atrocities of which I have been adjudged guilty. But it appears to me that the only remarkable features of the sketch are its frank and genuine good-humor, and the general accuracy with which I have conveyed my sincere impressions of the characters therein described." He concluded by announcing, "The author is constrained, therefore, to republish his introductory sketch without the change of a word."

I am no Nathaniel Hawthorne, and *Cultivating the Strategic Mind* is no *Scarlet Letter,* so, alas, the conservation of my edits cannot be attributed to perfection.

Indeed, I have updated a series of facts, contemporizing them. I have corrected a handful of typos and errors, surely creating new ones in the process. I have made current a few examples that had become grossly passé (having first published *Cultivating the Strategic Mind* the year the iPhone was invented), but done so quite sparingly, particularly with regard to corporate and technological examples, lest I delude myself about the merits of chasing shadows.

If we are fortunate to live another day, oh, how time flies, and the problems of yesteryear become so quaint.

Perhaps in another decade, when the text celebrates its 20th anniversary, I shall be compelled to tweak again, refreshing old bits and bytes and similarly correcting mistakes that stubbornly escape this jeweler's loop.

To the extent I possess peace, however, it is because *Cultivating the Strategic Mind* remains relevant. Hindsight being 20/20, it is clearer to me now — even more than at the zenith of my fevered and frenzied writing in 2007 — that *Cultivating the Strategic Mind* is primarily about *perspective*. In the years succeeding its publication, I have taught scores more classes and facilitated well over 100 additional strategy sessions or similar workshops. Through doing and teaching we learn the most, and if I have learned anything since, it is that *Cultivating the Strategic Mind* does indeed help leaders to become better strategists, thinkers to become more proficient practitioners, and virtually everyone to become even more creative.

We are each creative, often innovative, too, and I have found time and again — to my astonishment and delight — that *Cultivating the Strategic Mind* provides a suitable framework, a worthwhile holistic view, and a toolbox for people to behave anew and see more keenly, more sharply, and with altogether better eyes.

As a result, perhaps 90 percent of the text remains the same, its essence intact, its approach evergreen.

The names of corporations may combine or change, celebrity leaders may come and go or pass away, but the principles that animate strategy and effective leadership abide. They are timeless, because they are ultimately rooted in human nature which, for good or bad, and despite how the world may change around us, remains virtually unchanged.

In coming years, I shall turn my attention to something new, to a second work that reflects what is under me now and coming for all of us, but writing, and rightly, is an arduous task in this bombastic, bombarded world. To write, versus, say, to simply blog, I must become so completely and irredeemably possessed by an idea that only through my writing about it may it be exorcised. There is a current reality, upon us now for 10 years, that shall only get worse, not better in coming years. It comes to me and our entire team's consulting day after day after day. I feel its hands clutching at my ankles and clothing, bony and wanting like "the Ghost of Christmas Yet to Come" in Albert Finney's 1970 classic, *Scrooge*.

Meantime, *Cultivating the Strategic Mind* accomplished what I hoped it would, codifying a string of thoughts and practices important to me at the time, giving vocabulary and dance to my grunts and toe-stubs, and serving as a raggedy, tattered, besotted yet beloved field guide that users seem to enjoy and recite and apply with passion and pride.

I have seen the book in the most pleasantly surprising places, from oil fields and D.C. offices to start-ups in San Francisco and smokejumper training camps in Montana. Beyond North America, I have taught *Strategic Mind* workshops in Amsterdam, Beijing,

Lisbon, London, Seoul, Waterford, and countless points in between, and every month my wife and I receive tiny statements indicating its purchase in far away lands like Azerbaijan and Australia, so I have to believe the message in a bottle continues to bob its way across voluminous seas to distant shores.

When I originally tackled it, I hoped it would be fresh in the way any worthwhile scholarship should be, but also a stretch for me as a writer, and for others as implementers.

I am disappointed that, as time slides by, more and more of today's written words are derivative, superficial, or bound to be chopped for accommodation to sound bite. Where required, I shall evolve to avoid extinction, and where principled, I shall co-labor alongside others to stand for what is true, timeless, and essential, like thinking deeply about complex problems and working tirelessly — almost always in anonymity — to see that work gets done, and well.

By virtue of being human, we are all influential, and therefore we are obligated to be wiser leaders and better strategists.

That fact has not changed, remains immutable as far as I am concerned, and shall therefore stand the test of time.

The opportunities afforded us, and the problems facing us, demand nothing less than deep, critical thinking and introspection. Chess is child's play compared to what lies ahead for our world and each of us as participants in it.

Gird your loins, strap your helmet, and grab that sword and shield, because there are many good battles to be fought, both within ourselves and alongside others who cannot succeed alone.

Blake Leath
Hanover, NH
April 28, 2017

Contents

PART ZERO **POSITIONING**
Preface 1
The *Strategic Mind* Promise 5
Prologue 7

PART ONE **FOUNDATIONS**
Disillusionment 13
- Personal Case Study 22

Shortsightedness 24
Hope: Just What, Precisely, Is Strategy? 28
- Review of Representative Findings
  in the Literature 30
- A Few Points of Clarification: Strategic/
  Systemic Thinking vs. Strategic Planning & Strategic
  Management 35
- Beyond Origins, Etymology, and the Literature
  to Real Life 36
- Toward an Understanding of Terms:
  Strategic & Systemic 46

Strategy 48

PART TWO **TRIUNE**
The Strategic Triune 57
- Their Mind in Greater Detail: The Mind Map 65
- Their View in Greater Detail: The Omniscience
  Octagon 66
- Their People in Greater Detail: Inclusive Ownership 79

PART THREE **PILLARS**
Four Pillars of Strategic Organizations 85
- Leadership 90
- Culture 101
- Processes and Performance 105
- Sales and Service 107

PART FOUR **KALEIDOSCOPE**
Twisting the Kaleidoscope: A Few Perspectives
on Strategies and Systems 117
  I. Biology...118
  II. Physics..121
  III. Sociology..128
  IV. Psychology..130
  V. Mathematics..132
  VI. Astronomy...134
  VII. Religion...142

PART FIVE **IDEAS AND TOOLS**
  1. The One I Feed.. 147
  2. Two Principles of 1°... 148
  3. The Philosopher King.. 154
  4. The Importance of Solitude 156
  5. Solomonic Solutions.. 158
  6. Conscious Competence....................................... 162
  7. Visualization.. 164
  8. Transcending Politics... 168
  9. Principles of Hapkido.. 171
  10. Outcomes vs. Incomes 174
  11. Microscoping and Telescoping 178
  12. From Reconnaissance toward Renaissance 182
  13. The Archer's Aim... 184
  14. Self-Management and Burnout............................ 192
  15. Honoring the Fundamentals: VMV &
      Teleological Pursuits 198
  16. Turning Vision into Action.................................. 200
  17. Bluetooth Strategies... 205
  18. Unlearning and Learning: Mental Habituation
      and Ruts... 207
  19. Luddism... 211
  20. Behind the Curtain of Oz.................................... 213
  21. Four Types of Thinking 216
  22. MindTaffy: Methods for Transcending
      the Proverbial Box.. 220
  23. Three Types of Winning:
      The Competition Typology 224

PART SIX **TOMORROW**
Conclusion: From Simplicity to Complexity
& Difficulty to Ease 233

PART SEVEN **APPENDIX**
Strategist Matrix 243
Sources and Resources 251

ABOUT THE AUTHOR 259
INDEX 263

0
Positioning

Preface

The least important things, we think about and talk about the most, and the most important things, we think about and talk about the least.

Socrates

By the time my daughter turned three, she was in full-blown princess mode. Princesses and unicorns and fairy tales were the larger part of her world, imagination, and play. Her bedroom was an explosion of pink and purple and dresses, tiaras, wands, wigs, rings, necklaces, and tiny shoes heaped in random piles strewn across the floor. Inspired by a *Swan Lake* Barbie DVD, she informed her mother and me that she wanted to take ballet. Okie dokie; let's do it.

My wife enrolled her in a local dance studio, and now we had more and larger piles that included soft shoes, tutus, tights, headbands, and a microscopic yet stinky pink duffle bag that reminded me of every gym I've ever darkened in my life. But we loved it all, because we love our child as every parent does, and we got a real kick out of watching her leap and spin and stand agog as she watched the big girls *pirouette*.

You must forgive my ignorance of ballet nomenclature, as I'm not a ballet aficionado (just a ballet daddy), but as one particularly adept teen spun rhythmically and extended her leg and both arms, her body decelerated immediately, and as she drew her limbs in tightly to her body, she accelerated just as quickly. She would alternate this way endlessly...out — slow down, in — speed up. Whoosh, whoosh, whoosh. It was athletically elegant and my tiny daughter, all 30 vertical inches of her, stood nearby, hands down by her side and feet splayed open, with her mouth in the shape of a perfect O.

I share this story for two reasons. First, because none of us is immune to the kryptonite of greatness. Whether it's art, music, athletic performance, mental genius, social aptitude, mathematical prowess, transfixing literature, or the sheer grace that arises from pure selflessness, we each admire greatness, are moved by it, and become weak-kneed in its presence.[1] Second, because we can learn a great deal from physics and nature.

As members of humankind, we've all seen, in one form or another, greatness. And we each experience physics and nature on a daily basis. Having worked with many organizations and individuals for a number of years, I have witnessed great strategists in action. Not often, because they are quite rare, but often enough to know beyond the shadow of a doubt that they belong on a Mt. Olympus of sorts. To see a great strategist work his or her magic, summoning countless, seemingly unrelated data points and future possibilities and orchestrating them, is a feat of brilliance, and yet these savants generally make it appear effortless. It is indeed an elixir of science and art that boggles the mind.

Also, I believe that, just as it is with the pirouette, when the gifted strategist pulls everything inward, he accelerates, and when he pushes everything away, he slows down. And both are important. The pushing away, to analyze, detach, and avoid seduction when combined with the drawing near, to absorb, reform, and integrate allows the strategist to seemingly internalize the momentum of ideas and quicken himself and the organization he leads. It's a beautiful, simple demonstration — and yet, paradoxically complex — just like the human body. So much so that, like the human body, enigmas remain. Realities are occluded. What we think we understand, we often fail to understand.

In *Cultivating the Strategic Mind*, I do my best to share observations, research, and experiences that represent many best practices. This strategic manifesto won't be a panacea, and it isn't designed to save your life or make you the Mikhail Baryshnikov of strategy, but it may very well rekindle your and your organization's passion. It will certainly illuminate a path to exhibit your strategic capacities, and will leverage a scientific approach of diagnosis and prognosis that will complement an intuitive, artful reality that separates the winners from the also-rans. In short, I hope to pragmatize strategy for consumption and utilization by you and those you lead. We *must* learn to improve our strategic minds.

---

[1] Find Paul Potts' first performance on *Britain's Got Talent* for a literal example of what words inadequately communicate.

Can we capture lightning in a bottle? Is there anything new under the sun? You'll be the ultimate connoisseur, but I am certain of this: *There is a better way of strategy*. A *Tao* of strategy, if you will, and the following pages are submitted to tease it out of all seekers who dare to pirouette.

Socrates was onto something, you know. Drums of ink have been spilled onto the page in the analysis of strategy itself, but there is a glaring paucity of analysis regarding the strategists themselves. It's time now to study the behaviors of the greatest strategists as people, and see what they can teach us about ourselves, organizations and institutions, science, art, and ultimately, the potential of humankind.

The *Strategic Mind* Promise

I presume that two of the things most important to you as a reader are:
1. Your time.
2. Receiving tools you can apply immediately.

In less than a day's time, you should be able to consume *Cultivating the Strategic Mind* — and the payoff will include **more than 40 tools you can use tomorrow.**

I know what it's like to be the reader…you're standing there, caught by the cover, flipping through the book and reading the back to see if it's worth your time, or you're scrolling through images on a website, deciding if you should add this item to your cart.

Let me make this easy for you: *You must read this book.*
Why?

1. I promise to treat you as the intelligent, curious learner that you are. I'll give you the real deal — not some diluted, oversimplified pablum that wouldn't pass muster in an elementary school classroom.

2. I won't write in sound bites. I promise to communicate full, well-researched ideas that are valid. I'm not making things up here; I'm communicating what has been proven again and again in all sorts of settings.

3. I won't push a mnemonic device or acrostic solution on you. They're cute and memorable — they have their place and I use them, too. But *Cultivating the Strategic Mind* isn't a prescription — it's a new way of thinking about the world. I won't sell it short by embracing convention.

A book is special. It affords the opportunity to dive deep where we are otherwise superficial. In my *Strategic Mind* workshops, I'm forced to cover more in two to three days than I'd like — and although participants often hunger for more, time is precious and few of us can carve out more time than we already do. This is one of the reasons I'm so excited about this book. For the first time, I have the luxury of unspooling so many tools and ways of thinking about the world that will help you grow from leader to truly *strategic* leader. If history is any indication, most of my suggestions will resonate. Surely, however, some of them will fall flat — and that's okay, too. In the words of Mark Twain, "If we both agree, one of us is unnecessary." Feel free to dismiss me or my ideas, but only after you've finished the meal I've prepared and you've attempted what I've suggested. The outcomes just might surprise you.

If I'm *right* about my convictions — maybe you're the one who will form a *Strategic Mind* implementation book club and revolutionize your business or church or family for the better. If so, please send me a note in the coming weeks and let me know how this meal has nourished you.

Prologue

If you would persuade, you must appeal to interest rather than intellect.

Benjamin Franklin

The problem in too many organizations today is no real blueprint of *strategy*, and specifically, the lack of a *strategist*.

While *leadership* is a vital and obligatory chromosome in the DNA of any organization, it is not the same as *strategy*, and it alone is not adequate. I value leaders immensely; they occupy the second-highest tier on a pedestal within my mind. But the uppermost tier is occupied by the strategist: the progenitor of everything that follows. She is the one who first puts pencil to paper and sketches a blueprint that defines the entire space — its surroundings, its interior, and its inherency. I respect the strategist above all others, because it is the strategist who pioneers, who composes the music that leaders orchestrate.

Cultivating the Strategic Mind is a banquet table sagging beneath the weight of entrees, side dishes, and thirst-quenching beverages for the leader wishing to become an architect of strategy. There is food enough for all, including those who might not yet know they are famished or parched. **This book has only you in mind and is committed to helping you become the finest strategist possible in your current professional and personal roles, as well as those roles that may come with career or life transitions.** I cannot make you hungry or thirsty, but when that time does come — as it always does — *Cultivating the Strategic Mind* and its bounty will be right here, ready to satiate and help you become more strategic in whatever relationships you value.

We can all, as leaders and persons of influence *(the former being those with followers and the latter being anyone who can fog a mirror)* understand and employ strategy more rigorously at both the intellectual and behavioral levels. We can improve, and we must. Strategy and its execution can mean the life or death of an organization, and the chain from creation to implementation is only as strong as the interim links.

Clearly, there are millions of successful companies and organizations in the world today, but many survive in spite of themselves, and very few survive beyond the first generation's founders and immediate cohorts. Most failures can be attributed to environmental changes, decayed ideas, poor successors, disruptive technologies, consolidation, Organizational Darwinism,[2] and the sheer forces of chance, taste, time, and entropy. In the face of these afflictions, however, the following pages provide a bevy of ideas and tools built upon a *triune*[3] and *four pillars* — unified ways of thinking about the world, one's organization, and ultimately — *a system of strategy* predicated on proven truths that enable believers and adopters to create a robust means to a new and healthier end. As strategists, we cannot control the world or our environment, but there are ways of thinking and behaving within our reality to be addressed beginning with *definition* and running as far right as *new skills and a more formidable, integrated approach to strategic and systemic thinking.*

The three primary research questions we'll seek to answer include:

1. What is strategy, and why aren't more leaders better strategists?

2. While strategy is as foundational as DNA within the most exemplary companies, why are so many organizations missing it altogether?

3. What are the most prescient common denominators and best practices of strategists, and how can I apply these in pragmatic ways within my organization?

As a result of demonstrating a *Strategic Mind*, there are two intended payoffs:

1. For perhaps the first time, individuals will utilize a common language regarding *systemic strategies*, the result of which is an aligned, integrated approach to thinking about one's world and succeeding within it.

2. Adopters will demonstrate an organizational capability that is difficult to replicate, resulting in competitive differentiation and advantage.

---

[2] The notion of "survival of the fittest" occurring within the context of an organization.

[3] A triune is any three elements working harmoniously together to form a unified, coherent, systemic whole.

Though time itself more reliably judges such efforts, here are my secondary intentions for *Cultivating the Strategic Mind*:

1. To *satiate a deep, rumbling hunger that is fundamental in every way*. The would-be strategist hungers for more explicit methodology — we need to know how to implement those systemic strategies.
2. Second, to explore strategy in a way that is both *cognitive and sticky*. We'll explore strategy through applications drawn from sources as varied as biology, physics, sociology, psychology, mathematics, astronomy, religion, philosophy, politics, Hapkido, the Renaissance, Bluetooth technology, Luddism, competition, and the concept of MindTaffy. Essentially, this is serious, healthy trail mix with some M&M's sprinkled in to sweeten the pot.
3. Where successful, *Cultivating the Strategic Mind* should feel *fresh and fun*. Though deceptively prosaic, strategy should be invigorating.
4. Where applied, *Cultivating the Strategic Mind* should *increase competence*. The majority of strategic thinking is skill-based and choice-dependent, with the remainder subject to natural talent or giftedness. This is one reason why *Cultivating the Strategic Mind* should adhere.
5. *Cultivating the Strategic Mind leverages yesterday for tomorrow* by gleaning best practices from today's Baby Boomers and interpreting them for tomorrow's leaders. Implementing the great contributions of thought-leaders like Peter Drucker, Charles Handy, Warren Bennis, Ken Blanchard, Stephen Covey, Tom Peters, and more contemporary writers like Malcolm Gladwell, Patrick Lencioni, or Jim Collins, we can each become better strategists. Future generations must fervently commit themselves to the ongoing study of strategy.

Will these aspirations be met? While *Cultivating the Strategic Mind* will be no nostrum for your organization, of this I remain convinced: Within organizations and among leaders where these principles of understanding and emulating the *Strategic Mind* are woven into the fabric of everyday existence, more and better things become possible.

I
Foundations

When I was a child, I spoke as a child, I understood as a child, I thought as a child — but when I became a man, I put away childish things.

1 Corinthians 13:11

: Disclaimer

The stories I have recounted throughout this book are true. However, to ensure anonymity, names and identifying details of certain characters and organizations have been changed.

Disillusionment

Monday, December 22nd/3:50 p.m.

We stood on the cool marble floor within a quietly cavernous corporate lobby. With just three days to go before Christmas, there was an unusual urgency in the request to meet with a colleague and me. Generally, the last two weeks of our year are quiet, and while the prospect's corporate offices were an eerie ghost town, we took it on good faith the meeting could not wait. We were told it would be imperative to begin fleshing out some sort of strategy for this potential client prior to his year-end.

Momentarily, a purposeful-looking assistant exited the elevator and motioned us to step inside. We ascended soundlessly to the 25th floor and into the living-room-like office. Sinking deeply into the rich, warm leather chairs, we awaited our C-level executive at CorpBank,[4] a growing financial company with many divisions and thousands upon thousands of employees. Within minutes, a striking man in crisp attire entered and shook our hands firmly. He was tall and, though not the CEO, had silver "CEO hair," as a friend likes to say. Very quickly, we huddled around an intimate coffee table and my colleague and I became enraptured as Mr. Kane revealed the business challenges and aspirations of his organization. Arms flailing, knees bouncing, and periodically pacing across the plush carpet, Mr. Kane's overview ranged from a diatribe of CorpBank's missteps to an exoneration by way of its noble intentions. He passionately poked at every nook and cranny of the business, from his peer group to business development to paperwork hassles and ethical quandaries. By the time he completed exorcising many demons and outlining a few dreams, his muscular frame had begun to shine with the sweat of his effort. Our hair was blown by the wind of his rhetoric, and we had a fairly complete first impression of the business, its history, its outlook on the future, and the current state of employee morale and the culture.

---

[4] To preserve anonymity, a pseudonym has been created.

We arrived at five perceptions that we shared with Mr. Kane:

1. The industry was consolidating, and within five years it would likely be dominated by just three primary players, with also-rans being relegated to niche positions in the marketplace. The organization was committed to being one of these top three players.

2. The culture was atrocious, with exactly half of all newly hired employees leaving within six months. For every 1,000 employees hired, 500 would be gone within the first 180 days. Within one division alone, turnover costs topped $46,000,000 in 2001. The organization was viewed by most employees as a sweatshop, and there was an appalling paucity of leadership bench strength. Most employees described their leaders as supervisors or managers, not leaders.

3. There was significant churn at the highest echelons of the company, with transparent political jockeying and positioning occurring on a regular basis.

4. Employees were paid extremely well, and strictly monetary compensation had long been the only carrot to assuage the sweatshop culture.

5. There were many *undiscussables* in the organization, ranging from a hostile work environment, management by fear, employee fraud, ill-equipped individuals in positions of power, and total disillusionment among most employees.

As we summarized these themes, we described the importance of leadership and culture but found Mr. Kane uncomfortable with these topics. "*Culture?* I don't like that word. Too touchy-feely. If we engage you, you can't use words like that. Use *company*. And don't use the word *organization*. Too nondescript and airy-fairy. *Leadership?* This is a company that has thrived historically because of management practices, not leadership. I'm sure leadership has merit, but it's hardly part of our company and I don't know that anyone here could wrap his arms around what *leadership* means."

Like a bloodhound on a scent, Mr. Kane repetitively and pathologically chased quantitative metrics of the business. Most everything he alluded to as indices of success was numerical. I asked what I thought to be a necessary and fair question. "Does CorpBank value things that are immeasurable?"

"Like what?" he asked.

"Well, I don't know. Say…trust, direction, operating principles?"

"No. While I can't speak for anyone else, I — myself — wouldn't even know where to begin measuring things like that. I suppose I'd have to look at what the outcomes of those things are, then find a way to measure those."

"I find it interesting," I said, "working with so many organizations… um, *companies*, I mean…that adhere to an 'if we can't measure it, we don't do it' mentality."

"Why is that *interesting*? It seems only *logical*."

"Well, sure. Logical. But that's the point," I said. "Some of the most important aspects of the human condition — the things that define us as living critters — are immeasurable. Without them, life would be meaningless. And to ignore them, to de-value them because they're immeasurable, is to miss the largest puzzle piece, and frankly — creates a company with no soul. A company that, yes, though rooted in logic, fails to appeal to the most natural and intrinsic motivators available."

"Give me an example," he said.

"I'll give you ten. Faith, hope, love, justice, liberty, freedom, compassion, engagement, connectedness, purpose. Without these, and others like them, what sort of workplace does one create? A sterile, clinical lab — nothing more. As people — as employees — we hunger for elements like these, not for the metrics you rattled off. Sure, those are helpful, if only because they're measurable. But they're lame surrogates for what really matters. Consider this, for example. What's the difference between Nordstrom and JC Penney? Between Starbucks and Seattle's Best? Between Southwest Airlines and practically every airline? I hate to say it, Mr. Kane — because you won't like the answer. But frankly, the difference is leadership and culture and, as a result, the experience that is created…for both the employees who work and live there, as well as the customers who interact with them. Yes, these organizations have many measurables, and for good reason. But unlike CorpBank, they *get it* and understand that what you dismiss as *the soft stuff* is actually the hardest stuff, and they work at it daily."

Over the course of our dialogue, Mr. Kane became increasingly intrigued with our impressions. He agreed that our summary was on-target, but it would be a gross exaggeration on my part to say that he became a convert during our hours together. I remained disappointed by his reliance on economic and measurable indicators (to the exclusion of those more intangible factors that were clearly roiling beneath the surface). What he could not measure or point to within his massive three-ring binders held little interest or sway with him; this man was a metrics-guy, not an intuitive, visceral, gut-guy. I'm sure his *logic-only* approach had served him well throughout his career, but like many blind spots…we don't know what we don't know, and I sensed this absence of self-awareness might prove challenging going forward. Fortunately, in the current conversation, he was clearly distressed by the turnover, the politics, the "culture" — and although the organization was having an incomprehensibly wonderful financial year — I believe he became more open-minded about the softer underbelly of the organization (leadership and culture) being at the root of many of the business' ailments. In the end, however, these issues perhaps remained too trivial, as they eventually seemed to be eclipsed by things he could measure. This was a financial enterprise, after all, and without issues submitting to numerical inquiry, they were anomalous, and as such — unworthy of study and analysis. This is an all too common reality in business, both domestically and internationally, as we'll explore in greater detail later.

My colleague and I concluded the meeting with a few specific action items that would be addressed the following week and wished Mr. Kane a great holiday. "I'll be here while most of my employees are taking a day to spend with their families, so I'm not sure how great it'll be. We desperately need to turn this ship around though, or we're going to lose anyone who has alternatives. I look forward to your help and am ready to start as soon as you are."

We left carrying the ominous weight of Mr. Kane's concerns and fatigue. We agreed to begin work imminently, and Mr. Kane's organization contracted with us to bring our full resources to bear on the problems and opportunities.

I share this CorpBank story for many reasons, but primarily because it is a wonderful cautionary tale that is representative of the much larger reality: Too few leaders are strategists, and subsequently, few strategies are holistic enough to account for all the elements required by contemporary organizations. As the CorpBank project moved forward, Mr. Kane's commitments to us were more frequently broken, his attention waned, and he was embroiled in the ongoing issues he described to us weeks prior. He postponed appointments, became less available, and was altogether distracted with sales, volume, and economic interests. The market was great in 2004, the margins were healthy, and hundreds of individuals became quite wealthy. It was not unusual at all to see a 30-year-old employee without a college degree driving a Lamborghini, Ferrari, or Rolls Royce to the office. Thirty-somethings were frequently earning $600,000 to $2,000,000 per year, and we learned of one gentleman in his early forties who earned no less than $1,000,000 in commissions each month for 12 months in a row. Financially, the organization was an unstoppable juggernaut, the market was burgeoning, and those who survived thrived.

It was during this year of financial overflow that we were ultimately tasked with building a curriculum for leaders — a "rainy day" curriculum as Mr. Kane described it, "so when the market tanks, we'll have real leaders in place." Disappointingly, our advice to respect the Peter Principle and not promote people based solely on personal financial production went unheard, and more and more individual producers were promoted into the ranks of management. Cancer continued to spread clandestinely throughout the organization. Mr. Kane and the entire Learning & Organizational Development group viewed *training* as the answer, whereas we know from the field that real solutions arise from formulas that include job structure, special projects, role models, feedback, informal and formal coaching, mentoring, evaluation, linking behaviors to compensation plans, job rotation, developmental plans, and yes...external or internal training.

Detached from the organizational and operational processes that generally increase the likelihood of success, our leadership "project" devolved and we were handed-off to no less than four subordinates across the next 14 months. The Friday before our alpha-pilot for the new curriculum was unveiled to 20 participants who had flown in from across the country, Mr. Kane's right-hand man stormed out of a meeting and tendered his resignation. Mr. Kane continued leading (managing?) an extremely dysfunctional business, leadership staff, and management population through a declining market.

Where was the *Strategic Mind* in all this? It could not be found among the physicists at corporate who had designed the most sophisticated software in the industry. It could not be found along mahogany row, where politics and fear ruled the day. It could not be found in Mr. Kane's office four years ago, or today. This organization blossoms more like the poisoned rose or a Greek tragedy than anything else, with lessons and morality tales popping up week after week. There was no evidence of *systems thinking* or the *Strategic Triune* or the six elements of the *Mind Map* (each of which we'll explore in Part Two). Only hubris was demonstrated by ignoring the aspects of the *Omniscience Octagon* (also explored in Part Two, and which would have provided a roadmap for resolving CorpBank's many challenges with respect to culture, employees, and environmental realities and future), and CorpBank's culture continues to devalue and thwart employee involvement or constructive criticism. The *Four Pillars* (Part Three) of great organizations were largely ignored, with only one-and-a-half of the four pillars really mattering to this organization: *processes/performance* and *sales*. As a result, the customer service side of the organization has been downsized and complaining customers have fewer venues in which they can resolve their issues. Fascinatingly, CorpBank is so vilified by many angry customers and former and current employees alike that a hateful website sprang up that airs its dirty laundry on a real-time basis. I occasionally observed employees contributing to the website from within their cubicles — just feet away from their managers.

"You know, Blake," the right-hand-man said two weeks after he left, "you told us three years ago that turning a blind eye to leadership would be our downfall. We paid marginal attention to your input, mostly because we were successful in spite of ourselves. In hindsight, leadership should have been our primary focus, because it's clear to me today that financial success is not sustainable in a culture without strong, ethical leaders. Ironically, for years I had so many staffers tell me that CorpBank treats people like crap, but it wasn't until I experienced it in the past few weeks that I appreciated the gravity of their comments. If I had to do it all over again, and I know I will somewhere else, I would have spent 80 percent of my time building leaders and a healthy culture rather than focusing so exclusively on paying producers and selling my soul for the sake of volume and margin."

Today, CorpBank remains economically viable, albeit marginalized. It is not one of the primary players in the market as hoped, and with the retirement of key leaders looming on the horizon, its fate remains more precarious than ever. Turnover has increased as the juicy, red portions of the market watermelon have been consumed by the ordinary, and only the most savvy employees can survive while squabbling over the rind that remains. Literally thousands of employees have joined the exodus of the company in the past year, and the venomous website hosted by employees and irate customers denouncing CorpBank's leadership and cultural practices grows exponentially month after month.

Most of us know someone who has lived the experiences described in my recollections. Employers who focus solely on what's most measurable miss an important truth: *"People will forget what you said, people will forget what you did, but people will never forget how you made them feel."*[5] Companies that pursue extrinsic, financial rewards at the expense of something more meaningful build their house on shifting sands. From beginning to end, this story is a solid illustration of the *absence* of a *Strategic Mind*. We generally learn far more from our failures than our successes and from life's harder roads than its easier ones. This is true for all of us, and particularly for the strategist.

In subsequent months following our efforts to help CorpBank, we were approached by a half-dozen exiting executives seeking employment, and each of them had a journal-full of horror stories about the internal machinations of their former employer. Individually, each story would warrant a chapter unto itself. Collectively, they are discouraging commentaries on the sins of man, ranging from sexual escapades and blackmail to drug addiction

---

[5] The venerable Maya Angelou.

and customer identity theft. Where in this darkness was leadership? Shockingly, in more instances than I care to recall, we were told that many of these acts were committed *by* leadership, and it is likely that, in time, CorpBank's economic glory will be reduced to rubble like Sodom and Gomorrah.

The CorpBank story reveals some *good news* and some *bad news*. Among the *good news* are these morsels:

1. Thanks to the internet, we live in a world where *Information Leveling* and *Knowledge Parity* are omnipresent. Via Google, blogs, and grass roots websites like www.consumerdemocracy.com,[6] consumers can now have a united voice — and with voice comes influence and power. CorpBank and other large employers that have provided less than desirable service to employees and customers alike are frequently exposed on the world wide web. Skullduggery is now met with spotlights, empowering consumers by the millions to make more informed choices. With so much information at our disposal, the adage *caveat emptor*[7] is less foreboding than before.

2. The Sarbanes-Oxley Act (SOX), created in the wake of corporate scandals and investigations involving Enron, Worldcom, Global Crossing, Tyco, Peregrine Systems, iVillage, Adelphia, HealthSouth, McKesson, Qwest, and others, represents a watershed event in contemporary American business. Transparency and telling the truth are the orders of the day, and it is extremely hazardous for organizations to engage in even the most remotely questionable activities with regard to reporting their earnings and opening their books. I believe this transparency will permeate beyond accounting practices and eventually extend well into the practices of management and how leaders interact with employees. While there will be no equivalent to SOX

---

[6] See also, www.mouthshut.com, www.my3cents.com, and mainstays like www.consumerreports.com or www.epinion.com.

[7] *"Let the buyer beware."*

with respect to "leadership," the ongoing influence of unions in this country, combined with the war for talent and a general leader deficit following the Boomers will afford job candidates more choices than ever before, requiring leaders to not only be on their best behavior, but to be the best in as many aspects as possible.

The bad news is this: Despite being several centuries into the social sciences and study of organizations, more downfalls occur for timeless reasons like *the nature of humankind* rather than ignorance. As English historian J.A. Froude wrote in the 1800s, "Morality sees farther than intellect." This is a reminder that, despite our intellectual progress and capacity to access and perhaps even ingest more knowledge and best practices, it is our morality, not our cognition, that often betrays us. And so, while *Cultivating the Strategic Mind* and the preceding centuries' volumes of scholarly pursuits certainly steady our aim, it is our dark hearts that destroy. While we cannot leave such important discourses to the moral philosophers alone, I will limit my focus a bit herein, or else succumb to scope-creep, thereby diluting my aim with this book and unwittingly undermining its intentions.

Going forward, there are many changes astir that bode well for our collective futures and, specifically, that bode well for future strategists. The world is changing dramatically, and our children are being born into a reality that values interdisciplinarity more than ever before.[8] Whereas many educational systems in the prior century erred by creating graduates described as "an inch wide and a mile deep," progressive schools are seeing the light and returning to more traditional (which is to say, ironically, what some might view as more progressive) educational systems. Learners in ancient Greece, Rome, or during the Renaissance experienced tremendous cross-pollination of knowledge, but we somehow got off track in

---

[8] *The World is Flat*, by Thomas Friedman, is a great discourse on the value of interdisciplinarity. See also *How to Bring Our Schools Out of the 20th Century* pp. 52-56, TIME Magazine, December 18, 2006. One of the most progressive adult-education programs in the United States is provided by Union Institute & University, www.tui.edu. Sadly, because its rich, interdisciplinary, meaningful, and student-centric approach is unorthodox in the United States and doesn't readily lend itself to quantitative analysis, the school fails to appear on many prestigious academic lists. *Transformational education* is difficult to quantify using anachronistic scales.

recent years, pumping out students who knew everything about the pinhead, but very little about the world beyond. Sadly, this hindered society's ability to provide the ideal soil in which to grow strategists, because the best strategists are more likely to spring from well-rounded, fertile, and deep environments than from rocky, dry, or shallow ones.

Personal Case Study
Anticipate the Application

I recall a gentleman named John who shared a story with me about his first *plowing* experience. His father harnessed the horse, attached the plow, and handed the young boy the reins departing with: "I'll come back to check on you at lunch." Hours later, his father returned only to find the most unparallel rows of plowed soil he'd ever seen. John described his approach: "I was really focused, Pa. I studied the ground and worked really hard to keep 'er straight, but now that I look back across, everything's zig-zaggy." To this his father replied, "In the afternoon, just plow to the barn over yonder, son. Keep your head steady and your eyes fixed on the barn and you'll be able to keep 'er straight."

I love this story and have since the moment I heard it. It is such a simple reminder of the importance of vision and the weakness of fixating on things held too closely to us. I share it now for this reason: Before we hop entirely on this little raft together and push ourselves from the tranquility of the shore, it might be good to visualize a destination and pre-think what you hope to get out of our journey. *Cultivating the Strategic Mind* is not for everyone. I have worked tirelessly, not to create something light and airy, but rather, of substance. Sure, if I have succeeded in some small way at making the content easy and breezy like an Airwick commercial, that's fantastic and an added bonus, but by its very nature, strategy is a layered topic (though often made more complex than it should be). I have done my best to make the lessons portable and pragmatic, but there are certainly some chapters that will be much more meaningful if they receive your full attention and reflection.

To get started — *plowing to the barn* — please answer the following five questions before continuing:

1. What is strategy?
2. Why do I hunger to learn more about it?
3. Do I currently see differences between *leaders* and *strategists*? If so, what are the differences?
4. What are examples of strategy in my life…my organization…my community? Where do I see a need, opportunity, and/or compelling event(s) that necessitate(s) *strategy*? What is one strategy that I would like to improve as a result of reading and operationalizing the principles in *Cultivating the Strategic Mind*?
5. Who might join me in a study and application group of *Cultivating the Strategic Mind*?

Shortsightedness

In a conversation with Dean Lindsay, author of *How to Achieve Big PHAT Goals*, he echoed what I've heard so many authors lament over the years: "It's easy *to write* a book. It's pretty easy *to get an agent*. It's not even that hard *to sell a few copies* of your book. But what's hard — really hard — is to find people who have actually *read* your book! These people are priceless, because they are so few and far between." To Dean's points, I would add that it's even more rare to find individuals who have *applied* the concepts and tools and *reaped rewards* from their investments of time and energy.

> *What has been will be again, what has been done will be done again; there is nothing new under the sun.*
>
> Ecclesiastes 1:9

> *We are not voices, only echoes.*
>
> Dr. Mark Bailey

I reflect on those whose journeys were thwarted before they even began and I wonder to myself, "What if only they had tried? Just *tried*?" In ancient times, the edges of our known world were often demarcated with the foreboding and ominous phrase, "Here be dragons." Of course, we know today that such ignorance is folly and that as a species we hunger to know more, be more, do more. In many cases, we are *defined* by our pursuits moreso than our accomplishments. Consider the words of John F. Kennedy (quoting Robert Browning): "Man's reach should exceed his grasp, or what's a heaven for?" Or of Aristotle: "We are all teleological beings."[9] As a rule, nature abhors a vacuum and yet the best intentioned, well-informed, and respectable members of society can fall prey to *the presumptuousness of certainty* and believe the misconceived delusion that *the book is closed* on strategy. By way of proof, I submit the following 20 examples of closed-mindedness that, in equal parts, elicit dismay and laughter at the exhibited shortsightedness. I am

---

[9] From the Greek *telos*, which connotes *goal-orientation*.

not naïve enough to believe that you will read them all — but they're here, should you feel zealous. And yes, I had a bear of a time restraining myself and limiting the list to *only* 20.

Drill for oil? You mean drill into the ground to try and find oil? You're crazy.
Anonymous driller whom Edwin L. Drake
tried to enlist to his project to drill for oil in 1859

In a few years, all the great physical constants will have been approximately estimated, and the only occupation which will then be left to the men of science will be to carry these measurements to another place of decimals.
James Clark Maxwell, 1871

Louis Pasteur's theory of germs is ridiculous fiction.
Pierre Pachet,
Professor of Physiology at Toulouse, 1872

This 'telephone' has too many shortcomings to be seriously considered as a means of communication. The device is inherently of no value to us.
Western Union internal memo, 1876

The more important fundamental laws and facts of physical science have all been discovered, and these are now so firmly established that the possibility of their ever being supplanted in consequence of new discoveries is exceedingly remote; future discoveries must be looked for in the sixth place of decimals.
Albert A. Michelson, 1894

Heavier-than-air flying machines are impossible.
Lord Kelvin, 1895

Flight by machines heavier than air is unpractical and insignificant, if not utterly impossible.

> Simon Newcomb, 1902,
> 18 months before Kitty Hawk

Airplanes are interesting toys but of no military value.

> Marechal Ferdinand Foch,
> Professor of Strategy,
> Ecole Superieure de Guerre, 1911

Everything that can be invented has been invented.

> [Attributed to] Charles H. Duell, Commissioner,
> U.S. Office of Patents, 1899

The wireless music box has no imaginable commercial value. Who would pay for a message sent to nobody in particular?

> Anonymous associates of David Sarnoff in response to his urgings for investment in the radio in the 1920s

Professor Goddard does not know the relation between action and reaction and the need to have something better than a vacuum against which to react. He seems to lack the basic knowledge ladled out daily in high schools.

> New York Times, in editorial about Robert Goddard's revolutionary rocket work, 1921

Who the hell wants to hear actors talk?

> H.M. Warner,
> founder of Warner Brothers film studios, 1927

Stocks have reached what looks like a permanently high plateau.

> Irving Fisher, 1929

I think there is a world market for maybe five computers.

> Thomas Watson, Chairman of IBM, 1943

I have traveled the length and breadth of this country and talked with the best people, and I can assure you that data processing is a fad that won't last out the year.

> Editor in charge of business books, Prentice Hall, 1957

The concept is interesting and well formed, but in order to earn better than a 'C,' the idea must be feasible.

> Anonymous Yale University management professor in response to Fred Smith's paper proposing reliable overnight delivery service; Smith went on to found FedEx

But what…is it good for?

> Anonymous engineer at the Advanced Computing Systems Division of IBM, 1968, commenting on the microchip

So we went to Atari and said, "Hey, we've got this amazing thing, even built with some of your parts, and what do you think about funding us? Or we'll give it to you. We just want to do it. Pay our salary, we'll come work for you. And they said, 'No.' So then we went to Hewlett-Packard, and they said, 'Hey, we don't need you. You haven't got through college yet.'"

> Steve Jobs, founder of Apple Computer, Inc. on attempts to get Atari and HP interested in his personal computer

There is no reason anyone would want a computer in their home.

> Ken Olson, Founder/Chairman/President of Digital Equipment Corporation, 1977

640K ought to be enough for anybody.

> Bill Gates, 1981

Hope
Just What, Precisely, Is Strategy?

The beginning of wisdom is the definition of terms.

Socrates

Nothing you can't spell will ever work.

Will Rogers

Gimme:[10] *We are not all attracted to the same shiny objects.* I am a lover of language and context and, as a general rule, thrive on perspective and exploring the history and boundaries of topics. If you are not in this particular camp and do not wish to make a meal out of what might otherwise be a snack, I fully appreciate that and offer this reprieve: *Skip ahead and let's rendezvous at* **Beyond Origins, Etymology, and the Literature to Real Life.** (You simply may not have the stomach for this gluttonous excursion and I never want to be accused of not giving you an out.)

Go to the granddaddy of definitions and etymology, the *Oxford English Dictionary*, and here's what you'll find:

> **strategy**
> noun (PL. -ies) a plan of action or policy designed to achieve a major or overall aim: *time to develop a coherent economic strategy* | [MASS NOUN] *shifts in marketing strategy*.
> n [MASS NOUN] the art of planning and directing overall military operations and movements in a war or battle. Often contrasted with tactics (see TACTIC). a plan for such military operations and movements: *non-provocative defense strategies*.
> —ORIGIN early 19th cent.: from French *stratégie*, from Greek *strategia* 'generalship,' from *strategos* (see STRATAGEM).

---

[10] In golf, a **gimme** is that shot we agree *counts* without actually being played. For the diehard or academician interested in a somewhat full exposition on the confounding past of *strategy*, read on. For the reader interested in cutting more to the chase, please skip ahead a few pages and I'll catch up with you on the next shot.

This might seem encouraging, because whereas other dictionaries seem to zig and zag in their interpretations, the OED seems to clarify what strategy is by contrasting it with *tactics*, which it is not. But then (much to one's dismay), when flipping to the T's in the OED, here's what is found for tactic:

tactic

[noun] an action or *strategy* carefully planned to achieve a specific end.

n (tactics) [also treated as SING.] the art of disposing armed forces in order of battle and of organizing operations, especially during contact with an enemy. Often contrasted with STRATEGY.
—DERIVATIVES
—ORIGIN mid 18th cent.: from modern Latin *tactica*, from Greek *taktike (tekhne)* '(art) of tactics,' feminine of *taktikos*, from *taktos* 'ordered, arranged,' from the base of *tassein* 'arrange.'

Here's where the murkiness occurs. In the venerable OED, we see initially that *strategy* and *tactic* are contrasts — two ends of a spectrum — then moments later we see the word strategy used as part of the definition for tactic. Are they different, or are they one in the same? It's no wonder that in the midst of "strategic planning sessions," people's eyes glaze over and groups emerge (after *hours* together in the same room) confused and with multiple interpretations of what just occurred, what commitments were made, and what *strategies* and *tactics* were identified.

In 1964, U.S. Supreme Court Justice Potter Stewart tried to explain *pornography* and the definition of what is obscene by commenting, "I shall not today attempt further to define the kinds of material I understand to be embraced...*but I know it when I see it.*"[11]

This comment effectively summarizes the difficulty of trying to define obscenity and, for at least 53 years, the Supreme Court has been struggling with the meaning of it. Strategy suffers from the exact same ailment — and this explains a great deal of the variability regarding *expectations of performance* and *execution* among leaders and within organizations.

---

[11] http://en.wikipedia.org/wiki/Jacobellis_v._Ohio.

Review of Representative Findings in the Literature

There are many articles, white papers, books, texts, dissertations, and treatises on strategy, but fewer works on the attributes of exemplary strategists. Before proceeding however, it is important to familiarize ourselves with a few representative works made by pioneers whose efforts run the gamut from obscure to popular. If nothing else, these examples will shed some light upon whose shoulders we stand today and the scope of existing work that shapes our current understanding of strategy. Again, the thrust of *Cultivating the Strategic Mind* is to illuminate the practices of *strategists-as-individuals* and, ultimately, *systems thinking*, too. Neither of these inquiries is attainable without a shared understanding of *strategy* as a word, a body of work, and a field of study.

Table 1: *Sample Findings, Literature Review of Dominant Strategy Theories*

Author	Limited Summary
1. Sun Tzu (100 BCE)	*The Art of War* - Laying Plans, Waging War, The Sheathed Sword; Tactics; Energy, Weak and Strong Points, Maneuvering, Variation of Tactics, The Army on the March, Terrain, Nine Situations, Attack by Fire, Foreknowledge, The Use of Spies.
2. Carl von Clausewitz (1832)	*On War* - What is War, End and Means in War, The Genius for War, Of Danger in War, Information in War; Definitions of Strategy and Tactics, Elements of Strategy, War and Commerce, Politics, the Dual Nature of War.
3. Baron Antoine Henri de Jomini (1870)	*Art of War* - The Relation of Diplomacy to War, Military Policy, Strategic Lines & Points, Objective Points of Operation.
4. Michael Porter (1980)	*Porter's Generic Strategies* - Cost Leadership, Differentiation, Focus. Focus outward (on the enviroment) then focus inward and adjust.
5. Tom Peters and Robert Waterman (1982)	*In Search of Excellence* - Bias for Action, Close to the Customer, Autonomy and Entrepreneurship, Productivity Through People, Hands-on, Value Driven, Stick to the Knitting, Simple Form, Lean Staff, Simultaneous Loose/Tight Properties.

Author	Limited Summary
6. Kenichi Ohmae (1982)	*Mind of the Strategist* - Strategic Triangle: Company, Customer, Competition. Focus on the stream and the environment.
7. C. Wiseman, N. Rackoff, W. Ulrich (1985)	*Theory of Strategic Thrusts* - Differentiation, Cost, Innovation, Growth, Alliance Across Supplier, Customer, Competitor.
8. Gary Hamel and C.K. Prahalad (1990)	*Competing for the Future* - The Core Competence of the Corporation, Strategic Intent. Focus inward.
9. Robert Kaplan and David Norton (1992)	*The Strategy-Focused Organization: How Balanced Scorecard Companies Thrive in the New Business Environment* - Balanced Scorecard, Strategy Maps. Strategy Through Financial and Business Processes, Learning & Growth, and Customer.
10. N. Venkatraman, J.C. Henderson, S.H. Oldach (1993)	*Strategic Alignment Model* - Strategy Execution Technology Potential, Competitive Potential, Service Level.
11. Jim Collins and Jerry Porras (1994)	*Built to Last: Successful Habits of Visionary Companies* - Greater Degree than the Comparison, Arrived Syndrome, Heroic Customer Service, Clock Builder, Big Hairy Audacious Goals.
12. Colin Gray (1999)	*Modern Strategy* - Dimensions of Strategy, Politics & Ethics in Strategy, Strategic Culture, Legend of Clausewitz, Patterns.
13. Marcus Buckingham and Curt Coffman (1999)	*First, Break All the Rules: What the World's Greatest Managers Do Differently* - (1) Do I know what is expected of me at work? (2) Do I have the materials and equipment I need to do my work right? (3) At work, do I have the opportunity to do what I do best every day? (4) In the last seven days, have I received recognition or praise for doing good work? (5) Does my supervisor, or someone at work, seem to care about me as a person? (6) Is there someone at work who encourages my development? (7) At work, do my opinions seem to count? (8) Does the mission/purpose of my company make me feel my job is important? (9) Are my co-workers committed to doing quality work? (10) Do I have a good friend at work? (11) In the last six months, has someone at work talked to me about my progress? (12) This last year, have I had opportunities at work to learn and grow?

Author	Limited Summary
14. Robert Kaplan and David Norton (2000)	*The Strategy Focused Organization* - Strategy translated into organizational terms, Aligning organization to strategy, Making strategy everyone's day job, Strategy as a continual process, Change through leadership.
15. Jim Collins (2001)	*Good to Great: Why Some Companies Make the Leap and Others Don't* - Good is the enemy of great, Level 5 Leadership, First who then what, Confront the brutal facts, Hedgehog Concept, Culture of Discipline, Technology Accelerators, Flywheel, Doomloop.
16. Mike Freedman with Benjamin B. Tregoe (2003)	*The Art and Discipline of Strategic Leadership* - Strategic Time Frame, Strategy Implementation Thrust for Growth, Market Matrix.
17. David Morey and Scott Miller (2004)	*Insurgent Strategy* - Political Campaign Model, Do the Doable, Move the Movable, Play Offense, Communicate Inside-Out, Forget Reality (perception rules), Herd the Details (everything communicates), Deal with Crisis as SOP, Be Rebels with a Cause.
18. Jeffrey Liker (2004)	*The Toyota Way: 14 Management Principles From the World's Greatest Manufacturer* - (1) Base your management decisions on a long-term philosophy, even at the expense of short-term financial goals, (2) Create continual process flow to bring problems to the surface, (3) Use "pull" systems to avoid overproduction, (4) Level out the workload, (5) Build a culture of stopping to fix problems and get quality right the first time, (6) Standardized tasks are the foundation for continuous improvement and employee empowerment, (7) Use visual control so no problems are hidden, (8) Use only reliable, thoroughly tested technology that serves your people and processes, (9) Grow leaders who understand the work, live the philosophy, and teach it to others, (10) Develop exceptional people and teams who follow your philosophy, (11) Respect your extended network of partners and suppliers by challenging them and helping them improve, (12) Go and see for yourself to understand the system, (13) Make decisions slowly by consensus, considering all options, implement decisions rapidly, (14) Become a learning organization through relentless reflection and continuous improvement.

Author	Limited Summary
19. Saj-nicole A. Joni (2004)	*Habit of Mind* - Application thinking (mapping the known onto the unknown). A focus on planning and implementing well-understood methods in ways that yield replicable results. Expert thinking (invoking deep understanding of a specific subject). Exponential thinking (exploring new terrain with new frameworks).
20. W. Chan Kim and Renee Mauborgne (2005)	*Blue Ocean Strategy: How to Create Uncontested Market Space and Make Competition Irrelevant* - Red oceans represent all the industries in existence today. Known market space. In the red oceans, industry boundaries are defined and accepted, and the competitive rules of the game are known. Here companies try to outperform their rivals to grab a greater share of existing demand. As the market space gets more and more crowded, prospects for profits and growth are reduced. Products become commodities, and cutthroat competition turns the ocean bloody. Blue oceans denote all the industries not in existence today. This is unknown market space. Blue oceans are defined by untapped market space, demand creation, and the opportunity for highly profitable growth. While blue oceans are occasionally created well beyond existing industry boundaries, most are created by expanding existing industry boundaries (e.g., Cirque du Soleil). In blue oceans, competition is irrelevant as the rules of the game are waiting to be set.
21. Kenichi Ohmae (2005)	*The Next Global Stage: The Challenges and Opportunities in Our Borderless World* - New economics, Leveraging platforms for growth, Technology obsolescence (jumping ahead of it), Government in the post-national era, Leadership/Strategy/Vision.

What can we glean from this table? Numerous takeaways, I'm certain, but here are just a few thoughts that come to mind.

1. There are *many* great strategy-oriented concepts. Often, this is the problem. As strategists, it's difficult knowing which one(s) to engage.

2. There does not appear to be a one-size-fits-all approach that everyone can *plug 'n play*. Each organization must consider for itself what approach would work best. You've surely heard the sales maxim, "Make it easy for people to buy." Well, the selection hurdle of strategy makes "buying" quite difficult.

3. There are many redundant, overlapping, or complementary approaches. In some instances, these help us *see potential best practices*. Three particular models: *The Strategic Triune, The Mind Map,* and *The Omniscience Octagon* articulate great findings about strategic and systemic thought and execution.

4. Many existing approaches uncouple *strategy* from *execution* or portray the relationship between the two as linear and sequential. There is a *dynamic* relationship between strategy and execution with *nonlinear* and *concurrent* dimensionalities.

5. Across the literature, strategic thinking appears to come in what might be described as four common flavors:

    a. *Strategy as insight into industry dynamics and customer needs.* The focus with this flavor is striving to be novel, distinctive, analytical, or intellectual — ignoring results achieved.

    b. *Strategy as a long view.* The focus with this flavor is a stepped plan or vision of the future, ignoring immediate/current needs.

c. *Strategy as the province of the CEO, Board, and other Executives.* The focus with this flavor fails to optimally involve and mobilize the very individuals who will be tasked with implementation.
d. *Strategy as THE driver of decisions, organization, and operations.* The focus of this flavor often ignores core strengths, capabilities, competencies, and people.

A Few Points of Clarification: Strategic/Systemic Thinking vs. Strategic Planning & Strategic Management

All too often (in fact, almost always), I hear "strategic planning" used and described when people are wanting "strategic thinking." Let's contrast strategic thinking with terminology that occupies adjacent space — sometimes resulting in confusion.

1. Strategic Thinking involves Systems Thinking, which accounts for pondering value creation from beginning to end and understanding all interdependencies within the chain.
2. Strategic Thinking involves an *integrated perspective of the enterprise;* a view of the big picture and the operational implications.
3. Strategic Thinking is NOT formulating *strategies* to develop an *action plan.* This is *definitely* Strategic Planning.
4. Strategic Thinking is not *filling out forms.* Those annual gyrations that require one to think about next year do not remotely approximate true strategic thinking.
5. Strategic Thinking *is* creativity, innovation, exploration, thinking anew, identifying, questioning, challenging the status quo, surfacing, testing, proving, and disproving.

Beyond Origins, Etymology, and the Literature to Real Life

We have now looked at strategy through two keyholes. First, we considered it by way of definitions, but found ourselves still wanting. Second, we considered it through a literature review and, while our understanding of strategy is much richer now, we still find ourselves grasping for a bit more clarity. While I won't dive into as much detail as I did in the prior two keyholes, I will suggest that there is indeed a third keyhole through which one can view strategy: *examples from the field.*

How do we *measure* or *quantify* the success of strategy? How do we know if we're winning, losing, or just treading water? One way to broach a clearer understanding of strategy is to observe it in the real world, in realms where its success (or failure) is rather black and white. Beyond *business,*[12] consider these four realms in which strategy plays out daily, and wherein its results are often quite obvious: *Politics, Military, Sports,* and *Medicine.*

If we were to look at politics, we would see specific examples of strategies winning (or costing) elections.

For example, Bill Clinton's strategy in his '96 re-election campaign was to enhance differences between himself and his Republican opposition on issues that benefited Democrats (Medicare, Medicaid, education, environment) and to blur differences on issues that benefited Republicans (crime, taxes, balanced budget, welfare reform, family values). By enhancing differences on favorable issues, he was playing to his natural strengths. He was, in effect, mobilizing his base. By blurring differences on less favorable issues, and by co-opting elements of Republican rhetoric, he was able to take many of these issues off the table and, in so doing, opened the door

---

[12] Sure, we could dissect several common business examples utilizing the *case method* and explore such high-profile strategies as executed by Johnson & Johnson when they worked to quell customers' fears in the infamous 1982 cyanide scare or GM's efforts to meet a changing market by spinning off a new company called Saturn, but sometimes it's refreshing and insightful to look outside one's immediate sphere to expand our thinking. If we were to look for business examples of strategy, as so many of us have before, we would undoubtedly see examples of failed products, market research, and kite-high successes like Starbucks, Apple, The Container Store, Nordstrom, Southwest Airlines, and Google. We would also find evidence of good and bad strategies across non-profits, philanthropies, charities, churches, synagogues, mosques, and public and private organizations of all sizes and stripes, ranging from federal agencies to casinos on Native Americans' reservations.

to persuade swing voters that he was a reasonable, moderate, caring alternative to insensitive, extreme, overly partisan opposition. The tactics Clinton used to implement this strategy included early *positioning* TV spots in targeted markets ('Gingrich and Dole on Medicare') and a series of speeches ('the era of big government is over'), legislative proposals (school uniforms, opposition to teenage smoking) and bill signings (welfare reform).[13]

If we study military examples of strategy, as they do at West Point, the Naval Academy, the Air Force Academy, the Citadel, Virginia Military Institute, and so many other fine institutions, we see enough examples to fill volumes, bodies of work, and entire fields of research. As I write this, in 2007 and again in 2017, the United States and coalition forces remain mired in Iraq. The U.S. strategy, or perceived lack thereof, is an extremely contentious issue with no neat closure in sight. The same could be said of many military engagements throughout history.

The world of sports provides a forum where the outcomes of strategies are immediate and obvious. From teams that build dynasties to those who fail season after season, the strategy game is constantly, as Sherlock Holmes would say, "afoot."

Medicine, and medical research, too, provides an arena where keeping score is often possible by tracking the successes and failures of experimental drugs and protocols, as well as mortality rates and quality of life. We see examples each day of the toll taken on people's lives who fail to eat properly, care for themselves, or make wise decisions regarding their health. From *diets* (rather than sustainable, long-term *eating* strategies) and *exercise blitzes* (rather than sustainable, long-term *movement* strategies) to our ill-conceived attempts to offer treatment rather than create *health* or *wellness*, we see strategies operating as the invisible forces behind countless medical and medicinal efforts.

As any great strategist knows, there is much to be gleaned by looking beyond the confines of one's own fishbowl when searching for unique or eclectic solutions to recurring problems. We each possess personal and cultural worldviews and limiting beliefs that

---

[13] *Strategies That Win: Political Campaigning, Campaigns & Elections,* December 1997 by Ron Faucheux.

can become barriers to strategic thinking. Here are some fascinating trivia and examples of strategies from around the world — many of which hint at solutions to problems that plague numerous societies.[14]

1. Handford Road in Ipswich, England, is busy, and devoid of the usual stop signs, speed limit signs, lane lines, and plentiful traffic lights. Perhaps counterintuitively, their absence results in more polite drivers who graciously yield to others — bikers and pedestrians among them. By removing the usual *traffic management tools,* they have also removed the accompanying false sense of security. Nature has filled this vacuum with more eye contact, situational awareness, safety, and social responsibility. Holland's similarly designed *Shared Space* program is a fascinating strategy that reveals the notion of what can be described as the empowerment paradox: *To positively influence human behavior, don't try to control it.*

2. One in ten trips in Berlin is made by bicycle. In the Netherlands, it's one in four. Pollution, traffic, and overall transportation costs are less, health is up, and the biggest challenge is finding enough spaces for the thousands of bicycles left daily at local train stations.

3. In the Dominican Republic, baseball is more than a sport: It's a way of life, it's a form of play, and it's a promise. Since 1958, 440 major league players and nearly 25 percent of all minor league players were produced by this teensy-weensy Caribbean nation with a population of less than nine million. For D.R. youths, baseball is about honest-to-goodness *fun*...it's *play*. Yes, many children dream of making it out of poverty by way of the big leagues, but as children play pick-up games in fields and streets, one won't see coaches, scorekeepers, or explosive parents perverting the game. Ironically,

---

[14] *How They Do It Better,* U.S. News & World Report, March 26 - April 2, 2007. Contributing authors include Susan Headden, Andrew Curry, Peter Cary, David LaGesse, Lisa Moore, Will Sullivan, Eduardo Cue, Paul J. Lim, Beth Brophy, Angie C. Marek, Kim Palmer, Diana Cole, Adam Voiland, Thomas K. Grose, Elizabeth Weiss Green, Dean Clark, Linda Creighton, Alison Go, Todd Georgelas, Bret Schulte, and David E. Kaplan.

because many D.R. children play for hours each day and many days per week, the game has become life, and in doing so, remains purer. With less pressure and focus on winning, a disproportionately large number of *winners* derive from here.

4. In Colombia, rather than invest the millions required for a significant train infrastructure, the National Bus Rapid Transit Institute has found a way to make buses sexy, and even the upper-middle-class boards by hoards on a daily basis.

5. In Finland, thanks to egalitarianism, traffic fines (known as *day fines*) are calculated based on net income after taxes. The purpose is to align the severity of fines with one's disposable income. (For example, a local heir to a family fortune was fined $204,000 for driving 50 mph in a 25 mph zone.) The system is praised by most citizens who see it as an extremely democratic solution. Furthermore, the revenues generated help fund Finland's world-class services like free education and healthcare for all.

6. More kudos to Finland: According to the Program for International Student Assessment (PISA), Finnish students consistently score at the top in reading, math, and science and rank first among 40 industrialized nations in reading literacy, science (tied with Japan), and second in math. (The U.S. ranked 18th, 22nd, and 28th in those respective subjects.) Additionally, because Finnish classes are maximally heterogeneous, the gap between the strongest and the weakest students is negligible. In Finland, all teachers possess a master's degree and hold a status similar to that of doctors and lawyers in the U.S. Student textbooks, lunches, healthcare, and transportation come free. Because parents have tremendous freedom in selecting schools for their children, competition fosters best practices and ensures long-term high-performance among students and teachers alike.

7. In much of the Pacific Rim, one's *mobile* is much more than a phone — it's what we know it to be in America — *plus* a TV remote control and a debit/credit card, too. One can envision the day when it might function as a digital car key, replace the driver's license, retain personal measurements for the tailor, and much, much more.

8. Here's the *Quality of Life* top 10: Zurich, Geneva, Vancouver, Vienna, Auckland, Düsseldorf, Frankfurt, Munich, and Bern (tied with Sydney). (No U.S. city makes the top 20.)

9. In Japan, more and more homes and commercial facilities are replacing traditional toilets with *toilet-paper-free* versions.[15] Some makes-and-models go so far as to monitor one's weight, blood pressure, urine sugar content, and body fat.

10. In Japan, only 3.6 percent of adults are obese. In America, the number is 32 percent. Due to a fish-rich diet and smaller portions, overall Japanese health, vitality, and life expectancy set the standard.

11. In the Netherlands — a country no larger than Maryland — were it not for 10,000 miles of dikes, dams, dunes, sluices, and floodgates keeping the sea at bay, an estimated 65 percent of the country would be Atlantis. At a cost of $14.7 billion, the 50-year effort to create this infrastructure ensures the tiny country can withstand forces 50 times more powerful than a Category 5 hurricane — like Katrina, the behemoth that obliterated much of New Orleans.

12. Though initially surprising yet expectedly logical, aged prostitutes in Germany have been given a new lease on life as caretakers for the elderly. Think about it: *good with people, good listeners, and not afraid to touch people's bodies.* The trainees are part of an innovative effort to address a serious manpower shortage wherein a third of the population will be over age 65 by year 2050.

---

[15] Think *bidet*.

13. In Sweden, sex-ed begins at age six and the teenage birthrate is seven per 1,000 vs. America's 49. Twelve percent of Swedish girls are having sex before the age of 15. In the U.S., 14 percent do. Among American girls ages 15-19, there are 600 times as many reported cases of gonorrhea on a per capita basis than in Sweden. For six-year-olds, the curriculum begins with anatomical overviews. For teens, the curriculum addresses disease, contraception, and yes, even morality — where sex in the context of a loving relationship is stressed. Swedes view sex as a natural act, incorporating it into education and mainstream society in ways that remove the taboo and, correspondingly, the ignorance.

14. In Chinese medicine, naps are a good thing. As a result, 15 to 30-minute naps after lunch are commonplace in Taiwan. U.S. research published in the *Journal of Occupational and Environmental Medicine* indicates that fatigued and unproductive American workers cost $136.4 billion annually. Fifty-one percent of the U.S. workforce reports that sleepiness on the job interferes with the volume of work they do. In 75 percent of U.S. companies operating beyond 9 to 5, 3/4 explicitly disallow napping. The Exxon Valdez oil spill, the Union Carbide chemical explosion in India, and Chernobyl are viewed as having occurred, in part, due to employee fatigue.[16]

15. In Japan, thanks in large part to Buddhist traditions associating cleaning with morality, students pause for *souji* time — a period of about 15 minutes each day when students, teachers, and administrators pause and give everything a good scrub. Most schools don't employ janitors, and cleaning becomes integral to the varied web of activities that signal to children their value to their community and society at large.

---

[16] Also see *Take a Nap! Change Your Life*, by Sara Mednick, a sleep expert at the University of California — San Diego's Laboratory of Sleep and Behavioral Neuroscience.

16. In Singapore, antisocial behavior like spitting or dropping trash on the ground carries steep fines in excess of $1,000 plus community service that is designed to create shame. Needless to say, litterbugs are aberrations.

17. To say that Norway loves parents would be an understatement. Fifty-three weeks of maternity leave at 80 percent pay with assurance that one's job will be waiting afterward, five weeks of paid paternity leave, five weeks of vacation (the national standard), generous day-care options, a 37.5-hour workweek, and a government grant for a parent who stays home with his or her child from age one to two.

18. Bhutan is the first country to completely ban smoking. Twenty percent of the government's budget is earmarked for education and health, ensuring the king's (yes, the king's) plan for "gross national happiness" succeeds.

19. Politically speaking, Iceland, Finland, and New Zealand are the least corrupt countries in the world.[17] With upwards of 85 percent of the voting populaces politically involved, these small and quite homogeneous cultures foster record-high levels of accountability. Interestingly, these countries — particularly Iceland — possess stable, common languages and intergenerational stability, both of which facilitate unity and groupism...which are common predictors for stability. Simply put: There's a self-governing system in play (among citizens) that boosts self-governance (among politicians).

20. In the UK, Australia, and New Zealand, many students participate in international travel, work, and teaching assignments between high school and college. This *gap year* has become assumed and provides first-year college students with a global perspective, increased initiative, better decision-making abilities, and overall life skills.[18]

---

[17] See Transparency International's 2006 *International Corruption Perceptions Index* for more information.

[18] Visit www.gapyear.com or www.goabroad.com to learn more.

21. The top 10 in *Environmental Performance:* New Zealand, Sweden, Finland, Czech Republic, United Kingdom, Austria, Denmark, Canada, Ireland (and Malaysia, tie).[19] The U.S. comes in at #28.
22. Twenty percent of electrical needs in Denmark are met through wind power.
23. All European countries have a taxpayer-funded healthcare system. Britain spends $2,546 per person/year; the U.S. spends $6,102. Yes, Americans with healthcare receive much quicker responses from primary physicians and have more choices, but again, not everyone has healthcare. Britain trumps the U.S. in emergency and trauma care.
24. *Life Expectancy,* the top 11 (in years): Andorra (83.5), Japan (82.8), Hong Kong (82.2), Iceland (81.4), Switzerland (81.1), Austria (81.0), Sweden (80.8), Canada and Macau (80.7), Israel and Italy (80.6). The U.S. ranks 40th.

The purpose of my sharing these statistics and diverse examples of strategic solutions to typical societal challenges is to emphasize a point: Strategy is not some conceptual enigma, and it certainly isn't confined or defined by something as narrow as *business.* Strategy is ubiquitous and discernible; it is tangible and its consequences have volume, girth, weight. In so many cases, we can readily observe strategies play out, and we should exploit as many opportunities as possible to be students of successful and failed strategies in equal measure, that we might deepen and broaden our capabilities.

To amplify the omnipresence of strategy, consider *Selective Perception*. Selective Perception is the phenomenon whereby one's attentiveness to a particular stimulus or object is heightened corollary to one's newfound awareness of this stimulus or object. For example, if an individual were to decide he wanted to purchase a Jeep vehicle, he is extremely likely to notice or see Jeep vehicles disproportionately

---

[19] The index utilized accounts for air quality, environmental health, water resources, biodiversity and habitat, sustainable energy, and productive natural resources.

more frequently than prior to making this buying decision. I notice selective perception all the time and, logically, most readily in myself.

Mind-talk is the tape we each play in our heads all the time; some people *realize* these tapes are playing and can analyze and *reprogram* them, while other people play the tapes but don't realize they're playing. A common yet unhealthy example of mind-talk is seen among those unfortunate individuals who are victims of childhood trauma or abuse. It is not unusual at all for them to re-play very negative, angry, critical, self-destructive tapes for the remainder of their lives. One might wonder why the cycle of abuse is so hard to break when, in fact, the *software* in their minds has been programmed to repeat the loop of code continually. Fortunately, many people are able to record new and positive content over the old content, but its residue remains forever, just as it did on those cassette tapes some of us used throughout the '80s.

Here are some real examples of Selective Perception that should clarify what I'm striving to communicate:

- I remember (three years ago) my wife decided we should take our then two-year-old daughter to Disney World in Orlando. For the next several weeks, we each noticed *Disney stuff* everywhere — from commercials and magazine ads to plush toys in malls.

- After the passing of our son due to complications from Trisomy 18, as we dealt with the loss and grief and considered adoption, we noticed grieving and adoptive families everywhere we turned.
- I'm currently in the process of coming to grips with my aging yet beloved laptop whose planned obsolescence is imminent. You better believe I'm seeing Lenovos and MacBooks everywhere I turn.
- I was recently at a State Fair. While I've never been a health nut, I had recently watched a powerful TV show that described with harrowing gloom the future of America's children and the *obesity epidemic*. As I stood in the midway at the fair, I literally became repulsed by the pungent odors emanating from so many gypsy-like set-ups pumping out fried foods, corn dogs, ten-inch turkey legs, cotton candy, oversized colas, drippy buckets of popcorn, caramel apples, snow cones, eight-inch pretzels, and the like. As I walked, my shoes adhered to the asphalt, stuck to the grimy juices left by this culinary plague. Looking around, I noticed beer belly after beer belly, and looking down at my own expanding waistline, I committed to abstain from a third helping of crap.
- When I worked with a glassware manufacturer, I found myself turning every water glass upside down to search for their logo.
- When I worked with an airline, I found myself noticing the *cast of thousands* in every major airport required to pull off the logistical feats that I had formerly ignored.
- When I worked with an internet company, I noticed their commercials and collateral splashed all over the media on a daily basis.

When we are stimulated in some way by a new mental object, our attentiveness toward it increases correspondingly and our internal radar emits alarms with greater frequency. As strategists, it is important we notice the all-too-often *unnoticed* aspects of everyday life. I encourage you to and commend you in advance for seeing strategy everywhere in its natural habitats, for it is undoubtedly unfolding almost everywhere on a constant basis.

Toward an Understanding of Terms: Strategic & Systemic

> *Before I studied kung-fu, a punch was just a punch. As a student of kung-fu, a punch became much more than 'just a punch.' Now that I have 'mastered' kung-fu, a punch is just a punch.*
>
> Bruce Lee

As Mr. Lee indicates, when one is uninformed about a particular topic — unaware of its nuances or depths — it can appear utterly simple. In hindsight, I see this in my childhood with regard to most everything, and I certainly see it in my own daughter. The machinations of airplanes, gravity, chlorophyll, and fog would be handy examples. And as an adult the expression, *the more you learn the less you know,* proves accurate on a regular basis. But as Bruce concludes, he reminds us that (while even *he* acknowledged no *mastery* in kung-fu, but rather an ongoing journey of understanding) with competence, what was once simple — then complex — often becomes simple again.

Take this childhood recollection: I remember seeing letters as shapes, and knowing they had meanings but being ignorant of the meanings themselves. And yes, the shapes were simple. Circles, tails, lines, and squiggles. How hard could this be? With time, I noticed these shapes everywhere — on road signs, on the dashboard and instrument panel, in the books my parents read to me, on menus... they were inescapably everywhere. Eventually, I arrived at the age where it was time to learn their uniqueness, their topography, their sound...and how their shapes and types combine to form *different* sounds, and how syllables combine to form words, and how words combine to form phrases and sentences, and how sentences combine to form meaningful language. In time, every facet of language became a part of our collective, daily studies. Each of us has spent untold hours diagramming sentences, learning synonyms and antonyms, and writing short stories about what we did over our summer vacation. These building blocks and exercises were committed to memory in our subconscious, and we summon this second-hand prowess to navigate the world without thinking.

In other words, what was initially simple, then complex, is simple again — and yet, as a 'D' on a homework assignment reminded us perhaps 15 years after we'd begun this journey — what appears simple often possesses complexity.

It is against this truth that I repeat, *strategy appears to be a simple thing*. But, as we continue unpacking it together it will become more complex than before due to the appearance of some new, unseen facets. We will then re-assemble and re-pack, and while its compactness will facilitate portability, it will also make it richer.

Let's proceed.

Strategy:

A *systemic* means to achieve the desired *endgame* that leverages:
1. **philosophical and polymathic pragmatism** with
2. **holistic thinking** and
3. **inclusive ownership.**

Assuming we will adopt the above definition, we must have an agreed upon definition for *system,* too, because it is a lynchpin of strategy and, without both, we'll get nowhere.

System: *Our Working Definition for* **Cultivating the Strategic Mind**

A ❶ *dynamic,* ❷ *interdependent relationship* among ❸ **elements/subsystems** which ❹ **interact** and ❺ **generate** ever-changing ❻ **permutations**.

Systems can range from...
- **music** (notes and pitch combine to generate melody) and
- **business** (providers and consumers combine to generate markets) to
- **medicine** (symptoms and diagnoses combine to generate protocols) and
- **conflict** (constituents and ideologies combine to generate war)

Nothing of social significance occurs in isolation. Strategy is no exception and its DNA lends itself to holistic integration within an organization. *That's* why strategy cannot be entirely understood, much less executed without an appreciation of *systems.*

As defined above, **strategy** is *a systemic means to achieve the desired endgame.* In my mind, a system is comprised of six attributes:

(1) a *dynamic,*

(2) *interdependent relationship* among

(3) *elements* or *subsystems*

(4) *interacting with each other* and

(5) *generating constantly shifting/morphing*

(6) *permutations.*

While it may appear that I'm overcomplicating the simple, I am not. There is indeed method to my madness. As we did in high school biology, let's dissect the frog one tiny part at a time.

First, systems are *dynamic*. They are fluid. A system is not stagnant. As Heraclitus wrote, "Time is a river you cannot step into twice." Systems are no different; they are constantly flowing, and while they often re-circulate, that's no guarantee that what will come around next time is what came around last time.

Second, systems are denoted by *interdependent relationships*. In other words, systems are not about autonomy or independence but rather, by definition, are about the dance and interplay between — and defined by — the interaction itself. "Without each part, there is no whole," we might say.

Third, systems are comprised of *elements or subsystems*. Sort of the proton/neutron idea. The more we dig, as scientists and observers, the more we find there are no isolated parts, only parts within parts within parts and strings within matter. Think of the world as a series of nested dolls. Each larger doll is removed to reveal a smaller doll within, ad infinitum. This strikes at the very heart of systems, which are defined by such interrelatedness.

Fourth, systems are — as initially teed up through the notion of interdependent relationships — about *interaction*. Systems evolve, change, and in many instances of open systems, self-organize as we see with flocks of birds, schools of fish, swarms of bees (and termites and ants), rivers, spontaneous magnetization, turbulence, convection, avalanches, hurricanes, forest fires, tectonic shifts, traffic jams, critical mass, herding, groupthink, epidemics, fractals, friction, stock markets, poker games, eBay, and even social media, particularly items that go viral or trend within minutes.

Fifth, systems are *generative*. They are forces of creation and production. Whether it's waste or fuel, the systems I'm talking about throw off energy, build energy, and often violate two of the three fundamental laws of thermodynamics (the behavior of energy flow in natural systems). The Law of Energy Conservation states that *while energy can be converted from one form to another, it can neither be created nor annihilated.* The Law of Entropy states that *everything runs inexorably from order to disorder and from complexity to decay.* These two laws are truths in the purest respects, but haven't we all seen athletes, social movements, or miraculous efforts that have seemingly created new energy — that have evolved or re-animated from decay to life? I believe I have, and I hope you have too, because these phenomena lay waste to conventional thinking, and that can often be a great thing.

Sixth, systems yield new and often unexpected, unheralded *permutations*. They create things we never anticipated...never would have imagined. Whether we look at systems of animal cloning or memes or values like *liberty* introduced to countries in shackles, few people can predict what will come of all the tomorrows that stretch out before us.

It is within these six nerves — within this circulatory system of features — that our little germ of strategy takes root. This is profound, because we begin to see unfolding before us the elegant simplicity and sophistication of strategy and the realization that its cradle is an ever-changing picture, clicking along like the Zapruder[20] film in our collective consciousness. The more we study, question, and speculate via leaps predicated upon growing evidence, the more we see and understand the big picture. It is not some one-dimensional, stagnant photograph we can trim and paste in our scrapbook or annual report. Quite the contrary, it is lightning we hope to capture in (or at least direct toward) the proverbial bottle.

Strategy is vastly more than the intersection between *vision* and *tactics* or some *long-term means to an end*. These approach the truth but miss it by 1°, and by anyone's math, that's a long way from the bull's-eye. A sniper aiming at a target 1,000 meters away with a four mph crosswind will attest to this, as should any leader striving to be a strategist crafting five-year organizational plans in a dynamic, globally compressed marketplace the size of a BB. Off by a little? Might as well be off by a mile. Stay at home and sleep in; there's no use trying if you're just spitting in the wind anyway.

Next, we've got to peel back the thin layers of strategy even further and investigate the aspect of *endgame*. For starters, the idea of *endgame* has not been an omnipresent word in the lexicon of leaders. That's changing, as I have heard the word used with

---

[20] The infamous footage by Abraham Zapruder captures the presidential motorcade of John F. Kennedy through Dealey Plaza in Dallas, Texas, on November 22, 1963. The amateur film is the most complete visual recording of the assassination of President Kennedy.

greater frequency in the past three or four years. This is promising, because I believe it signals a revelation that there is something more than the idea of vision itself — and for me, at least, much of that realization has to do with endgame. So, what exactly is endgame? In his brilliant book, *Anatomy of Motive*, FBI profiler and pioneer John Douglas explains at length that serial killers, for instance, can be differentiated in several ways, not the least of which is whether they kill randomly, in a disorganized fashion, or purposefully with some orchestrated, organized, highly-ritualized endgame in mind. Similarly, throughout the past century of economic work and game theory, there is frequent dialogue about the notion of endgame and scenarios. Criminology and economics might initially appear unrelated, but the parallels are strong, starting with a shared focus on human motive.

Beyond vision then, the farther stake in the ground is endgame. For our purposes, let's define endgame as *the likely, significant reality looming in the contextual distance within which vision occurs.* It is paramount for leaders to understand this concept if they are to begin the leap that will transform them to full-fledged strategist status, because armed solely with vision and without a strong grasp on the endgame, a leader is a dreamer and optimist, but not a Stockdale Paradox-practicing realist who understands the consequences of and context in which visions unfold.[21] More to the point, a leader with vision and without endgame is Pollyanna.

Time Out

We've unpacked a lot in the past few pages. Let's summarize, acclimate, and re-group before we go any further.

1. First, there is clearly a substantive difference between the function, role, and person of *leader* and *strategist*. Indeed, the former are not always the latter. Similarly, we often relegate strategy to strategists, when many strategists fail as leaders. This conundrum illustrates my point that leaders and strategists are not synonymous. Whether the gap between a leader and a strategist is subtle (as in, perhaps

---

[21] Essentially, *reality-based fortitude* vs. naïveté. See Jim Collins' *Good To Great,* chapter 4, pages 83–85.

only 1°), it can also be dramatic, as in the case of the leader who mistakes *strategic planning* with *strategic thinking*.

2. It makes no sense to contemplate strategy without incorporating *systems thinking*. The two are intertwined, and I believe that strategy cannot be defined or understood without integrating the realities of what a system is.

3. There is an anatomy we're exploring here — *six aspects of a system* and eventually *three attributes of archetypal strategists* — that proves extremely useful and implementable in all organizations by leaders aspiring to become strategists, too. Having sketched out the six aspects of a system, I will introduce the three attributes of archetypal strategists in Part Two of our travels together.

But what of the six aspects, and where to now? If one heads far enough north, he eventually winds up turning south across the apex of the globe and yet, if one were to head east, one would never end up heading west. This puzzler is subtle yet instructive. Societally, it often feels as if we continue flying east hoping to somehow wind up heading west. Fly, fly, fly. Always buzzing, but never arriving anywhere different. We've each heard, "The definition of insanity is doing the same things, in the same ways as before, yet expecting a novel outcome next time" (variously attributed to Rita Mae Brown, Einstein, a Chinese proverb, and Rudyard Kipling, among countless others). Aren't we doing the same thing in terms of strategy? Don't we seem to repeat the same errors based on similar assumptions? Isn't it time for a dramatic course correction?

In 1960, Douglas McGregor published his work on *Theory X* and *Theory Y*,[22] and he described something that is often misinterpreted. McGregor wasn't writing about managers-as-people being Theory X or Theory Y — he was writing about their assumptions being X or Y. Notice the subtlety. The heart of McGregor's work is about assumptions: Managers making Theory X assumptions about people perceive the world quite differently than those who make Theory Y assumptions.

---

[22] *The Human Side of Enterprise,* 1960. See also *The Triune for Attraction & Retention: Creating a Culture of Good Leaders, a Great Workplace, and Sustaining Employer of Choice Designation,* yours truly.

A similar yet more labyrinthine phenomenon occurs with leaders-as-strategists. A leader who assumes *strategic thinking* is about his organization exercising itself through an annual *strategic planning* process is equivalent to a child playing dress-up. When we play at something with more depth than we perceive, we're lost in an illusion. As leaders, the dress-up that we mistake for strategic thinking is based on the impression that thinking and planning are one in the same, but they are not. Such assumptions drastically hamstring our potential. You see, the magic elixir of strategy is elemental, as foundational and basal and simple as movement, and yet when performed and demonstrated and seen at its peak, strategy is as rare as perfection, new world records, or selflessness. The questions must be asked by all of us, "What assumptions define our strategic gyrations? Are we exercising really hard, once a year at the corporate or executive level alone, or wisely and daily and throughout the organization as if everyone were the CEO or owner?"

Strategy, at its height, stands our neck hairs on end. When experienced, a collective hush befalls a group as all the air is sucked out of the room. Time slows down. Hearts beat louder, harder. We freeze, wondering if what we think we experienced really happened. Did it? Did it? Yes, and it can for you and your organization, too.

Societally, we stand on a precipice. From country to country, below the equator and above, to the east and to the west, deeply problematic issues await us in the days and years ahead. But so does greatness. The hard work of so many — *from quiet scientists and scholars to philanthropists and missionaries to volunteers and backbone contributors from the poverty level to the middle class to the billionaire benefactors around the world* — can transform us, and the times in which we live. Thinking anew, strategy can be our maidservant rather than an aristocratic monarchy, and by serving us better we can, in turn, serve each other more fully. We can weave the newest findings from all fields of research and commerce and religion and all points in between into a new, unheralded tapestry that will further our work to eradicate world hunger, enable third-world countries to bootstrap themselves out of their impoverished and desperate realities, or run our businesses as more ideal corporate citizens. We can hand the baton to a new generation with more choices than ever before, affording *freedom* and its sisters to all tomorrow's children.

As Keith Ferrazzi describes in *Never Eat Alone*, impoverishment of any kind is less about financial resources, and more about lacking access to the many resources that enable a person, a country, or a society to make something more of itself. And strategy, because it is so fundamental yet extraordinary, can undergird all pursuits in these areas, and many more.

We must not sell ourselves short. As leaders, we are obligated to not only improve, but to exert ourselves in pursuit of greatness. As Maslow asked, "If not you, then who? If not now, when?" We must each commit ourselves to better thinking, to better use of our minds and hands and hearts. Our children, our spouses, our peers, our followers, and all the generations that will build their lives upon ours are counting on us, just as we relied on those who preceded us.

Take up arms; gird yourself with insatiable curiosity and commitment to be more, to be better, to be great — and together, brick by brick and day by day, we will build a better future — the one our parents hinted at through fables, the one prophets trumpeted in the great and holy books, the one that is seared into the depths of our souls and the heights of our dreams. Together, like founding mothers and fathers setting out to create a new nation, we can chart a course for a new destination and, along the way, learn how to arrive west after departing to the east.

II
Triune

The problems we have created in the world today will not be solved by the level of thinking that created them.

Albert Einstein

The real voyage of discovery lies not in seeking new landscapes, but in seeing with new eyes.

Marcel Proust

The Strategic Triune

I landed in Albuquerque on a crisp September morning. The sun radiated through the window as we coasted on the tarmac to the gate. On the drive to Sante Fe, I reflected on what my client had asked me to help his team accomplish in the coming days. Brian was a VP of HR at a regional Citigroup call center, and he was interested in facilitating the development of a strategic plan for the organization. He had also asked if I wouldn't mind walking his group through some contemporary leadership, change, and collaboration concepts. "We're always hungry for learning," Brian had commented, "but we seldom have the time to read or keep up with what's out there."

I thought about his words as I navigated the rental car north. I had an overnight bag with two days' worth of clothes in the trunk, my trusty MacBook, and a few mental anecdotes to convey regarding some of the more popular thinkers of the late 90s — Senge, Peters, Covey, Hamel, Collins, Handy, Peck, Blanchard, Ohmae, Wheatley, Kotter, Pinker, Gardner, Welch, et al. Ninety minutes of blue sky later I arrived at the beautiful, rustic resort where we would spend two full days and three long nights together and where — unbeknownst to me — I would be asked a simple question that would germinate in the dark recesses of my mind for the next several years. It would grow from a tiny seedling of curiosity into a full-grown, call the kids, grab the camera, look at that 367' tall California Redwood mental possession.

The question emerged gently enough on day one, rising from the fertile soil of an exposition on leadership concepts and strategic planning.

"Blake, beyond the identification of strategies and the tactics comprising them, **what is strategy really, and why aren't more leaders better strategists?"**

Hmmm. That is a great question. ***A really great question.***

Several years, 41 states, 27 countries, and 14,000 leaders later — I'll cut to the chase and tell you that — yes, based on my own experience and the work of our team — it is a *flamingly* wonderful question, and it is indeed meritorious of deep exploration and navel-pondering. But you know this, because you're a reader, you're curious, and the question is pregnant with implications for anyone who strives to influence others or think strategically.

Our dinner that evening was a lively one, and the dialogue tickled that tiny seedling in my brain for well over three hours. As Brian's team of eight executives enjoyed their wine and gathered around the roaring outdoor fire pit that crackled in the cool night air, we pulled on personal observations regarding the disparate interpretations of the word *strategy* itself, on the chasm between leadership and strategy, and on the difficulty many leaders have implementing strategy.

I knew in my gut there was value in solving this riddle, because for several years I had observed hundreds of leaders with strong convictions and robust self-assurance who, in the face of *strategizing* and developing strategic plans with their teams had, in a word, failed. More completely, they became increasingly unsure; they wobbled to and fro as they brainstormed visions, BHAGs,[23] purpose statements, and goals, and when striving to define strategies and context and meaningfulness...they struggled and fumbled and fell.

In an organization, the Chairman, CEO, COO, CFO, EVPs, SVPs, VPs, directors, managers, and supervisors all have strong primary responsibility for strategy and strategy development, but the extent to which strategy becomes a living, breathing, organic idea is governed by the extent to which it is pluralistically socialized throughout an organization.

Think of it this way, multiplicatively. $10 \times 10 = 100$. Similarly, $10 \times 0 = 0$. To use an analogy, executives who fail to create an organization wherein *strategy* becomes currency that's traded across all castes, levels, rungs, locations, functions, divisions, or departments are inadvertently hindering the potential of a capitalistic economy predicated on stewardship, participation, ideas, and growth. *The organization that succeeds at making strategy everyone's business often dominates the marketplace.*

---

[23] *Big, hairy, audacious goals,* as described by Collins and Porras in *Built to Last.*

Are You a Strategist?

It's time now to begin describing the person I've referred to throughout as *strategist*. It's also time to study the *three attributes of archetypal strategists* that revolve around their *Mind*, their *View*, and how they perceive and interact with *People*.

Endgame: Inhabit, Indwell, Embody

At their core (see Figure 1), great strategists are like those FBI profilers with regard to the ability to perceive one's endgame (or lack thereof) by inhabiting, indwelling, or seemingly embodying another's thoughts. In some cases, there may be no endgame — only reaction. *(A shopper's unplanned purchase at an end-of-aisle beer display would be an example.)* In other cases, there may be a very

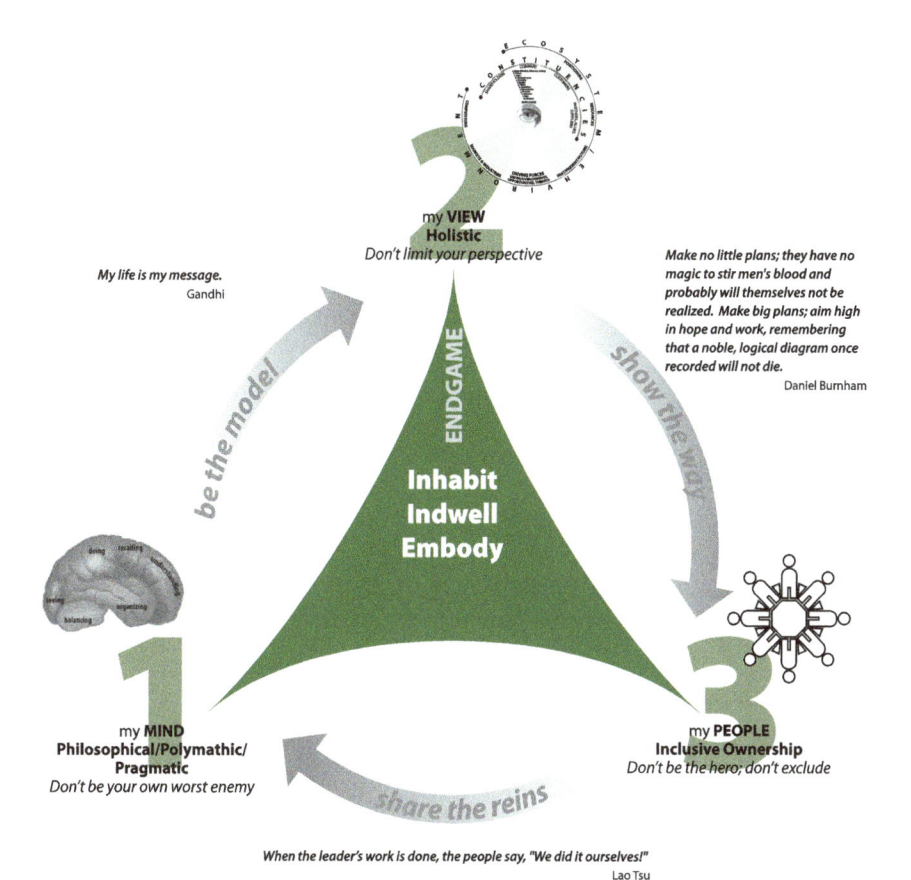

Figure 1: *The Strategic Triune*

serious endgame involved, and knowing this is equally helpful. *(A COO who purposefully deceives board members in order to oust his CEO would be an example.)* Though I'm reaching a bit here, we could equate the first instance with *self-defense* ("I saw the beer and couldn't resist.") and the second example with *murder in the first degree* ("I knowingly and willingly orchestrated the coup."). As you can imagine with these examples, perceiving another person's or party's endgame can be invaluable.

The success of an organization's strategy, as crafted by strategists, is largely defined by the extent to which it works and is *accurate*. Leading or merging with a constantly changing world requires attentiveness, but certainly not telepathy or the ability to literally read the minds of industry players, competitors, and consumers. I'm not a believer in telepathy, just as I'm not a believer in clairvoyant quacks or alleged feats of telekinesis by crazies like James Hydrick[24] (whose claim to fame was his defrauding by both James Randi on *That's My Line* and Dan Korem in *Psychic Confession*). Genuine attentiveness, however, and the ability to think as others might think, is valuable. Think about it this way: If I create a strategy that unfolds too early or too late, I fail. If I create a strategy for a demographic that has yet to exist or has passed, I fail. If I create a strategy that is overly simplistic or complicated, I fail. Overpriced, underpriced? Failure. Too exclusive or too inclusive? Failure. Too large or too small? Failure. Too short-term or too long-term? Failure. The opportunities for failure are bountiful.

Because the stakes are usually life and death, professional profilers take seriously their ability to get into the minds of others and mentally cohabitate with them. As strategists, we should do the same. In most cases, like the manufacture and distribution of firearms, tires, vehicles, scuba tanks, airplanes, car jacks, space shuttles, explosives, medicines, and even humdrum household appliances and children's toys, the decisions made by strategists affect *huge* populations on a constant basis. And beyond these examples involving product safety, the decisions of strategists affect the livelihoods of employees and shareholders, upping the ante even further. Considering the federal government invests the appropriate time and money to

---

[24] http://en.wikipedia.org/wiki/James_Hydrick.

develop profilers, shouldn't we expect the same — or better — in the private sector? From focus groups and ethnographic field studies to psychographics, demographics, typologies, taxonomies, and so much more, there are many options at the disposal of an inquiring mind to improve one's understanding of other players in the game. Competitor reconnaissance, market research, and industry trends should be the fiber of every strategist's diet.

Shakespeare was a tremendous observer of humankind; it's one of the many reasons for his resonance and longevity. He had a breathtaking ability to capture the comings, goings, and ruminations of the widest spectrum of people representing all walks of life — so much so that each of us can see bits of ourselves in his works. **If you wish to be a better strategist, commit yourself to understanding people.** It's a powerful capability, and one that demonstrates the curiosity about the world and its inhabitants that is shared by all successful strategists.

> *Cassius: Tell me, good Brutus, can you see your face?*
> *Brutus: No, Cassius; for the eye sees not itself*
> *But by reflection, by some other things.*
> *Cassius: 'Tis just,*
> *And it is very much lamented, Brutus,*
> *That you have no such mirrors as will turn*
> *Your hidden worthiness into your eye,*
> *That you might see your shadow.*
>
> William Shakespeare,
> Julius Caesar
> (I.ii.51-58)

Moving from the center of the Triune illustration outward, we see three recurring *hubs* or commonalities that present themselves in our research and fieldwork with great strategists. These commonalities comprise *The Strategic Triune* and at their core are the features that differentiate great strategists from great leaders. They include a strategist's:

1. **Mind** (how it operates),
2. **View** (of the world in which one operates), and
3. **People** (and how one engages them).

Let's continue with a thumbnail overview introducing each third of the Triune, starting with the strategist's mind. As is true with *talents* (those abilities that come naturally, that we don't recall learning, and which bring us joy), we are each gifted with some (rather than gifted with "all"). To certain leaders, strategic thinking comes easily and richly. To others, it comes rarely and in tiny doses, if at all. By studying and applying the many findings presented in *Cultivating the Strategic Mind*, you will indeed become a more purposeful and cogent strategic thinker and leader.

Their Mind

Great strategists are intrapersonally aware and think in three important ways. First, they are *philosophical*. This means they are comfortable living in "What if?" questions and thrive in a world of ambiguity needing clarity. Second, they are *polymathic*. The greatest strategists are lifelong learners, avid seekers, and observers of the world and those operating within it. Strategists are sponges, and their insatiable quest for knowledge knows only distant bounds. As a leader in business, for example, they might be able to draw on findings from chemistry, physics, mathematics, history, or other fields to make sense of their own organizational issues. Third, great strategists are *pragmatists*. After all the pontificating, philosophizing, and polymathy, they are able to apply their ruminations to real world needs and excel where others remain either earthbound or etherbound.

Their View

Great strategists think *holistically*. Their view is appropriately broad, and they generally consider multiple issues integratively rather than in isolation. For example, they might be viewed as Kasparovian chess masters, never thinking only three or four moves ahead but, rather, a dozen moves ahead and with great consideration of every component of the chess board, the table upon which it rests, the opponent across the table, the bird in the tree 30 feet away, the wind rustling the leaves overhead, the boys shooting baskets nearby, and the approaching car at the nearest intersection to the park. (This is not dissimilar from what militarists often describe as *situational awareness,* or "SA.") In an organizational example, when they consider a marketing strategy, they will consider it contextually in relationship to an entire value stream across all functions, departments, geographic locations, customer demographics, and longitudinally based on past moves, future moves, the reactions to those moves, and so forth but without analysis paralysis or debilitating hesitation.

Their People

Great strategists are interpersonally successful. They have the ability to create *inclusive ownership,* whereby their ideas become others' ideas, and followers see their own image or DNA in the decisions and efforts of the organization.

My late father-in-law told me a story about my wife, Dawn, that typifies the importance of people seeing themselves in the solutions we, as leaders, create.

"One day, I was sitting in the family room flipping through a photo album. Dawn came skipping across the floor and hopped onto my lap. She was three. As we sat together and I turned the pages, she pointed excitedly at a photo of a young girl on a Big Wheel.

'That's me! That's me!' she squealed.

'No, no, Sweetie. That's your big sister Kim when *she* was three.'

'Oh,' she said, and I turned the page where she saw another photo of a young girl standing by a pool.

'Hey, that's me! That's me!' she screamed.

'Oh, no, Sweetie. That's Kim.'

Hesitantly, I turned the page again, only to reveal a third photo of Kim. This time she was standing in the driveway with her hands on her hips in a cute 'aren't I cool?' pose.

'Is *that* me, Daddy?' Dawn implored.

My heart broke as I revealed the truth. 'I'm sorry, Sweetie. But that's Kim right after we moved into this house.'

Immediately, Dawn hopped out of my lap and shuffled across the floor and out the back door to play by herself. She hadn't seen herself in any of our photos, and I was kicking myself for having slacked on the photo-ops. With our firstborn, we had been continual shutterbugs, snapping live-action photos of spittle, the eating of solids for the first time...we captured even the most routine happenings. But with Dawn, the novelty was gone, and we just hadn't been as disciplined as before. I *learned* from the *photo album incident*. We immediately resumed taking photos, and when we had our third child, Jason, we took a *ton* of photos!"

I hear my father-in-law's wisdom ring in my ears every day, and I do my best to ensure that people see themselves in as many solutions as possible. It's what *I* hunger for when I'm asked to contribute or participate on a board, an advisory committee, or the like. If one doesn't have a voice, it's difficult to engage and invest. This ability to create collective buy-in (and equally important, to do so without yielding to political correctness or myopic or exclusively near-term interests) is significant and differentiating, because most strategists are viewed as great mentalists when, in reality, they must excel equally at involving others in order to bring their ideas to fruition.

I'll err on the side of exposing many U.S. and European based companies' bias for Western approaches by submitting their argument that *involvement* has proven successful in numerous performance settings, from politics (democracies vs. dictatorships) and economies (capitalism vs. communism) to education that affords choices (private schools or voucher systems vs. many public school systems) and even software platforms and web entities (open [*e.g., Linux or Wikipedia*] vs. closed platforms [*e.g., Microsoft or most commercial web sites*]) — with regard to what value has been created through a self-organizing, grass roots, collective methodology.

Participative, involving strategy is a green field of opportunity. For organizations to thrive and achieve a breakthrough, it's critical to engage, encourage, and enable the multitude of leaders and employees whose insatiable thirst for knowledge compels them to learn more, know more, and be more for themselves and the others in their life. This idea of extending leadership into the realm of strategy is about much more than business or organizations. We need, at the most foundational of levels, a way to see our world anew, to actualize our strategic intentions more effectively, efficiently, and altogether grandly.

Their Mind in Greater Detail: The Mind Map

The Mind Map (Figure 2) is a deeper exploration of the first element in *The Strategic Triune* (expectedly, one's *Mind*) and identifies the six primary functions at which great strategists excel: *Seeing, Recalling, Understanding, Organizing, Balancing,* and *Doing.*

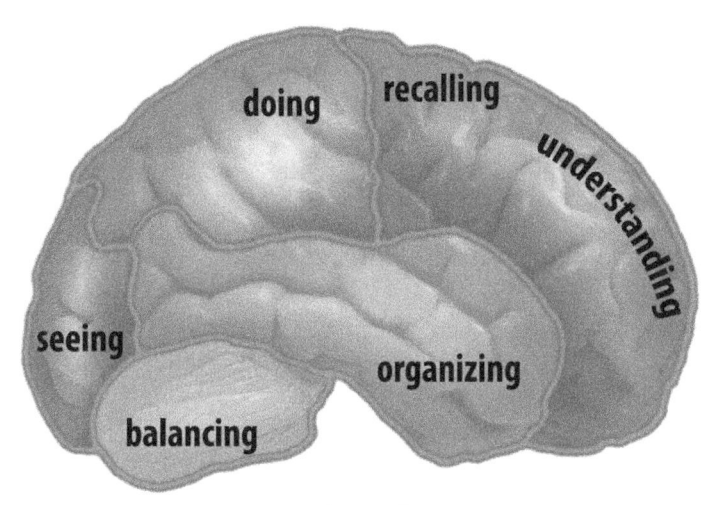

Figure 2: *The Mind Map*

First, great strategic leaders are seers. They generally envision important variables, organizational chess moves, and future states that others do not.

Second, great strategic leaders have fly-trapping minds that reveal astonishing recall. They remember the when's and lessons learned, are able to draw on the past for insights to the future, and do not typically repeat history's mistakes.

Third, great strategic leaders possess an impressive level of understanding. From polymathy to integration, their minds allow them to track what the vast majority of people are telling them, whether it's a technician on the shop floor, a salesperson in a region, a manager in IT, or a scientist in the lab across the Pacific, the great strategist possesses the breadth and depth of understanding necessary to actuate strategies on a daily basis across most disciplines, functions, levels, and demographics.

Fourth, great strategic leaders are organized. They're flexible and dynamic and nimble; they have their act together — their capacity for personal organization allows them to manage multiple strategies simultaneously.

Fifth, great strategic leaders are balanced. They can sprint, multi-task, and perform seemingly Herculean tasks, but they also realize they're running a marathon and are able to avoid burnout through self-management and discipline.

Sixth, they are doers. They're experienced, application-oriented, and eager to roll up their sleeves and get their hands dirty. They don't live in glass houses, eat solely in the executive cafeteria, or while away entire weeks on mahogany row within the isolated and removed conclave known as *corporate headquarters.*

Their View in Greater Detail: The Omniscience Octagon

The Omniscience Octagon (Figure 3) is a tool that has been used successfully within many industries by ensuring that organizations consider their constituents not in isolation or in theory, but in the context of the real-time ecosystem or environment. Just what, exactly, does this mean? Clearly, no person is omniscient, but the *Octagon* puts — front and center — the elements in a company's universe that warrant attention in order to think holistically. In today's hurly-burly, rapid pace environment, it is all too common to be distracted by immediate crises on our windshield, losing sight of what might be around the next turn or approaching us from behind. The *Octagon* serves as a simple yet powerful checklist to ensure we see and reflect upon the big picture.

The *Octagon* is comprised of eight overlapping slivers. Because the greatest organizations are employee-centric, I have placed employees in the interior. Surrounding *employees* is a center ring that accounts for the four remaining *Constituencies.* Regarding constituents, who are they, and why are they important? They are important, because without serving them, failure is the certain outcome. Constituents frequently include *employeess, shareholders,* the *company* itself, *customers, partners/allies,* and *suppliers.* (In the social sector, they may include congregants, voters, representatives, and the like.) Let's explore all five constituencies in more detail.

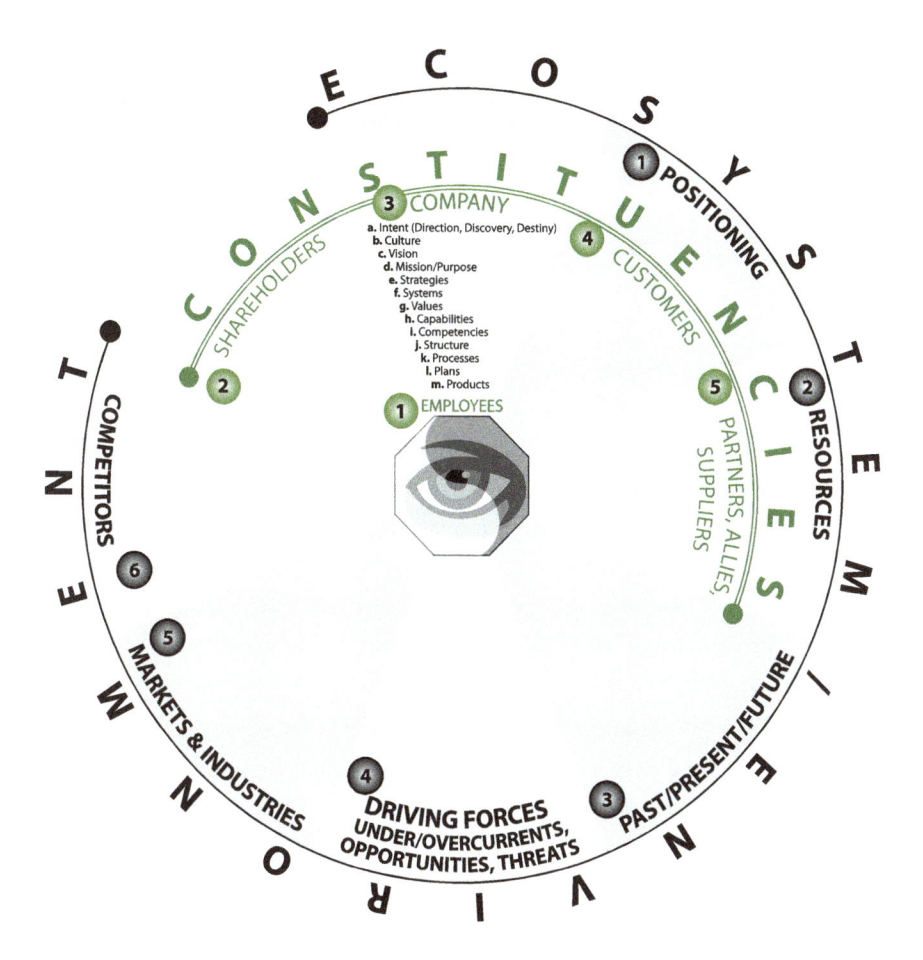

Figure 3: *The Omniscience Octagon*

1. **Employees (overlaps with Company)** — Much to my chagrin, I still find countless organizations who believe *the customer comes first.* Correspondingly, most of these organizations believe *employees exist to serve leaders.* Of course, I understand such employers are well intentioned and grasp the reality that without customers, there are no employees...but building an organization that is customer-centric rather than employee-centric is an antiquated worldview whose time has passed. I consider employees to be the primary constituent in any organization, followed by customers who are secondary, leaving all others as tertiary. If an organization focuses first

and foremost on its employees and their performance, well-being, and engagement, great customer satisfaction and loyalty will follow. As the late, great, and always prescient Peter Drucker wrote, "All organizations now say routinely, 'People are our greatest asset.' Yet few practice what they preach, let alone truly believe it. Most still believe, though perhaps not consciously, what nineteenth century employers believed: People need us more than we need them. But in fact, organizations have to market membership as much as they market products and services — and perhaps more. They have to attract people, hold people, recognize and reward people, motivate people, and serve and satisfy people."[25] *As a leader striving to be a strategist, I encourage you to always focus primarily on the type of culture you are creating, because this is the flame that attracts employees and keeps them near, warm, connected, and in the right mindset to elate customers with whom they interact.*

2. **Shareholders** — It goes without saying that in publicly traded, for-profit companies, shareholders are an ever-important constituency. Great strategists see their force for what it is, and work purposefully to engage and coalesce this powerful base of supporters.

3. **Company (aka Organization; overlaps with Employees)** — The organization is, to my mind, simply an extension of its people. Like a fractal, what one sees at the employee level represents what one should expect to see at the organizational level. As a customer at Nordstrom, for example, the salesperson with whom I interact *is* Nordstrom, and the impression he or she makes on me will be what I carry with me when I think of Nordstrom. It is important for the strategist to realize this and to help employees see that the organization-at-large is simply a larger representation of each employee and how she presents herself. Simply put, *to change the company, start with the employee.*

---

[25] *The New Society of Organizations,* Harvard Business Review, September — October 1992.

a. **Intent: Direction, Discovery, Destiny** — This *company* sliver of the octagon reminds us that a company's intentions and aspirations are extremely important: Specifically, its direction — where it's heading; its Discovery — what it's learning, and its Destiny — what it will one day be. This is an important line of inquiry in which strategists engage leaders and employees alike: "What are we moving toward? What do we know about ourselves that will facilitate or impede our aspirations? What are we called to be in this world several years hence? Among our constituents? Within our environment?"
b. **Culture** — Culture, and the seven elements that comprise it, will be discussed in great length in Part Three. Suffice it to say that by now, I presume you anticipate that culture is important — immensely important — and a great strategist understands that culture literally defines an organization and must, therefore, be an integral part of any strategic efforts.
c. **Vision** — Release whatever baggage you may have about *the word itself* and remember its intent. When people can see where they're going, they're far more likely to get there. Whether you choose to create a *Vision,* or you disguise it with any of the other clever synonyms like *Strategic Intent, Primary Aim,* or *Big Picture Focus,* just do it — and know that when done right, your people will thank you. One of the primary causes of employee stress is *ambiguous employer expectations,* and Vision is a great means to decrease ambiguity. A useful definition for Vision is: *a realistic (doable), worthwhile (adds value), desired (wanted) future state that is better in significant ways than what exists today.* When you vision-cast something that's five years away, and people believe in it, see its merit, and want it — you're golden, and the organization stands a much better shot at aligning and moving in the right direction.

d. **Mission/Purpose** — The daily purpose of an organization may appear obvious, but the great strategist takes nothing for granted. I describe mission/purpose as *our everyday reason for existence, beyond profit*. By removing the economic element, your organization is liberated from restating the obvious and can be much clearer about why it exists and how it might differentiate itself from similar organizations. (If your only reason for existence is money, then perhaps you should be in another industry or another business — because there are often easier ways to *just make money* than the ways most organizations go about it.)

e. **Strategies** — These *systemic means to the endgame* should be inclusive enough to account for the efforts that enable your company to achieve its Vision. For example, *people strategies* (to attract, develop, compensate, retain, promote, etc.), and *visibility strategies* (like branding, marketing, advertising), and *financial strategies* (including sales targets, individual quotas, profit margins, etc.) — whatever they are — should all work like the spindles of an umbrella to support the fabric of an organization's daily purpose, its mission. Strategies are, at the granular level, various means to the end.

f. **Systems** — As described in Part One, systems are all about *the generative dance between elements*. The strategist appreciates that as people, ideas, functions, projects and the like collide, interact, or merge... they change each other and are themselves changed. Systems are an important aspect of any organization or company, and the strategist must work hard to ensure they work in a complementary and connected way at every turn.

g. **Values** — The word itself derives from the Latin *valere*, which means *to be of strong worth*.[26] Both

---

[26] *Oxford English Dictionary*.

relational values (like trust and respect) and operational values (like efficiency, safety, and profitability) are intertwined with an organization's culture and, as a result, it is important for the strategist to help his employer align *espoused* values with the inherent *real* values. For example, some companies may espouse they value *respect,* when in fact they do not, and there is no evidence they do. I always think about it like this: If you were called to the stand as a witness in a trial and asked under oath, "What proof do you have that your employer values *respect?"* what would you say? Would you have enough evidence for the jury to judge you truthful? When there is dissonance between espoused and real values, common outcomes include distrust, disengagement, and overall skepticism. Better to not articulate any values than to pontificate about values that people disbelieve.

h. **Capabilities** — Capabilities are generally *organizational* in scope — *the extent of our power or ability to do something.* They are broad, often long-term abilities required for an organization to succeed, compete, and thrive. An important aspect of capabilities is the difficulty that competing organizations have at replicating them. As a result, capabilities are a strong and enviable source of competitive advantage.

i. **Competencies** — Competencies are generally *individual* in scope — *the skill to do something effectively and efficiently.* They are more narrow, immediate skills seen in current employee performance. While an organization might have great *engineering competence* at the individual level, that doesn't always translate to *engineering prowess* at the organizational, capability level. Returning to an airline example, we see that while every airline understands the blueprint of a successful airline (its capabilities), mashing all the appropriate building blocks together (competencies) does not equate to a great airline. People often ask, "If Braniff, Pan Am, and Eastern understood...and today's American Airlines or Delta understand what is required to create a great airline, why don't they all *just do it?*" Unfortunately, whether it's Delta's *Song* or *JetBlue,* it isn't as easy as it looks, and having the right genetic elements doesn't necessarily translate to a healthy organization if they're not assembled carefully, in the right order, at the right time, and with that seemingly elusive alchemy of leadership, culture, and employee attitude.

j. **Structure** — Structure is a component of culture, and as such, will be discussed in more detail in Part Three. It is an extremely important chess piece for the strategist, because *how people are organized* says a great deal about what one values and also reveals a lot about how we expect people to interact with each other.

k. **Processes** — The methods and protocols of an organization, whether tribal or refined, reflect an organization's values as well as its potential. While tribal, loose, and unreplicable processes may *feel good* or *easy,* with growth and maturity must come more rigor and repeatability. Processes, or the lack thereof, speak volumes about an organization's life cycle relative to a typical ogive (J-curve, S-curve, or sigmoid curve), revealing whether the company is in Phase I (infancy), Phase II (adolescence), or Phase III (maturity). The strategist works hand-in-hand with leaders to appropriately advance processes concurrently with an organization's evolution, and especially during times of transition and bifurcation.

l. **Plans** — The plans or blueprints for organizational progress remain one of the simplest and most important tools in the strategist's toolbox. *Identifying options, then priorities, then plans to accomplish goals* affords the strategist a very tactical opportunity to explain to people "how we'll get from Point A to Point B." Remember, strategic planning is not the same as strategic thinking, but the former benefits from the latter.

m. **Products** — **(and Services)** remind us of our deliverables and what it is we're expected to produce or deliver. It's important for a strategist to always inquire, "Is there a better product, a more ideal final result, or a more desired deliverable than the one we're creating?" Partnering with customers to identify more perfect current and future needs is an invaluable, regular practice that every strategist should employ. Seeing customers not as *receivers*, but as *part of the family,* goes a long way toward providing a clear view of what is needed, wanted, appreciated, and possible.

4. **Customers (Overlaps with Positioning)** — In his article, *Be a Better Liar,* Seth Godin[27] explains the phenomenon whereby customers come to know an organization as a specific entity and believe particular things about it. When people attempt to change their minds or what they believe about the organization, it's almost as if they perceive the organization is lying to them in its attempts to change what they have already come to accept as truth. Godin explains:

> You cannot succeed if you try to tell your competition's story better than they can. You can't out-Amazon Amazon. The natural instinct is to figure out what's working for the competition and then try to outdo it — to be cheaper than your competitor who competes on price, or faster than the competitor who competes on speed. The problem is that once a consumer has bought someone else's story and believes that lie, persuading the customer to switch is the same as persuading him to admit he

---

[27] *Fortune Small Business,* p. 90, May 2005. Also, see Godin's *All Marketers Are Liars,* published by Portfolio, a Penguin Group, in May 2005.

was wrong. And people hate admitting that they're wrong. Instead, you must tell a different story. If your competition is faster, you must be cheaper.

To my way of thinking, this is a wonderful illustration for the importance of *positioning* (and *Hapkidoing*, which will be described in Part Five), because there can be a sort of chicken-or-the-egg conundrum when it comes to our customers. As Tom Peters and others have noted, it's harder to unlearn than to learn.[28] In the eyes of customers, we come to occupy a certain position in their worldview, and as time marches on, it becomes harder to displace these perceptions. Take the example of Kmart, Sears, or JCPenney.[29] Perhaps a generation from now, these brands might come to reposition themselves more effectively in the eyes of customers (that is, if they all survive). But as of today, Kmart and Sears have come to occupy the lowest echelons of retail in this country (and JCPenney, although they've been on quite a hot streak recently); these retailers have much to overcome if they aspire to move up the proverbial retail food chain. As Jim Collins admonishes us with his adage about *facing the brutal facts*,[30] the strategist will do well to see *reality* from the *perspective* of the customer and work to exploit that space, rather than fly a kamikaze mission by trying too quickly to change customers' expectations and thereby one's position in the marketplace. A successful example of telling an improved "lie" was GM's Saturn. Rather than simply launch another product line, GM created a separate entity — initially emancipated of GM's shackles — in order to give the runt upstart a viable shot at occupying a fresh market position. The same can be said of Lexus, Toyota, and Scion. Rather

---

[28] In the words of Mark Twain, "Habit is habit, and not to be flung out of the window by any man, but coaxed downstairs a step at a time."

[29] Kmart acquired Sears, Roebuck and Company in 2005. The combined organizations are now known as *Sears Holdings Corporation*. I am describing the retail presence of each brand (which still exists as of this writing), not the corporate entity.

[30] The prolific Jim Collins, *Good to Great*, 2001.

than marketing three *product lines,* Toyota works hard to create the illusion of *three separate car companies* vying for three unique market segments. This "lie" is much more palatable to customers than would be the notion of paying $20,000 for a $50,000 car or vice versa.[31]

5. **Partners, Allies, Suppliers (Overlaps with Resources)** — Given their importance to our success, I would argue that partners, allies, and suppliers should occupy a position nearly as important as our own employees, and certainly as important as customers. When a strategist sees the system for what it is...an interconnected, cyclical flow of mind share, effort, time, money, and resources — flowing from employees, customers, and partners, it becomes obvious that the chain is only as strong as its weakest link. Whether turnover is high (in which case, managers can be the weak link), or customer loyalty is low (in which case, customers can be the weak link), or partners are unreliable, myopic, only self-interested, or play win/lose (in which case, they are clearly a weak link), we see an equation where $10 \times 10 \times 10$ is the goal, but often one of the multipliers is zero, in which case the entire result is nothing. Of course, in reality, 0 is less frequent than something like 5 or 3, but the logic remains the same — the effects of the weakest link can be seen in the aggregate. Given this reality, the strategist collaborates with partners, allies, and suppliers to ensure that all necessary resources are brought together in a win/win way toward a common outcome that benefits the entire system.

Proceeding to the periphery of the *Octagon*, what are the things that an organization must be aware of and purposeful about within its Ecosystem or Environment, and why does this matter? It matters because many organizations have died because they lost sight of the reality in which they perform and of the changes occurring

---

[31] Let me state for the record: Neither Godin nor I are endorsing lying. This is a discourse about what people come to believe and the difficulty of displacing that, regardless of whether what they believe — or any organization espouses — is true or not.

around them. They became the boiled frog that didn't perceive environmental changes until it was too late. The outer ring accounts for the six primary elements of any organization's Environment or, more preferably, its *Ecosystem* — preferred because it reminds us that it is dynamic, ever-changing, growing, mutating, dying, re-birthing, etc.

Six aspects of the ecosystem or environment that will be considered here include *positioning, resources,* the *past/present/future, driving forces* (under- and overcurrents, opportunities, threats), *markets and industries,* and *competitors.*

Let's explore these elements in detail.

1. **Positioning (Overlaps with Customers)** — As hinted at prior, *positioning* is about the identity one creates in the minds of customers.

2. **Resources (Overlaps with Partners/Allies/Suppliers)** — As introduced earlier, partners/allies/suppliers are the resource-lifeblood of any thriving company.

3. **Past/Present/Future** — While far from easy, the strategist strives to be both a formidable historian and prognosticator. Indeed, the world is replete with recycling (not in the eco-sense, but rather, in the sense that what was en vogue 30 years ago will likely be en vogue again soon), and the strategist is a student of these trends. However, in addition to paying attention to such cyclical patterns, the strategist is keen to historical failures and blunders that serve as reminders of what should not be attempted again. Equally important are the strategist's attempts to forecast and foresee what is coming next month, next year, and in the coming decades. The strategist who helps leaders become historians as well as futurists is worth his weight in gold.

4. **Driving Forces (Over/Undercurrents), Opportunities, Threats** — Like a spider minding her web, the strategist is ever-sensitive to the driving forces, overcurrents, undercurrents, opportunities, and threats within her company's ecosystem. By these, I'm meaning the forces at play within a market like expansion, contraction (often

manifested by consolidation), regulation, and so forth. Overcurrents, as I see them, are quite obvious...very *in your face* as it were, while Undercurrents are subtle, if not altogether unsensed or invisible. The field of economics is rife with excellent examples. While the effects of supply and demand in a free market system are readily apparent even to a novice, there are other phenomena, like inflation, that may increase or decrease due to an array of potential, explanatory (suspect) causes that often defy explanation even by sages like John Kenneth Galbraith or Alan Greenspan. Try as economists might to agree, they often disagree, and their inscrutable explanations elude us. By *Opportunities* and *Threats,* I'm referring to the future potentials and pressures that are, by definition, inherently desirable and undesirable respectively.

5. **Markets and Industries** — Essentially, this is the *arena* within which we compete. Generally, I consider an *Industry* to be defined or driven mostly *from the inside-out;* for example, Toyota is in the automotive industry, because it designs, manufactures, distributes, and services automobiles. I consider a *Market* to be more accurately defined or driven *from the outside-in.* For example, there are many markets for which Toyota and its industry competitors (e.g., Honda, BMW, Ford) vie, and because of somewhat natural/existent/inherent/unique segments, Toyota is currently responding with that three-tiered strategy comprised of Scion, Toyota, and Lexus. One could argue that Toyota or any company *creates* these markets rather than *responds* to these markets, and there is certainly a great deal of truth in both camps, but I perceive that where there are natural markets a strategist can exploit, he or she will succeed, and where there are illusory or imagined markets that he or she tries to create, a fad will follow rather than a lasting and robust market that can be mined for decades. By way of example, I have heard some people argue that Apple has *created and defined* any number of markets,

populated by the iPod, iPhone, etc. While they have clearly dominated in these markets, I would argue that these markets have existed for a long time, and Apple merely met the obvious need that we all have for reliable, elegant, and powerful devices that unify and simplify entertainment and communication. This hardly seems revelatory; though it is perhaps disruptive in some ways, it makes all the sense in the world.

6. **Competitors** — In a zero-sum game where there are finite attention spans, customers, and dollars, the strategist is constantly at work to gain and retain market share. In this timeless scenario, *Competitors* are simply the other guys seated at the table fighting for the existing slices of pizza.

As an exercise in the workshop version of *Cultivating the Strategic Mind*, I provide posters of *The Omniscience Octagon* and ask participants to gather in groups of four to six and populate the document by identifying all the many elements — from constituencies and all the sub-components of 'company' to the ecosystem and all the elements at play therein. While each 1/8th of the *Octagon* seems so blindingly simple to each of us, it never ceases to amaze me how meaningful the conversations become in the process. I encourage you and your colleagues to carve out a half-day to complete your own *Octagon* and see how helpful it can be at providing you with a holistic and broad view of your *Ecosystem/Environment* and *Constituents*.

Learning Lab: Idea(s) in Action

Tube Balance

To experience the power of seeing the entire picture — perform this exercise with your family, friends, or employees.

Set-up:

Construct a tube out of a flipchart sheet or newspaper — approximately 36" long and 1" diameter.

Instructions:

Round 1: Place the tube, vertically, in the palm of your hand. *Stare at your palm and balance the tube.*

Round 2: Place the tube, vertically, in the palm of your hand. *Stare at the ceiling and balance the tube.*

Round 3: Place the tube, vertically, in the palm of your hand. *Look wherever necessary to balance the tube.*

Summary:

Round 1: Too often, we focus on tactics to the exclusion of long-term vision. This is especially common in publicly traded companies who are fortunate if they ever focus beyond *the immediate quarter's performance.*

Round 2: Equally problematic is focusing so long-term that we fail in the near-term. Or we get so future-focused that we lose site of the day-to-day.

Round 3: Ideally, we want to move fluidly and constantly between long and near-term focuses. We look up, we look down...up, down. At the center...back up, then down. *This* is what great strategists do. They don't lose site of the entire picture — and *that's* what *The Omniscience Octagon* is all about: seeing the whole, constantly.

Their People in Greater Detail: Inclusive Ownership

As we round the horn and approach the final third of the Triune — this time, focusing on people — it wouldn't surprise me at all to learn that you're thinking, "Come on, Blake. It's the 21st Century, man. Surely we don't *still* need to talk about involving people! Isn't this a no-brainer? What sort of caveman hasn't received *that* memo yet?" Uh, well, many. Truth be told, the idea of including people in *strategy development* is light-years away from being a no-brainer. As a general rule, the people typically privileged enough to participate are C-level executives (e.g., CEO, CFO, COO, and closely orbiting colleagues).

Entire fields and professions make untold **billions** of dollars each year reminding these leaders that employees matter, reminding one spouse that the other matters, and reminding individuals of all sizes and shapes that we each matter on this giant, revolving hairball of ours. From training and development to psychiatry, psychology, therapy, marriage counseling, coaching, mentoring, and all points in between, *not-so-cottage* industries are at work 24/7 pumping out wisdom and constant reminders that still...inarguably *a very long time indeed since our creation,* we remain, in too many cases, complete goobers when it comes to working with other people.

Who among us can claim (within the last seven days) to have:

1. Understood everyone with whom I've interacted?
2. Not hurt someone else's feelings?
3. Anticipated everyone's reactions?
4. Adjusted my approach, pace, verbals, and nonverbals to provide a comfortable and attractive environment for everyone around me?
5. Perceived the mind-talk[32] experienced by those around me?
6. Effectively interpreted the motives and aspirations of those around me?
7. Adequately listened to and incorporated the ideas, suggestions, needs, and requests of those with whom I've worked?

See — there are so many constant signals and meta-messages bombarding us each day that it's a miracle if 10 percent of them penetrate our cranium. Sure, by way of the human sciences, we've made colossal strides in recent decades, but like exercise, we've got to work regularly to keep our muscles — in this case, our social muscles — limber, strong, and responsive. Around the world, many strategists are encumbered by a heroic paradigm of leadership that, while effective to a point, sets a limiting example. After current generations have retired from the workforce en masse, this paradigm will change a bit, but what replaces it may not be any better...only different.

The heroic paradigm can be explained by recalling *Zorro*. Here's how the model of heroism works. One day, a barn down in the village in the valley catches on fire. As the blaze grows, the village people (!)

---

[32] Mind-talk was introduced on page 44.

holler, "Zorro! Zorro!" As if on cue, Zorro (imagine Antonio Banderas in all his glisteny, muscular radiance) hops out of bed, runs to the stable, hops on his trusty steed, and rides down the mountain to save the hapless locals from the burning barn. He douses the flames, hops on his horse, gallops off, and grabs a damsel by the hand, pulling her quickly onto the saddle as they ride back to the villa…the lair…the Batcave…the mansion…the ranch…the *Daily Planet* newsroom (feel free to insert nearly any other American heroic paradigm here). This cycle repeats itself over and over again. *Crisis, helpless victims, loner/misunderstood hero, rescue, maiden/damsel, happily-ever-after.* Now, in this self-perpetuating cycle and self-fulfilling prophecy, who gets rewarded? Well, obviously the villagers do (because they get their barn extinguished), and the hero does (because he gets to do what he does best and gets rewarded for it on multiple fronts), and yes, the gals do (because they get the guy). *There is one theory floating around that the maidens in the village are arsonists.* But I digress. So how does this paradigm conclude? In our Zorro example, in the years that come, Antonio begins to resemble Anthony Hopkins, fewer fires arise, and a peace falls upon the land. Coincidence? Perhaps. But then, one day many years later, a young, new hero arises to take Zorro's place/sword/cape/persona and the balance of the universe is restored.

Back in the real world, things aren't much different. Who usually gets promoted? Too often, it's the people who excel at swift action and problem-solving — in a word, firefighters.[33] It's seldom the consensus-builders, the listeners, the champions of ideas and teams and professional development; nay…it's the heroic types who thrive at moving quickly, putting out fires, and moving on. These are the John Wayne archetypes that we still look to, often in our subconscious, when we think *leader*. Granted, one's stereotype of *strategist* might be different — for example, the introvert working at DARPA or RAND — but in either case, the pitfalls are the same, because perhaps neither stereotype is prone to involving people or ensuring everyone's images and DNA are in the picture, and that's a shame. Remember, nothing of lasting significance thrives in isolation, particularly ideas, people, and certainly not their strategies.

---

[33] No, I'm *definitely* not dissing firefighters, who occupy one of the most venerable roles in any society; I'm just using a well-known colloquialism for descriptive purposes. Ironically, firefighters are versed in much strategy despite our vernacular that would infer otherwise.

Unfortunately, one of the facts that resurfaces repeatedly when changing these approaches is *unlearning is harder than learning*. To disassemble and cast aside a habit is much harder for most people than adopting or embracing an altogether new or different habit. Because the heroic archetype is so firmly welded into our collective psyche, nuancing it for future generations will take just that... generations.

I encourage you to work daily to foster inclusive ownership by enacting the following steps:

1. **Anticipate** — First, anticipate resistance to ideas grown in the seclusion and secrecy of your own mind. Many people have an immediate aversion to ideas not their own. Interestingly, a similar or identical idea, when it originates with them, is bloody brilliant. Check your ego at the door. The creditor doesn't care where the money comes from, as long as the checks don't bounce, and neither should you. Just be thankful for the deposit and the interest.

2. **Inquire** — Seek people out, track them down, invite them in, and genuinely demonstrate that their input does have unique value.

3. **Engage** — Share your vision and/or the sideboards/constraints (e.g., time, money, people, other available resources, expected outcomes), then let others' minds do the rest. People are attracted to blank slates and raw clay, as long as they know what winning looks like. Once their energy is in the equation, strategy and inclusion and ownership are imminent.

4. **Implement** — Don't ask for suggestions, input, or participation if you're not willing to accept or support the consequential contributions. You'll train people to wait for your answer and to disengage and indulge you rather than commit. The great strategist surrounds himself with people who want to be the pig at breakfast, not the chicken. While the pig makes the ultimate sacrifice, the chicken just calls it in.

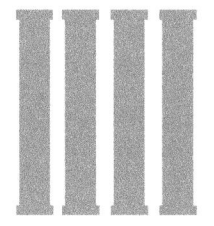

III Pillars

If our executive training programs look fifty years ahead then we should think about the kindergartens being of the right sort in order to create the future bosses and generals and managers and leaders that we will need in the next century.

Abraham Maslow

Four Pillars of Strategic Organizations

While there are certainly others, I do believe there are four main pillars that undergird every successful business and, with a bit of tweaking, every organization. These pillars — *Leadership, Culture, Processes and Performance,* and *Sales and Service* also define a nice, chronological architecture that I'm passionate about. Obey the chronology, and chances of thriving increase. Disregard or violate the elements and their chronology, and the chances of thriving decrease. Let me provide a thumbnail sketch of each pillar, followed by a detailed explanation starting on page 90.

Leadership is first for all the obvious reasons. Without it, organizations flounder. Without vision, strategies, core ideologies, and the people to pull the organization forward on a daily basis, organizations waffle, wander, and wonder. There is limited alignment without leadership, and while *organic/grass-roots efforts* are fascinating and sometimes as pervasive as ivy, their effects can be multiplied when accompanied by leadership's pulling and top-down efforts. This may sound contradictory, but it's not. Where a hybrid approach exists — a combination of *Evolutionary* Leadership (grass-roots, organic, emergent) plus *Revolutionary* Leadership (top-down, orchestrated, inculcated) — leadership in total is the most profound, gaining traction from both the earth and the skies.

> ***Archetypes:*** *When I think of leadership, I often think of the United States' founding fathers: Benjamin Franklin, George Washington, Thomas Jefferson, James Madison, John Adams, Alexander Hamilton, Samuel Adams, Patrick Henry, John Hancock, Thomas Paine, Roger Sherman, John Jay, James Wilson, and the like. Despite tremendous stress, limited resources, disparate constituents, and fragile international relationships, they created a country from scraps. Granted, the U.S. has numerous complex challenges, and is still finding its footing on a world stage, but within its first 241 years, its contributions are, in many ways, nothing short of amazing.*

Culture is next, because it is a direct reflection of Leadership. Where there are strong, purposeful, healthy leaders, there is strong, purposeful, healthy culture. Where there are weak, misaligned, unhealthy, or accidental leaders, culture evolves accidentally, haphazardly, dysfunctionally, and much as the proverbial lab accident...with sometimes disastrous, unforeseen, and undesirable results.

> *Archetype: Southwest Airlines. Fun and on-time because of no assigned seating and outstanding operations, this no-frills, low-cost airline remains the most consistent David in a field of struggling Goliaths. When you fly Southwest, visit their headquarters, or chat with employees, you can practically smell, feel, and taste the culture.*

Upon the bedrock of culture, an organization can more adequately turn its attention toward the **processes and performance** that will advance all existing and new efforts. It is at this third pillar that efficiencies can be maximized, waste can be removed, repeatability can be refined, and performance management soars.

> *Archetypes: Toyota and McDonald's. The former, for popularizing and perfecting total quality management, lean manufacturing, and consistent processes across product lines, languages, and cultures around the globe. And the latter, for proving repeatability and predictability each and every day, from Des Moines to Seoul.*

As processes and performance mature, the creativity with which organizations **sell and service** becomes an important focus for continued longevity and differentiation. Too often, organizations perceive that the sale itself is the end-all, but of course, this is wrong. The sale is the beginning. It's the "I do" that initiates many opportunities to deliver and improve again, and again, and again. I remember the day my wife bought her first Lexus. The young salesman (no more than 30 years old and having been hired just a few weeks prior) looked earnestly into my wife's eyes and said, "Ms. Leath, I don't want to sell you *this* car. I want the privilege to provide *every car* you'll ever drive. Today is our first day to prove ourselves, and we'll do it again, and again, and again, because we want you to love your Lexus and the Lexus experience. If you ever feel that you're not getting the quality you expect or the service you deserve, call me, my manager, or anyone in this organization, 24/7. Thank you for the opportunity to serve you." Wow. Okay; sold. And I can guarantee you that this young man has kept his promise, several years hence. When my wife buys her next car, you better believe it's going to be a Lexus.

__Archetypes:__ Other sales and service archetypes include the almost-too-easy name-drops like Nordstrom, The Container Store, and Dell. These organizations respect customers' time, intelligence, and tastes. They make it exceedingly easy to buy, they work hard to provide personalized service in a dense world, and they always deliver.

I cannot let the moment pass without sharing my own Nordstrom experience. Many years ago, in the throes of an out-of-town client project, I was re-assigned mid-week. I had been working with a company that necessitated I wear blue jeans and steel-toed boots in the field. In addition to these simple wardrobe items, I had in my bag an oxford shirt, a pair of khakis, a few flannel shirts, t-shirts, socks, underwear, and toiletries. My re-assignment required that I fly to the northeast and "wear something nice." While my suitcase held the *potential* for something nice, I was missing one key ingredient: the shoes. On the way to the airport, having just completed two days *in the field,* I passed a Nordstrom. I had — literally — 15 minutes to spare, but being without many choices, I grabbed a parking space and darted inside, hoping to avoid being waylaid. I entered, found the wall of shoes to the left, and quickly selected a pair. The shoe department sales manager approached me, and we had a rapid exchange.

"May I help you?" he asked quietly and calmly.

"Yes," I blurted rather loudly and hurriedly. "I have 10 minutes to buy these. Can we hurry?"

"Of course, Sir. What size do you wear?"

"Ten."

"Great. Let me check the back. I'll be right back."

One minute passes. Two minutes pass. Three minutes...I'm dying here. He floats out through the curtains. "I'm sorry, Sir. We don't have this style in your size. I could call one of our other locations for you and see if they have this shoe in stock. Would that be acceptable?"

"Uh, no. No. I now have about seven minutes or I'll miss my flight. Maybe I should find another shoe."

"A flight you say? I'm sorry; I didn't realize. I tell you what, can you wait right here? I'll be right back. Let me just check something."

And with that, he was off — he jogged toward the wall of shoes and dashed around the corner out of sight.

One minute passes. Two minutes pass. Three minutes. I thought I was dying before, but now I'm about to bolt. This guy's clueless. It appeared that he understood my urgency, but now, I'm beginning to think he's forgotten me entirely. Just then, I hear the clippity-clop of his strides; he's sprinting through the center of Nordstrom, heading straight toward me. He stops a meter away; breathing heavy, red-faced, sweat cascading down his forehead. He reaches for his handkerchief and wipes his brow. "Here you are, Sir. I'm so sorry for the delay. Size ten, right?"

"Uh, yes. Ten. Are you okay, man? Where did you get these shoes?"

And with that, he responds with one word...a name. A name that, to this day, blows my freakin' mind: "Macy's."

Macy's. I'm incredulous. Completely dumbfounded. Here I was, my mind-talk devolving into, *surely he's forgotten me.* But in reality, he was sprinting through the mall, sliding into Macy's, and using his relationship and goodwill with his Macy's buddies to snatch me a pair of shoes. Man. It just blew me away, and I still get goosebumps thinking about. *But wait.* There's *more.*

"Since you're in such a hurry, how about this: If you have a business card, just give it to me, and when you land tonight, you can call me then and I'll collect your credit card number."

"Are you kidding me?" I ask. Seriously, is this guy for real?

"No. It's no problem. Got a card?"

And with that, I hand him my card, shake his sweaty hand, and head for the airport. And yes, I did catch the on-time departure, and the shoes were perfect. I still have them, in fact, a decade later, just to remind me that kind people do exist, that some strangers are willing to trust other strangers, and that, yes — there are organizations that value people over rules, regulations, and forms. Rules, regulations, and forms make a lot of sense, and they keep organizations out of trouble, but they can also create a black and white world in which repeatable protocol trumps situational logic, the big picture, and doing what's right in a given scenario. We've all been victims of entities who demonstrated outright stupidity and either incurred more cost or lost revenue, *because* they followed the rules. From the airline industry (where making exceptions often requires a miraculous intervention) to your post office or local department of motor vehicles, employees are often put in positions without the training, development, skills, or permission to do what's right and ensure repeat customer elation. As strategists, we must do better than straw-narrow-vision and empower employees with adequate training, sight, and permission to excel at balancing what's right for the customer and the organization.

I can tell you this much. My shoes cost $300 — which is a sizeable amount, but I've spent perhaps ten times that in the past decade as a result of the young man's service, responsiveness, and trust in me. Moreover, I've shared his story with untold thousands, and have heard similar tales in return from dozens of people; people who have been elated by their dry cleaner, their auto mechanic, the manufacturer of their hard drive, and yes...on a number of occasions, even their airline.

I once took a brand-new watch to an authorized repair center, because the crown was difficult to turn, and I couldn't synchronize the chronograph features (month, day, hour, and lunar cycle). To make a long story done, the repair center lost an employee, then the watch, and three years later after a BBB complaint and the manufacturer's involvement, my watch was returned to me along with a bill for $160, "because the warranty has lapsed." To this, all I can say is, "I'm sorry; you suck." And away we go.

You will notice the first two pillars are focused internally (in the mirror, as it were), while the last two pillars are focused externally (out the window). It's my observation that without the internal rigor of self-management, leaders generally fail in many external relationships with others, from staff and peers to customers, suppliers, and partners. This reality has been commented upon a number of times in other literature, but we'll continue it with our own vigor through a more detailed pass at each pillar, starting with leadership.

Leadership

What is true leadership, and how do strategic leaders come into existence? By what process (nature/nurture or a bit of both) do they get birthed and evolve?

It is my belief that to varying extents and in different ways, everyone is a leader, because everyone influences those around him. The person sitting quietly in the corner cubicle looking like nerdy Peter Parker or docile Clark Kent may really be a leader or strategist waiting to break out. It is the collective calling and responsibility as members of humankind to facilitate such transformations and usher new leaders and strategists into our midst. But we should not limit our focus to just developing leaders at work. For example, remember the precious, sweet-smelling tyke sleeping in that tiny bed down the hall in one's home. And that wonderful human being who has agreed to spend his or her life alongside another. And that difficult child at the back of the classroom — the one who always seems to be getting into trouble. Maybe, with a little direction and positive encouragement, a great leader or strategist shall emerge from these places, too. In a moment, we'll investigate three supporting items to ensure this happens: *the Pygmalion Effect, the Potential Envelope,* and *the Seven Questions Every Life Must Answer.*

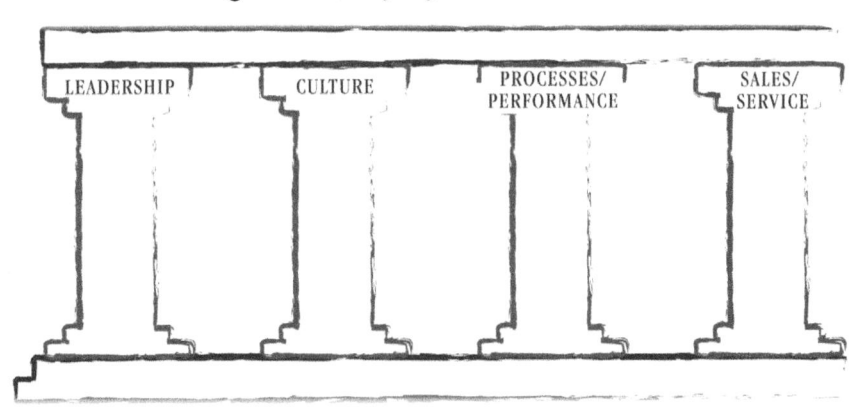

Figure 4: *The Four Pillars of Strategic Organizations*

Context

Hollywood has perfected for our collective consciousness the "it moment" in film. You know the one I'm talking about. It's when a character sees his potential for the first time or is altogether transformed in an instant. Many of the greatest scenes that come to my mind are in the category of mentor movies. Specifically, *Mr. Holland's Opus, Dead Poets Society, Lean on Me, Stand & Deliver, Dangerous Minds, The Emperor's Club,* and *To Sir, with Love* with the peerless Sidney Poitier. These movies, in particular, include what we might call the *butterfly moment* as the individuals emerge from the dark husk of a chrysalis that defined them for so long. They probe their way out of the shell, pulling and thrusting their new, broad, fluffy, powerful wings for the first time. The mentor/teenager/young adult movie category is perfect for this butterfly moment, as that's what young people are — chrysalis-dwellers awaiting their awakening. Recalling these films, I observe that sometimes young adults are achievers, but generally, they are not — were not before — and that's why the transformation is so radical, so welcomed, so exciting, so rewarding for the audience. It's the juxtaposition of the *after* against the backdrop of the *before.* Often, the transformation is the result of two or three key factors: *undesirable/difficult circumstances,* an *encourager/mentor/coach/professor/teacher,* and *some C4 explosive turning point*...specifically, a combustible event that clangs, bangs, and ignites the big boom that yields a new being. I get giddy just thinking about it. Remember *The Natural* when Robert Redford's character busts the lights with a fantastic smack of the bat? Or when Tom Cruise lures Jack Nicholson's ego out in *A Few Good Men?* Or when, in what must be the best guy-movie ever — *Braveheart* — Mel Gibson's William Wallace gallops along on his horse, converting a motley crew of Scottish and Irish ragamuffins into a force with which the English army must reckon? As far as film goes, I just don't think it gets any better than these moments.[34]

I've had many interesting conversations, more than I care to count, with people who have espoused that leadership falls in the *nature* column in the *nature/nurture* argument. *Leaders are born, not made* summarizes their stance. While there are indeed many leaders who are born possessing that x-factor, that charm, that attractiveness, that aura, that gravitational pull that draws followers to them, my livelihood has hinged on the reality that there are also many leaders

---

[34] My wife, on the other hand, is a sucker for *The Princess Bride* of all things, and that eludes me as much as my favorites elude her.

who are the result of purposeful development and work, rather than the sole act of being born. When asked by a client, "Do you think we can develop leaders?" I reply, "Of course. I've seen it happen again and again."

The cell of raw potential helps immeasurably, but it isn't always necessary. I think it's a crime to write-off potential leaders because the individuals are shy, introverted, quiet, amiable, goofy, or ill at ease. Whatever stereotypes we attribute to great leaders can be shattered by historical and contemporary examples of individuals who were not born or perceived as leaders right out of the womb but, rather, developed over time — often blossoming very late in life.

Having participated in thousands of coaching sessions over the years, I've come to approach the sessions with a sense of anticipation and excitement, often like a spelunker, detective, or forensic scientist eager to locate and identify the leaders who have thus far flown under the organizational radar. During the initial relating phase of a client engagement, I've often asked the questions, "Who are your leaders? Who will people identify as leaders and potential leaders in the organization? Who are the 'persons of influence?'"

Following the typical recitation of the folks at the top of the org chart, subtler speculations will follow, "Oh, and maybe John Salvo, Tom Mitchell, Heather Greenley. Yep, they're probably seen as leaders also." Needless to say, we'll often identify dozens of employees within the population who are perceived as leaders. But surprisingly, and pleasantly to this explorer, we often work with many individuals not perceived as leaders, only to witness their emergence as butterflies from that chrysalis. Before? An employee. After? A leader. And how do they develop? How do they migrate from being an employee to being perceived as a leader by their many peers?

In some cases, the individual simply needed encouragement to speak her mind. Or, he needed coaching to improve his self-management skills, effectively slaying his own worst enemy. Or, she needed direction or purpose to bootstrap into new territory. And certainly, in some cases, circumstances unfolded that defined the individual or ushered him into a new realm of influence, not unlike the case of Abraham Lincoln.

And what is the result when these individuals transform into a leader, emerging from the confining chrysalis that defined them prior? All the air is sucked out of the room, time stands still, sounds muffle, and neck hairs salute.

The Pygmalion Effect

A friend of mine (who is a professional educator) tells the story of Michael.

"When I was just starting out as a teacher, I took a job at a high school. There were a few ways to make some extra cash. You could coach, be the sponsor of a student organization, or supervise the kids in detention! Since I'm not an athlete, and given my immaturity, I didn't feel up to making the commitment as some sort of sponsor, I chose detention.

After doing it a few afternoons in a row, a tall, lanky sophomore shuffled in. He was very quiet — kept to himself a lot. Frankly, I didn't pay much attention to him other than to just get his name and ask him to sign-in. He came back, day after day. After a while, and perhaps due to boredom, I started to pay more and more attention to Michael. I noticed that he was always focused, and while some of the other kids were always screwing around and getting in trouble, Michael sat quietly at his desk, read a lot of books, and completed all the assignments his teachers had given him. To be honest, I just assumed he was one beer short of a six-pack, but after a while, I started to realize that Michael was a pretty bright bulb. One day, maybe three weeks after I'd first met him, we struck up a conversation.

'You seem pretty focused; what are you working on there?'
'Just homework, Sir.'
'Homework. Yep. It seems like you're always doing homework.'
'Yes, Sir. That's true.'
'Hey, Michael. Can I ask you a question?'
'Sure.'
'You've been coming in here for three weeks now. But I never see you doing anything...*wrong*. Why, exactly, are you here?'
'I think I uh...I have a reputation.'
'A reputation?'
'Yeah.'
'Can you tell me about it?'

'I suppose,' he said softly, 'When I was in fifth grade, I lost my temper. I sorta pushed a teacher.'

'Okay. Fifth grade? Michael, that was what — six years ago or so? What the heck are you doing in detention TODAY?'

'I guess the label stuck.'

'What label?'

'Problem child.'

'Okay, but still — what have you done *lately?*'

'I'm not really sure. I've been in and out of detention pretty much ever since. Teachers are always findin' somethin' wrong: *You don't participate in class; you're not paying attention.* Stuff like that.'"

This feeble, seemingly hollow explanation, really intrigued my friend. "I started digging, Blake, and I'm telling you, there was nothing to it. Michael, for whatever reason, had this big bull's-eye on his chest. Turns out, he was really bright — MIT bright, but the teachers, starting with his fifth grade teacher, thought he was a threat, thought he had anger management issues, thought he didn't care, *and they essentially wrote him off.* I began to counsel him, encourage him, and before it was all said and done, I suppose in hindsight I had become a sponsor after all."

Michael graduated from Rice University in Houston, Texas — *a very good school,* indeed.

This story about Michael could be about many teenagers. At its essence, the Pygmalion[35] Effect is about *people rising to our beliefs in them.* Put another way, *we get what we expect.* Whether it's the child or teenager we write off, the spouse we write off, the employee we write off, the neighbor we write off...sometimes by writing them off in our mind, in our deeds, and in our relationship and expectations of them, they write themselves off, too. Our expectations become so low, these individuals actually meet them.

As strategists, the extent to which we believe in people and talk straight with them, engage them, keep our commitments, are honest

---

[35] In Greek mythology, Pygmalion was a king of Cyprus who fashioned an ivory statue of a beautiful woman and loved it so deeply that, in answer to his prayer, Aphrodite (Roman name, Venus) gave the statue life. The woman (at some point named Galatea) bore Pygmalion a daughter, Paphos. In 1968, Dr. Robert Rosenthal proved The Pygmalion Effect in an elementary school; see also *Eye of the Storm* for the controversial Blue Eyes/Brown Eyes study involving Jane Elliott (www.guidanceassociates.com/collegeeye.html). Pygmalion was the basis for George Bernard Shaw's play of the same name, the musical *My Fair Lady*, Woody Allen's *Mighty Aphrodite*, and other works across art and literature.

with them, listen to them — and expect much of them — determines what typically comes of them. Yes, there are people who behave as slugs and, try as you might to rehabilitate them, they stay slugs. There are saboteurs who, try as you might to trust and empower them, will assassinate you from miles away or stab you intimately like Brutus. There are those employees who, as David McLelland discovered in his research,[36] simply don't possess much need for achievement. It is my discovery, however, and the general consensus among most people I meet, that erring on the side of high aspirations, trust, and inclusion pays off far more than it fails.[37]

The Potential Envelope

Many years ago, I found myself sitting on a plane next to a sports psychologist. I was heading home, and he was heading to work. He was going to meet with a professional athlete — an athlete (who shall remain anonymous) who played for an NFL team (that shall go unnamed). As we chatted, he drew this on the page of his notebook:

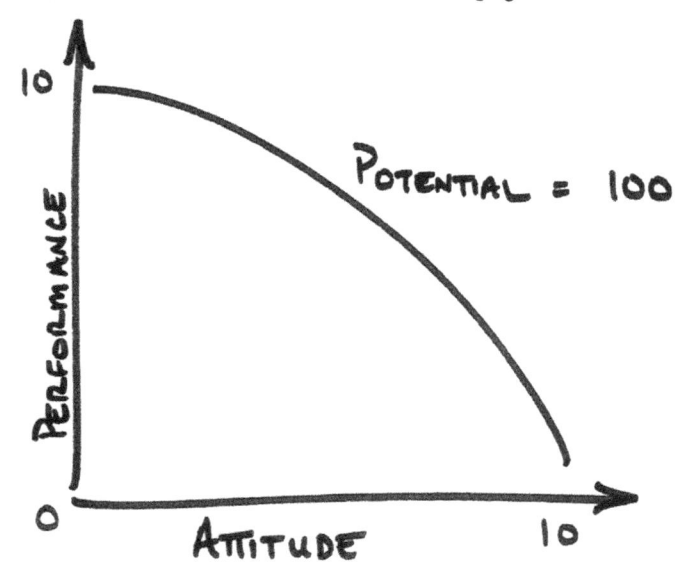

Figure 5: *The Potential Envelope*

---

[36] Visit http://en.wikipedia.org/wiki/David_McClelland or download *The Triune for Attraction & Retention: Creating a Culture of Good Leaders, a Great Workplace, and Sustaining Employer of Choice Designation*, yours truly.
[37] Remember Maya Angelou from page 19.

"Here's how it works," he began. "This fella I'm going to work with...he's a criminal. Simple as that. He's violent, he does drugs, he sleeps around, he gambles. And on Sundays, he's a superhero. Usually. But lately, he's gotten sloppy. My assignment is to stop that and start helping him pull his life back together. He's an investment, and the investment is at risk."

"Yeah, I suppose so," I managed.

"So this model here, it explains that, in many respects, an athlete's potential is the result of his *attitude* and his *performance*. His attitude is that 'tude he shows up with and maintains over the long haul. Take Michael Jordan. Wow, what a Godsend. He's a coach's dream. He shows up for practice, coaches from the floor, leads his peers, and makes other people better than they were before they met him. He builds champions and dynasties. This other axis here, this performance piece, isn't just about what the athlete does on game day; it's about the whole package — his relationships on and off the field or court or track, his finances, his addictions, his diet, the whole deal. Again...Jordan? He's a gift. But a few of these guys? Think about it. They're young, wealthy, in and out of hotels and different cities week after week, and they've got groupies and hangers-on everywhere they turn. No wonder there's trouble."

"And that's where you come in."

"Exactly. I listen, but I don't take any crap. These guys'll talk a good game, make promises, tell you what you wanna hear to get gone, or just blow you off altogether. But this fella I'm going to see? He's gotta clean up his act, or he'll be gone, and that...*THAT* is an ugly scene. Broke, crippled, washed-up. *Not* good."

In a matter of seconds, this man rattled off a dozen names. Names of millionaire-criminals, the ones on their last leg. I would share the list, but you know it all too well, and frankly, I don't want to wake up with a horse head in my bed or death threats at my home. But as so many times before, I digress.

The point of my discourse is about the model — the image in the notebook and all that it represents. Such a profoundly elegant image that I've shared it a hundred times since. On one occasion, I shared it with a room full of engineers, and one of them burst out, "Hey, that's a 'potential envelope.' We use something like that in our field, too, but it's not about human potential; it's about the work we do here. The key, Blake, is that it's a model that emphasizes the importance of multiplication. 10 × 10 = 100, and that's 100 percent of something's aperture...its potential. Michael Jordan was, in reality, all that he was in potential. Some of these other guys...they get a 3, a 2, a 1, or a 0 for attitude, which would make 'em a zero."

As strategists, inculcate The Potential Envelope into your thinking and interactions with others. Too often, we focus exclusively on performance dimensions (which are important) and ignore attitudes (which are equally important, and often diminished or altogether ignored).

Seven Questions Every Life Must Answer

Strategic thinking starts early, at least for some. Eugene Brown (aka *Chessman*),[38] a man I admire greatly, teaches the value of chess to youths in inner city Philadelphia. He takes children and young adults through the basics (pieces' names and rules), but his intent is to teach life lessons. Pleasantly, chess is a great metaphor for life.[39] There are roles, rules, strategies, and an appreciation for *thinking ahead*. Eugene shares a story about a boy who is planning to murder his mom's boyfriend. He shares a story about a boy who wants to steal cars. In both stories, his retort is the same: "Then what? What are you gonna do *then*?" He plays these scenarios through to their logical conclusion. In Eugene's mind, and eventually in each child's mind, the final scenario is not peace, resolution, or a *happily ever after*. It is loss, misery, and a lifetime of institutionalization and incarceration: living in a concrete cube for the rest of one's life, condemned to an existence of second-guessing and wondering, "What was I thinking?"

I love what Eugene is doing, especially in today's world, because we have become so myopic, so immediacy-focused, so selfish, and so conditioned to take what we want. Many of us have become so entitled. As much as I wish it were otherwise, life is *not* a free, all-you-can-eat buffet.[40] It's necessary to be reminded of this; it's a public service that Eugene is providing. While there are millions

---

[38] ABC News' *Nightline Up Close*: 8/13/02.
[39] Read *How Life Imitates Chess*, by Garry Kasparov, or see the tremendous example of Dr. Jeff Bulington in Franklin County, Mississippi (CBS News' *60 Minutes*: 3/26/17).
[40] Unless you're lucky (or cursed?) enough to be born into royalty.

who are indeed doing the right thing, working for what they want, giving back and into communities and those in need, there are also millions with open hands and unexercised minds and muscles.

To contrast that problem, let's take a look at an opposite extreme: imbalance, dissatisfaction, and joyless lives resulting from *overwork*. When I was a senior in high school, our student council brought in a speaker by the name of Mark Scharenbroich. He's still around, living in Minnesota.[41] Let me tell you something. This man kept 400 of us enraptured for 90 minutes. We were 18. Do you remember being 18? When I was 18, there wasn't much that anyone could say to me that sounded right, wise, or insightful. But Mr. Scharenbroich? He kept us mesmerized for an hour and a half. I heard him about 10,950 days ago, but his words echo in my ears some 30 years later. Here's a recollection of what he said:

"Listen to me. You're each invincible, and you have your whole life ahead of you. And when you leave this place, you'll scatter to the winds. Some of you will go to college; some of you won't. Some of you will marry, some of you will divorce, and some of you will do neither. Some of you will make promises to yourself. You'll say, *'When I get this degree, then I'll be happy,'* or *'When I have that car, then I'll be happy,'* or *'When I marry this type of person, then I'll be happy,'* or *'When I make so much money, then I'll be happy.'* Well let me ask you something. When, exactly, do you think these people will be happy?"

"Never," we whispered.

"That's right. Never. Do not, please, *DO NOT* become one of these people. Strive, yes. Achieve, yes. Contribute, yes. Earn, yes. Give, yes. Help, yes. But *do not* live a life of misery, of bargaining, and of promising yourself happiness when such-and-such happens or when you have this or that. Because these people, my friends, are among the most unhappy people in the world."

His words made so much sense then, and they make even more sense today. I am, unfortunately, a slow learner though. It took me about 12 more years to grasp the razor-blade sharpness of what Mark was telling us. I have a Type A personality,[42] and it all came to a head one day, standing across the kitchen island as I listened to my wife

---

[41] www.nicebike.com.

[42] http://en.wikipedia.org/wiki/Type_A_personality.

implore, "When will it be enough, Blake? When will you have learned enough, experienced enough, accomplished enough, or helped enough clients to be satisfied with your life? I can't live like this, Sweetheart. You have got to figure this out. I can't go another seven years listening to you say, 'When this happens or that happens, then… .' You've got to learn to be content, or you're going to drive both of us into the ground." Wow. With tears streaming down her face and her hands trembling, I saw it all slipping away. Everything I had worked so hard for — security, education, clients, co-workers, my boss, my in-laws, my parents, my future — all jeopardized by the driven pursuit itself. What irony. In trying to have all, to do all, to be all, I would lose all. I will say that, at least for me, the completion of my formal education (the following year), was the point at which I finally felt at peace. Only then could I (at least in my own way of rationalizing) finally ease up on the gas pedal and drop 'er down from 90 to 60 mph. Upon the birth of our daughter and the loss of Will, I have dropped 'er down from 60 to 55 mph, but I'm a living example of someone who has to work daily at relaxing. More irony. As Laurence Sterne wrote, "Men tire themselves in pursuit of rest." Indeed.

While it took some sense of *having arrived* to bring me a modicum of self-gratification and peace in my professional life, I do believe that we can do better for our children and young people. While it may take them years to internalize the message, that shouldn't stop us from delivering it. As I see it, one of the greatest ironies of all is that at a time when they are the least prepared, teenagers are required to make some of the most determinant choices of their entire lives. Specifically, (1) *How will I earn a living* and (2) *With whom will I spend my life?* Equally important questions that precede, coincide with, or follow the teenage years include:

(3) *What will I believe in or place my faith and trust in?*

(4) *Where will I go? Live?*

(5) *Who will I be?*

(6) *How will I contribute?*

(7) *What will I stand for?*

A great leader answers these seven questions for himself — and helps others do the same. Like the chess player, the strategic thinker sees several moves ahead, grounded in who he is and where he's going; the ineffective leader struggles with personal contentment and direction across his lifetime. As it's often been said, *You can't lead others if you can't lead yourself.* As adults, these questions *continue* to beg answers and face challenges frequently, but we should do all we can to help the Michaels of the world think upon them. We should, as strategists ourselves, work to help tomorrow's leaders think several moves ahead and answer these seven immensely pivotal questions before they get answered by circumstance or folly.

I'll conclude this section with a few related quotes that continue to inspire me many years after reading them.

The crowning fortune of a man is to be born to some pursuit which finds him employment and happiness, whether it be to make baskets, or broadswords, or canals, or statues, or songs.
Ralph Waldo Emerson

Do what you love. Know your own bone, gnaw at it, bury it, unearth it, and grow it still.
Henry David Thoreau

We do not go to work only to earn an income, but to find meaning in our lives. What we do is a large part of what we are.
Alan Ryan

In the end, it is important to remember that we cannot become what we need to be by remaining what we are.
Max DePree

Let us so live that when we come to die even the undertaker will be sorry.
Mark Twain

The most elusive key to satisfaction is not getting what you want ~ but wanting what you get.
Anna Muoio

He has the most who is most content with the least.
Diogenes

As long as we think that we don't have enough money, we don't ask the important questions about our lives. We use that rationalization to protect ourselves from the fearsome fact that we do have choices…and they must be made. Sometimes we hate to admit we'll never be happy with what we have. It's time to be happy with who we are.

Shoshana Zuboff

Many people today are hungry ghosts. Bottomless stomachs, small mouths. Always wanting…and nothing is enough.

Elizabeth Gibson-Meier

Only the educated are free.

Epictetus

It requires a very unusual mind to undertake the analysis of the obvious.

Alfred North Whitehead

Culture

The second pillar differentiating strategic organizations from ordinary ones is *culture*. Sure, strategic leaders consider the external ecosystems in which their organizations operate, but they first emphasize the cultural context internal to their own organization. This makes sense for a number of reasons, the primary reason being a matter of influence and the realization that while leaders might be able to anticipate or mitigate their environment, they can generally influence and sometimes approach a degree of control within their own culture. This tract identifies seven elements or levers that strategic leaders pull in efforts to grow the desired culture. Leveraging all seven proves influential to a purposeful strategist and is elemental to the deployment of the *Strategic Triune*.

Seven Elements of Culture

¹B	e	l	i	e	f	s							
	²L	a	n	g	u	a	g	e					
³B	e	h	a	v	i	o	r	s					
⁴P	r	o	c	e	s	s	e	s	/	S	y	s	t	e	m	s
										⁵T	o	o	l	s
				⁶S	o	c	i	a	l		S	t	r	u	c	t	u	r	e	s
			⁷E	n	v	i	r	o	n	m	e	n	t	/	E	c	o	s	y	s	t	e	m

Figure 6: *Seven Elements of Culture*

The first cultural lever is *Beliefs*. Beliefs are the wellhead of any culture. Consider, by way of example, the myriad forms of *theism* (e.g., atheism, monotheism, polytheism, or even animism) and their impacts on any given civilization. The belief in the supernatural (or absence of belief) shapes culture in countless ways, from the important (what happens when one dies) to the mundane (what holidays are observed). Similarly, an organization's beliefs equally affect and determine its own culture.

Here's an example. Just this morning I was working with an organization comprising 30,000 employees across 12 countries. In conversation with a senior leader, I was told this: "Our CEO and EVP of HR don't value our people. Essentially, they're missing that gene. It affects everything around here. Rather than considering how people will feel and react to changes we're going through, they — and the CFO is the worst — just focus on the dollars and the operations." An entire book could be (and many have been) written about this single reality.

The second cultural lever is *Language*. Beliefs must be communicated, and the ways in which language unfolds and reflects culture are well documented. From the Chinese languages that are character-rich (depicting relationships and visual phrases) to the Western languages that are words surrounded by words comprised of bits and bytes and letters, the effects of beliefs on language are ever-present. Organizationally, consider an example regarding engineers. While they all have a common language predicated on logic, math, structure, and the like, each field of engineering has its own unique language. Electrical engineers, mechanical engineers, chemical engineers, production engineers — they all have their own nomenclature, and this influences the ways they communicate with each other and across bridges to other engineering tribes. Another rich example would be the military (and paramilitary organizations with multi-layered hierarchy) and their acronyms. On no fewer than a dozen occasions, I've been handed a list of internal acronyms within the first week of working with a military group or paramilitary organization. *Oy vay,* it's enough to make me *verklempt* just thinking about it.

The third cultural lever that any strategist should acknowledge is *Behaviors*. Every culture has its norms, taboos, and overall expectations for behavior. From touching and secrecy to spitting or urinating in the street, what is normal or accepted in one culture may be abnormal or unacceptable in another. The same is true for any organization. What goes over like gangbusters at Apple might go over like a lead balloon at IBM. Be sure you know your audience and learn to merge gently before stretching too hard or too fast. Behaviors, while elastic, often become rigid and fragile with age. To become an effective change agent, you must immerse yourself adequately and earn credibility and trust. Once people know you're the real deal and sincere about your strategies and suggestions, they'll be more inclined to indulge you and your nonconformist suggestions that challenge the status quo.

The fourth cultural lever is *Processes/Systems*. As behaviors and various organizational efforts evolve and become more ideal, they typically become practices that are institutionalized through various processes and systems. This is an important evolutionary leap for any organization, because it reflects a passage from "one offs" to defined, repeatable best practices that solidify a culture even further. Granted, some specific organizations — by their very nature — resist the institutionalization of best practices, but most pine for them, because they yield greater efficiency with less effort. Examples of such processes and systems include *performance appraisals* and *material acquisition processes* and *quality assurance methodologies,* to name just three of what is potentially a limitless list.

The fifth cultural lever is *Tools*. Tools can run the gamut from hard to soft, with hard tools including literal, obvious examples like computers, smartphones, shovels, wrenches, scalpels, and soft tools including processes, methodology, systems, software, goals, training, and so forth. Lean and Six Sigma are great examples of soft tools (since they are more esoteric and cannot be held in one's hand or weighed on a scale), as are the protocols followed in group meetings or when conducting employee performance reviews. As instruments to accomplish tasks, tools come in many forms and cannot be ignored, although they are often overlooked. Every organization employs both hard and soft tools, and their existence, mix, and usage partially define a culture.

I was listening to a leader who said, "Our employees' computers and software programs are five years old, at best. Our customers think we're glossy and shiny and contemporary. One of our worst fears is that one day, they'll pull back the curtain and see that all their data are held together with twine and spit."

The sixth cultural lever is *Social Structure*. Organizations can be designed in many ways, from traditional, hierarchical, top-down arrangements to organic, fluid, embryonic, practically structureless arrangements. Similarly, some organizations are paternalistic, while others are maternalistic; some are dictatorial, and others laissez-faire, and some possess peacocky power structures, while others reveal invisible undercurrents of power that can only be seen upon careful inspection by the most astute, informed, or intuitive observers. As social creatures, we quickly perceive social structure and adapt if we are to avoid extinction.

To create images in your mind that reflect social structure, consider the Catholic Church and contrast it with what you know about Ben & Jerry's Homemade Ice Cream company, or BMW and how it varies from Nordstrom. Social structure is the result of many things (though predominantly beliefs and habits), but what is most important is why a particular structure is reinforced, and therefore, still in operation. This provides the strategist a very large, clean window into the soul of an organization.

The seventh and final lever is *Environment*.[43] While context is not everything, it is indeed something determinant — and understanding the environmental context in which an organization exists is key to appreciating the dynamics and interplay of variables affecting the daily life of a business, synagogue, tribe, etc.

---

[43] This element was first introduced in *The Omniscience Octagon*.

In Jared Diamond's Pulitzer Prize winning tour de force, *Guns, Germs, and Steel,* we are sensitized to the importance of one's surroundings and the effects of resources on tool-creation. Likewise, when traveling, one sees the consequences of raw materials on architecture and construction. Where there are trees, there are many wooden houses. Where there are fewer trees, there is stucco or adobe. Where there are quarries, there are stone or brick homes, and so on.

Whether it's architecture, as just mentioned, or factions warring for table scraps of limited resources, a culture's environment is a cog that interacts with all the others, driving certain predictable loops or outcomes.

These seven elements of culture are vitally important for a strategist to be aware of if for no other reason than to provide a clear view of the relevant tissue that holds an organization together.

Processes and Performance

The third pillar differentiating strategic organizations from the rest is *processes and performance.* In the wake of great leadership and healthy culture, there is an increasing pull toward optimization, efficiency, discipline, rigor, replicability, and continuous improvement. Likewise, with burgeoning improvement and maturity, there is a declining tolerance for non-performance. Perhaps surprisingly, however, there is a yang to these yin. While processes and performance hint at greater standardization and alignment, there should also be processes and performance for innovation, creativity, challenging the status quo, or hosting sacred cow barbeques. A reticence to jettison the old and adopt the new has proven fatal for countless organizations. Atari and Wang are handy examples, though there are countless more. Last time I saw the statistic, approximately seven of ten U.S. companies that are launched fail within the first 12 months, and among family businesses very few survive beyond the first generation — and even fewer beyond the second generation, so the odds of failing far exceed those of succeeding. To learn from those who succeed and fail, we study many clear patterns. Chief among them is the need to build a replicable, focused machine that is, where appropriate, supple like the willow.

Figure 7: *The Algebraic Bike*

Here's a specific way to think about what I'm describing. Even the most ordinary bike has two tires that work in unison. They each provide distinct purposes — e.g., steering or propulsion — and each purpose is best served by working together. The tires are joined by this algebraic x, representing the *secret sauce* for which all organizations hunt. Great organizations appreciate that *processes and replicability* must congeal in some way with *innovation and breaking molds*. There are myriad wonderful methods for refining organizational processes, from TQM and Lean to Six Sigma, as well as great methodologies like TRIZ to think beyond the proverbial box. What matters most to me, in the context of this particular rant, is that employees are afforded both the opportunity to refine their world along with encouragement to re-invent it when it is mutually beneficial to customers and employees alike.

They say in the South, "You gotta dance with the one who brung ya." Unfortunately, a blind commitment to the wrong partner (in this context, the product, service, brand, image, slogan, etc.) can prove disastrous. There are more examples than can be mentioned in these pages, but consider any organization that holds on to its declining slice of a declining market. Like the stubborn raccoon in Wilson Rawls' *Where the Red Fern Grows,* any organization that reaches into a hollow log to grab a shiny silver object may very well starve with its riches in one hand. Learn from those who have preceded us and work tirelessly to shape an organization that questions itself, its past, its means, and its ends.

Sales and Service

The fourth and final pillar of strategic organizations is *sales and service*. In both the for-profit and not-for-profit sectors, money is a requisite fuel and so it is not unusual to focus first and foremost on funding and generating revenue before valuing leadership, culture, processes, or performance. This is understood and yet remains one of the most common chicken-or-the-egg dilemmas. Many organizations elect, often by necessity, to focus predominantly (if not exclusively) on making money, generating revenue, meeting payroll, and maintaining cash flow. Other organizations elect, for various reasons, to focus on leadership, culture, processes, and performance, believing that sales and service will follow and will enable the organization to meet its many financial commitments.

Obviously, these two ends of the same spectrum are just that — the extreme ends. Most organizations swing more toward the middle, constantly working to balance seemingly intangible elements like leadership and culture with the more quantitatively oriented aspects of processes, performance, sales, and service. It is the responsibility of a great strategist to appreciate the choices along this continuum and lead the organization in the right direction at the right time. Failure to do so ensures a most calamitous future, while respecting the best practices of great strategists dramatically increases the odds of organizational excellence.

When I think upon sales and service and the experiences that have shaped my sense of each — from the vantage points of *consumer/end-user* to *moderator of marketing focus groups* to *facilitator of product design* to *decision-maker about pricing* to *victim of misrepresentation and fraudulent practices* — I, like you, see an endless corridor with infinite doors on either side. Truth be told, there is more to the conversation about sales and service than I hope to address in our limited time together, so please allow me to communicate the following with respect to the strategist's responsibilities and imperatives as they relate to the sale and support of one's products and/or services:

> First, I believe it's important to be a realist about one's widget(s). It's extremely easy as an employee to believe your own press or become drunk at the corporate water fountain

and succumb to internal hype. Imbibing is good and necessary if one wishes to *lean forward and live into the future* rather than die bit by bit via repetitive work in a prairie-dog town of cubicles. But too often, after becoming the boiled frog within an organization, one comes to view the water as the fountain of youth — immaculate, rare, magical...when in reality, it's a whole lot like the one in Seattle, Chicago, and Tampa. In other words (and this is heresy, so brace yourself accordingly) *it's a commodity* — just as a tissue is a tissue, whether I call it a Kleenex or Puffs, and a photocopy is a photocopy, whether I call it a Xerox or a Canon, and a phone is a phone, whether I buy it from Verizon or AT&T. Imbibe, yes, but remain adequately detached to be an objective scientist. Objectivity is paramount for strategists if they are to help navigate followers through inevitable fogs and resulting delusions. Yes, I'm all for loyalty and getting employees lathered-up and stoked-out about how great one's employer is...how unique... how irreplaceable...how indispensable; these are normal desires that we all share — to be part of a *special* enterprise. But retain perspective; imbibe — but also be the designated driver. Differentiation, while it certainly occurs through product design, function, quality, etc., is wonderful — but the chasm between your product/service and the next guy's or gal's may not be as broad and deep as you perceive, and it's seldom enough to warrant complacency or egotism. To fight commoditization in a world that is compressing to the size of a BB, invest in your people — and differentiate through them. *Any organization's greatest assets wear shoes.* Outside of a Steinway or Bösendorfer piano, nearly every other purchased good depreciates or is sensitive to market fluctuations. But like the finest pianos in the world, people are appreciable assets that, if cared for, invested in, and nurtured, will be worth far more tomorrow than they were yesterday. Trust me in this — you'll thank me and so will your customers who reap the benefits of high quality and great service and will happily pay your and your employees' paychecks.

Second, I want to acknowledge the importance of consultative or partnership-based selling. The day a salesperson realizes he is a *solver-of-problems* rather than a *pusher-of-product* is a momentous day indeed. In working with scientists in national laboratories following 9/11, whose organizations were pursuing the dollars flowing into Homeland Security markets, I observed a great deal of trepidation. Scientists do not perceive themselves as salespeople, and they were very reluctant to engage in and pursue sales, despite the money that was flowing in the streets. Rather than going against their nature and attempting to make them salespeople *per se*, I encouraged them instead to view sales as *problem-solving with a quantitative indicator of success at the end:* money. A sale. In due time, the light bulbs went on and I'm happy to say that scientists can be formidable salespeople.[44]

There are tremendous resources available today for anyone interested in learning more about — or improving as a salesperson or provider of service. Again...an endless corridor, so I will conclude with this third point: True strategists don't see the cost of a problem, they see the value of a solution.

Why, when I point to the moon, do you stare at my finger?
Chinese Proverb

Having seen the innards of hundreds of companies, I'm often flabbergasted at the blinding myopia that handicaps good decision-making. For example, I observed a $12 million problem with a $60,000 solution get waylaid, nitpicked, delayed, then ultimately kiboshed by a 24-year old newbie in the finance department.

I sat in a plane at the gate for two hours — along with 184 other passengers — as flight attendants waited for a member of the ground crew's union to arrive with gloves and a trash bag to remove a broken plate that had been found in a seat-pocket in first class. There's a $20,000 problem with a $7 answer if I ever saw one. You see, where

---

[44] This is an example of Hapkidoing human energy and will be discussed in detail beginning on page 171.

tacticians see costs, strategists see the price of a problem. Here are two examples that may help illustrate the point; the first is from a professional colleague and the second is hearsay — but makes the point nonetheless.

A company's new Operations personnel were having difficulty getting a piece of equipment back up and running. It had changed over the years to a computer-based operating system and, despite bringing in the *experts,* the equipment continued to break down.

One of the newbies remembered hearing about a guy named Frank who had left as part of a re-org after running the Operations department for a number of years. Being desperate, they gave Frank a call. Frank said that, although he was enjoying playing a lot of golf and while it might require him to push back his tee-time, he would see what he could do to help. The manager said he would make it worth Frank's while.

Frank arrived at the plant, went to the unit, and asked everyone to leave the room while he listened to the equipment. After about 10 minutes, he pulled a piece of chalk out of his pocket and placed an X on the equipment before calling the manager back in the room. Frank told the manager if he opened up the shell where he put the X, got down on his knees, and looked up at a 25° angle underneath the pulley, he would find where an arm had broken and that everything would run just fine after the arm was replaced. In a matter of another 15 minutes the machine was repaired and running great.

The manager asked Frank how much he owed him. Frank thought about it for a minute and said, "$100,000." The manager was shocked but didn't want to show it, so he decided to ask Frank to itemize the work and deliver an invoice to him in the morning so he could submit it to his boss for payment. Not only did he want to pass the buck, the manager thought Frank would see how unreasonable that amount of money was for the short period of time he spent on the job.

The next morning he found a handwritten invoice with Frank's name and address at the top. Underneath it read:

One white chalk *X*:	$	1.00
Knowing where to put it:	$	99,999.00
Total:	$	100,000.00

Moral of the Story: Strategic leaders see the price of a problem rather than the picayune cost of solving it. As an organization once told me: "We don't charge by the bullet, we charge for the kill."

Here's the second story to drive home the importance of selling based on value-based pricing rather than costs. *(I've adopted dollars instead of francs to make the value obvious.)*

A young mother and her daughter ran into Picasso in a Paris bistro. "Would you be so kind as to draw a picture of my daughter and me?"

"Certainly," he replied. With that, he grabbed a piece of paper and sketched away. A few minutes later, he handed the mother the paper and smiled warmly. The mother looked at the drawing and thanked him.

"It's beautiful!" she exclaimed. *"Thank you so much.* How can I repay you?"

"You cannot. The picture you hold in your hands is worth $10,000."

"$10,000?" she gasped. "How can it be worth $10,000? It took you less than ten minutes to do this!"

"Actually, it took me 50 years."

Summary of Parts One and Two: The Strategic Triune and Four Pillars

We began with three problem statements, among them: *Strategy is a core strand of DNA within excellent organizations, and far too many organizations are missing it.* Whereas most literature on the subject has focused on strategy itself — its inherent anatomy, purpose, relationship to vision, etc., our quarry also includes the person behind the strategy. Our first clue was a footprint that revealed this: Great strategists think, see, and interact differently than managers and most leaders.

Unpacked, this observation conveyed two observations, one individual (illustrated through *The Strategic Triune*) and one organizational (illustrated through *Four Pillars of Strategic Organizations*). Using *The Strategic Triune,* we learned that true strategists demonstrate six mental aptitudes, each of which can be improved by using *The Mind Map*. Second, strategists view the world integratively. We explored how each of us can do this more adequately through *The Omniscience Octagon*. Third, the most exemplary strategists succeed at making sure that ideas are *others' ideas*.[45] They achieve this through *Inclusive Ownership*.

Finally, strategists demonstrate a successful orchestration of *leadership, culture, processes and performance,* and *sales and service*. Through these *Four Pillars,* inquiring strategists see a prioritized chronology for use in their own organization.

Committed leaders will achieve a more robust mastery of strategy through deploying the resources described thus far, but the kaleidoscopic perspectives provided in Part Four and the philosophies and tools provided in Part Five will equip practitioners with even more radical, concrete, and proven methods used by some of the greatest strategists around the globe to build indomitable organizations, to feed a hungry world, and to achieve more modest though equally worthwhile aims closer to home.

You ain't seen nothing yet.

Al Jolson

---

[45] This has also been described as the *reflected glory principle*.

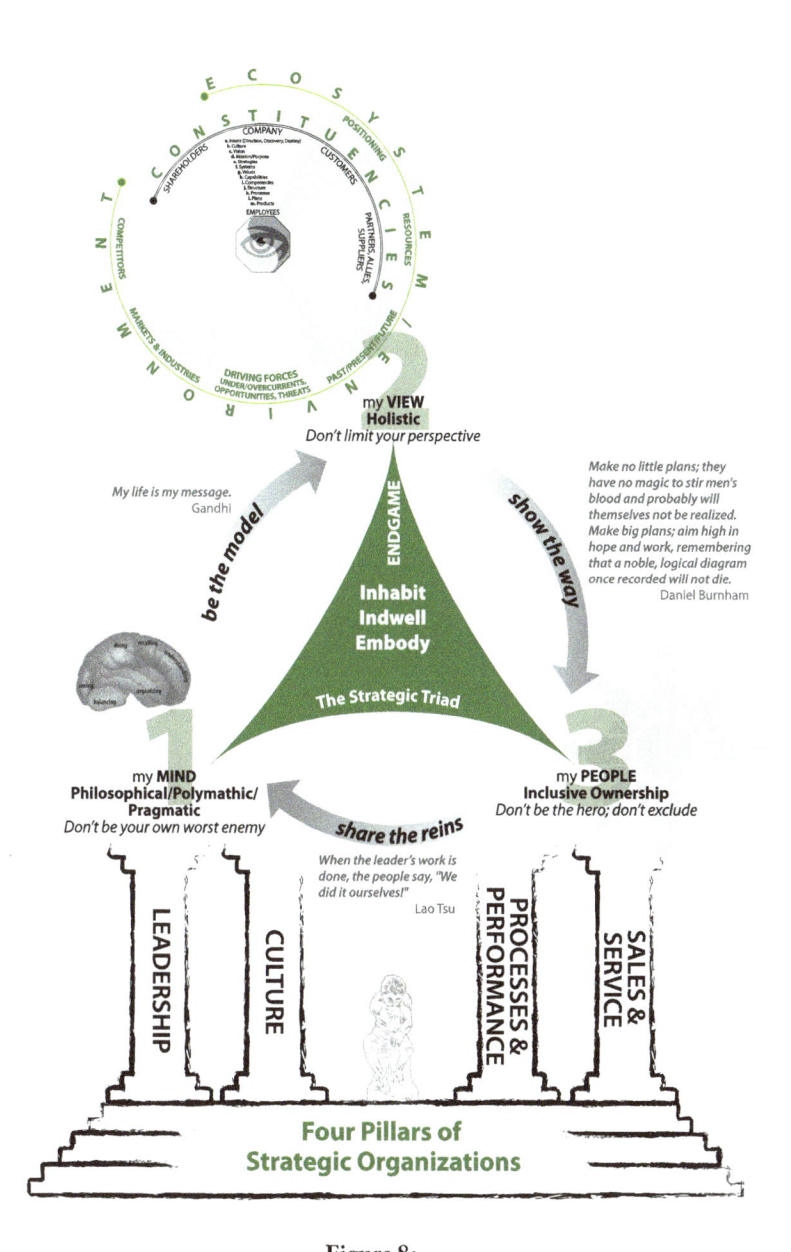

Figure 8:
Cultivating the Strategic Mind, Integrated Models: Strategic Triune (The Mind Map, The Omniscience Octagon, Inclusive Ownership) and Four Pillars of Strategic Organizations

IV
Kaleidoscope

One's mind, when stretched by a new idea, never regains its original dimensions.

Oliver Wendell Holmes

If the only tool you have is a hammer, you will see every problem as a nail.

Abraham Maslow

Twisting the Kaleidoscope
A Few Perspectives on Strategies and Systems

Time to shift gears. We're going to take what I hope will be a fascinating and equally oblique turn. We're going to zag into random, brief scraps of ideas designed to make you think[46] and make potentially unexpected connections. (In the *Strategic Mind* workshop, this section of content is accompanied by a dozen experiential activities, brain teasers, and kinesthetic puzzles. In lieu of being together face-to-face, we'll be working without that advantage, but I'll do my best to try and bring the ideas to life through explanation.) The phrase *twisting the kaleidoscope* is mostly a fun way of describing our attempts to explore and probe the boundaries of creativity and ideation in hopes of seeing strategy through fresh, unexpected lenses.[47] It's more than *thinking outside the box;* it's about thinking upon things other than the box in hopes that, upon returning to the box itself, we'll perceive it freshly and altogether differently. Creative strategists do this all the time anyway, usually by accident, but doing it knowingly, intentionally, and with purposefulness[48] elevates one's game to an entirely new level.

In the following sections, the anatomy will be as follows:

1. **Outline to the Flake**[49] (as in, the flakes within the kaleidoscope — these will be major concepts and new ways of thinking upon common problems) with **Observations** (where I'll add my 2¢ commentary or more detailed explanation)
2. **Reflections** (where I'll share one example on usage)

---

[46] And hopefully, about things you don't *normally* think about.

[47] If we were together in person, you'd be reclining in a bean bag by now and staring at PowerPoint slides on the ceiling through a kaleidoscope. The purpose of this would be to change your perspective.

[48] With "conscious competence," as Maslow might say.

[49] Each flake provides a creative, polymathic, new way to think about strategy through different lenses.

Remember, the brain is an organ, but it functions much like a muscle. As we cover the ideas, constantly ask yourself this strategic question: "Is there anything here that *informs me*, helps me see *beyond my current worldview*, or serves as a *useful analogy?*"

Outline to the Flake

I. **Biology: Neo-Cortex, Limbic, and Brain Stem**

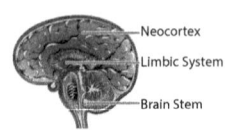

   A foundational building block of Strategic and Systemic *Thought* is the process of *THINKING*. There are differences between the mind and the brain and the way the two are conditioned societally. The brain is an organ, yet it functions much like a muscle — especially in the most formative years of childhood. So how does the brain (and consequently, what we think of as the mind) work? The "triune brain"[50] is comprised of three main parts:

   A. **Cerebrum** (contains **Neocortex**): Complex thoughts, reasoning, language, judgment.

   B. **Limbic System**

   1. Feelings, emotions, mood, attitude.

   2. Panic response (dodging a car without thinking).

   3. When people are emotional, the limbic system dominates reasoning, temporarily rendering people irrational. The neocortex is clouded, and limbic responses generate black/white reasoning at best. Crude thinking handicaps us, we get more flustered and frustrated, and the emotionality thwarts us further.

   4. Memories of *abuse, trauma, tragedies*...or *graduating magna cum laude* or the *birth of a child* would be stored here.

   5. Sense of smell is the only sense that doesn't go through the thalamus to be processed first. This is why smells evoke such strong memories and emotions.

---

[50] Google this to learn more.

6. PMS: 5-10 days prior to menstruation, the limbic system is inflamed.

7. Limbic system is slightly larger in females. (Evidence: smell, bonds with children, etc.)

C. **Brain Stem:** Basic functions. Often called *reptilian brain* because it's found in lower-level critters too, aka lizards, etc. Body temperature, heartbeat, breathing, blood pressure.

D. **Observations**

1. What implications and effects does the triune have on strategy? What surprising contradictions impede strategy? What seemingly counterintuitive strategies are actually right on target?

    i. We value (and need) logical, rational, well-reasoned thinkers and strategists in our organizations.

    ii. Our school systems are predominantly designed to educate children in logic: math, sciences, reading, writing, SAT, ACT, LSAT, MCAT, and courses on philosophy. Culturally, there is still traditional "IQ Bias," meaning, despite all the chatter about the importance of multiple intelligences (among which, EQ is one example),[51] IQ still trumps everything else.

    iii. And yet, the limbic system:

    a. Can lay waste to our best efforts when people's negative emotions engage.

    b. Should be leveraged, if we want to tap feelings.

If you would persuade, you must appeal to interest rather than intellect.

Benjamin Franklin

---

[51] For more information, read anything by Howard Gardner (www.howardgardner.com/books/books.html). For more on EQ ("Emotional Quotient") read anything by Daniel Goleman (www.danielgoleman.info/blog).

Reflections

At first blush, the overriding importance of logic makes total sense, because it is simply an extension of what is valued in education as well. Similarly, strategy around the world is rooted in logic, and yet logic constitutes only a portion of the equation of exemplary strategy. Humans are sentient beings, often gloating and taking pride in being *higher-level primates* and *rational thinkers*, but conservatively speaking, we are profoundly affected by the limbic system — the feelings, emotions, and moods that wash over us constantly. Can you begin to imagine the consequences of this subtle, often overlooked, yet profound reality? To begin, acknowledge the dichotomous pull across most Western schools of thought that is retarding the development and nurturing of great strategists. How do the greatest of strategists think and operate in the world, and why is the pull between the cerebrum and limbic system hamstringing the education and production of strategists?

Organizations (and educational systems) emphasizing predominantly logic-oriented strategies that fail to breed passion, excitement, and connectedness often fall short.

Most ordinary organizations drown in mediocrity while their leaders focus on logical strategy alone without leveraging the limbic system and tapping into the wheels of performance turned by attitude, motivation, excitement, and feelings. Darkly, the limbic system can also undermine our best strategic efforts when people's negative emotions engage (for so many pedantic reasons like *we discount people by excluding them from strategy development sessions and are then forced into a selling/buy-in mode, we don't deliver on commitments, etc.*). When an individual is emotional, the limbic system overrides reasoning to the extent that the neocortex is clouded. What began as logic succumbs to emotion and now swirls in a cloud of confusion. A logical, well thought out, well intentioned parental argument with a hormonal, angry teenager typifies this scenario. Similarly, when we ignore the brain stem and reptilian instincts of self-protection, survival, or routine, the most rational strategies often fail, because we omit how they threaten one's status quo or challenge comfort zones.

The biology of the brain is just one consideration for great strategists. Leveraging the cerebrum (to craft logical, well-reasoned strategies) while leveraging the limbic system (to imbue cold strategy with heat, passion, and emotion) is a trait shared by strategic thinkers. Despite vehement protests, the truth remains — emotional supersedes rational — and leaders who fail to imbue *strategic ideas* with *feelings* fail to give strategy an emotional imprint or tattoo. In return, this makes it quite difficult, if not impossible to generate significant, long lasting buy-in and momentum.

1. What are you doing...can you do...should you do...to drive *strategy* deep into others' brains?
2. How can you tattoo strategies on people through more emotionality?
3. How can you include people more fully/wholly to bring strategies to life and make them more memorable?

Outline to the Flake

II. **Physics: Thermodynamics (Conservation & Entropy), Gravity, Chaos Theory**
We can learn much from the field of physics that helps us conceptualize key phenomena in strategies.

  A. The field of **thermodynamics** studies the *behavior of energy flow in natural systems.*[52] Two of the Three Laws of Thermodynamics[53] are helpful here:

   1. **Law of Energy Conservation:** While energy can be converted from one form to another, it can neither be created nor annihilated.
      i. *Lesson: People have energy; the strategist's challenge is to direct it.*
   2. **The Law of Entropy:** Everything runs inexorably from order to disorder and from complexity to decay.[54]
      i. *Lesson: Keep things simple; over time strategies can break down and the strategist's responsibility is to keep the wheels on the wagon, especially during tumultuous change.*

---

[52] Sometimes, systems are idealized as closed systems, in which there is theoretically no transfer of energy in or out, such as in the proverbial vacuum, or perhaps in a biosphere or greenhouse.

[53] As summarized by Dr. Isaac Asimov. See Google for his many appearances and explanations.

[54] Entropy is constant or increases in closed systems. The entropy of an open system can decrease, which would be a measure of the increase in order.

3. **Reconciling "Laws 1 and 2" with "Self-Organizing Systems" (SOS)/Emergence/Complex Systems:** Self-organization refers to a process where the internal organization of a system, normally an open system, increases naturally without being guided or managed by an outside source. Generally, for SOSs to occur, four characteristics must coincide:
    i. Thermodynamically Open
    ii. Many Parts with Local Interaction
    iii. Nonlinear Dynamics
    iv. Emergence (new/coherent items that aggregate over time)
        a. Examples of open systems (or "processes"):
            - Flocks of birds, schools of fish, swarms of bees (and termites), rivers, turbulence, convection, avalanches, hurricanes, forest fires, tectonic shifts, traffic jams, critical mass, herding, groupthink, epidemics, fractals, friction, stock markets, poker games, eBay, and viral and/or trending social media.
            - Spontaneous Magnetization: As a bar of iron cools, ferromagnetic particles magnetically align themselves with their neighbors until the entire bar is highly organized.
            - Water particles, suspended in air, form clouds.
            - An ant grows from a single-celled zygote into a complex multicellular organism and then participates in a structured hive society.

The fascinating part: The organization seems to emerge spontaneously from disordered conditions, and it doesn't appear to be driven solely by known physical laws. Somehow, the order arises from the multitude of interactions among the simple parts within an environment.

b. *Lessons: First, acknowledge that nature abhors a vacuum. Second, realize that people prefer open systems that welcome participation rather than closed systems that exclude (Yes, "the haves" like exclusivity and memberships, but that's a different topic). Third — and this is the cool news — open systems are self-organizing, which means they're no harder than closed/controlling systems, and they generally add much more value, because a greater percentage of each person's energy within the system is voluntary, and therefore, more plentiful.*

B. **Gravity**[55] — "Just because you can't SEE it doesn't mean it isn't there." Sometimes we see only the effects.

   1. *Lesson: For many employees who are farther from strategy and closer to its tactical execution, it can be difficult to see the strategies themselves. A strategist's responsibilities include educating employees about "the big picture" and how it relates to them.*

---

[55] Motion due to gravity, before and after Sir Isaac Newton:

1. Aristotle taught that heavy objects fall faster than light ones.
2. According to Galileo, all objects fall with the same acceleration (rate of change of velocity), unless air resistance or some other force slows them down.
3. Newton showed there is a connection between the force that attracts objects to the earth and the way the planets move. Newton showed how the sun's gravitational attraction must decrease with distance. Newton's theory of gravitation says the gravitational force between two objects is proportional (related directly) to the size of their masses. That is, the larger either mass is, the larger the force is between the two objects.
4. Einstein's theory of gravitation, widely known as *the general theory of relativity,* states that gravitation is an effect of the curvature of space and time. Einstein's theory involved a complete change in ideas about gravitation. The general theory of relativity is based on two assumptions. The first assumption is that space and time are curved wherever matter or energy is present. The second assumption, known as the Principle of Equivalence, states that the effects of gravity are equivalent to acceleration. To understand this principle, suppose you are in a rocket ship at rest in space – that is, without gravity or acceleration. If you drop a ball, it floats and does not fall. If the rocket accelerates upward, the ball will appear to you to fall to the floor exactly as if gravity had acted upon it. Thus, acceleration produces the same effect as gravity. The Principle of Equivalence predicts that gravity must cause the path of a light ray to bend as the ray passes near massive bodies, such as the sun, that curve space. This prediction was first confirmed in 1919 during a total eclipse of the sun. The sun also bends and delays radio waves. This delay was measured by sending radio signals between the earth and the Viking space probes that reached Mars in 1976, providing the most precise confirmation yet of general relativity. General relativity has also been applied to cosmology, the study of the universe as a whole. The theory predicted the universe must either expand or contract. Observations such as a shift in the wavelength of light from distant stars indicate the stars are moving away from us and the universe is expanding.

C. **Chaos Theory**

1. Three key theories of the 20th century: *Quantum Mechanics,*[56] *Relativity, Chaos.*

2. **Misconception:** Chaos theory is not necessarily about disorder, but rather the driving pursuit to find order (and patterns) where there often appear to be none.

3. **Chaos Theory** is a blanketing misnomer that is often used to describe multiple phenomena of science, from mathematics and physics and biology to finance and music. Where the classical sciences end, chaos is only the beginning. The terms *complexity theory, complex systems theory,* and *complex nonlinear dynamic systems* provide a better description of the subject matter, but "chaos theory" is the more widely utilized term.

   i. Focused on the study of **nonlinear systems** (not straight lines, not easily predicted, and not always easily modeled through mathematics).

   ii. **Systems:** The understanding of the relationship between things that interact.

   iii. **Modeling:** Systems can be created which will, theoretically, replicate the behavior of the original system. Through modeling, we can be predictive to the point of mathematical models (e.g., Newton's law of gravity helps us understand how a pile of stones might interact when stacked and toppled).

   iv. **Noise:** When studies of linear systems result in strange/anomalous findings, failure is often blamed on experimental error (noise)…originally, noise was referred to as chaos. Today, studying the noise is a major component of chaos research.

   v. **Complexity:** Defined by the complexity of the model required to effectively predict a system's results. (Weather — can only be modeled with an exact duplicate of itself; hence, very complex.) A simple system would involve predicting the time

---

[56] The branch of physics that deals with atomic and subatomic systems.

it takes a train to travel from point A to point B, assuming there are no stops in between. The formula is simple: miles/mph (distance and speed are the only required data points). Modeling a pile of stones, perhaps surprisingly, is a very complex system. Predictability is hard, hence the system is complex.

vi. **Chaos Theory in *Real Life*:** Systems of dynamic equations have been used to model everything from population growth and epidemics to arrhythmic heart palpitations and the stock market.

vii. *Lesson: Life is complex, and finding patterns can be quite difficult — but that's an aim of a good strategist. Realizing that few things are altogether linear, try to build diagrams and models to make strategies palpable and tactile. Don't disregard noise (for example, employee complaints or followers who ask the same questions repeatedly — this is instructive noise, and the latter is usually a statement disguised as a question). I know you appreciate the complexity of life, but be encouraged that there are perhaps more patterns to be discovered than we readily acknowledge.*

Learning Lab: Idea(s) in Action

The Numbers Game

To experience the power of pattern — perform this exercise with your family, friends, or employees.

Set-up:

Provide a copy of the document that follows.
Participant will need a pen or pencil.

Instructions:

Round 1: Connect the numbers as quickly as possible using a solid line from #1 to #2 to #3 etc., through #60. *No one has ever failed.* Go! By 30 seconds, you should be at #15. By 60 seconds you should be at #30. By 90 seconds you should be at #45. By 2 minutes you should be at #60.

Document the time to complete. How long did it take?

Instructions:

Round 2: The goal in this second round is simple: Beat your last time. Before beginning, however, study the page for a moment. Do you notice a pattern?

You will notice that *even numbers* are on the right, and *odd numbers* are on the left. You may notice other subtler patterns, but this observation is adequate to cut your time by at least 30 percent.

Begin.

Summary:

We learn from chaos theory that as a strategist, a primary aim is to identify patterns. *The Numbers Game* is a simple, fun way to reinforce the importance of patterns — and how knowing the pattern can dramatically improve accuracy, performance, and efficiency. As a strategist, make it a key goal to coach and mentor others to find the patterns at play in their organization, their team, their family, and their life.

Reflections

1. What are some ways you can engage people's energy more fully?
2. What has become *too complicated* that you should simplify?
3. How can you create a more *open, inclusive system* as a leader?
4. How can you help people see, hear, smell, taste, and feel strategy? How can you make it more real and palpable to others?
5. What squeaky or disruptive noises in your organization should you be paying more attention to/responding to?

Outline to the Flake

III. **Sociology: Culture, East/West Variances**

As strategic and systemic thinking must occur in some context — let's extend the seven elements/levers of culture and apply them to two real scenarios, followed by a brief exposition on sociological implications of the Eastern and Western worldviews.

A. **Seven Elements of Culture**

1. To what extent do we account for *Beliefs, Language, Behaviors (and Processes), Tools, Social Structure,* and the *Environment* when we develop strategies? (And why might this matter?)

    i. In their first decade, heart transplants failed for a brutally ironic reason: The very body they were meant to save rejected them.

    ii. Many mergers and acquisitions fail — not because of external factors, but because of the internal *white blood cells* that attack from within and destroy the foreign, new, unrecognized *intruders.*

    iii. *Lesson: A strategist benefits greatly when he accounts for the seven elements in all his work and creations.*

B. **Eastern and Western Worldviews**

 1. **Cartesian Thinking:** Among his many scholarly contributions to Western thought, French philosopher Rene Descartes introduced the notion of *reductionism: the breaking of things into parts.* Reductionism works brilliantly for the watchmaker, but limitedly for the strategist.

 2. **Eastern Thinking:** Eastern thinking is different in a number of ways, among them its expressions of holism. The consideration of yin-yang (Chinese), um-yang (Korean), in-yo (Japanese), and its many variations permeate all aspects of Eastern culture. The inclination to think systemically, with consideration of opposites, and holistically, with consideration of all the parts, is a complementary worldview that strengthens any strategist's reductionist tendencies.

 3. *Lesson: There are times to be a watchmaker (pardon the pun) and times to be systemic in the broadest sense, accounting for the interplay between all the cogs in a machine, organization, or culture. It is imperative the strategist does not discount the importance of culture, particularly as it varies around the globe and within diverse social groups.*

Reflections

1. How can you help disparate or competitive groups within your organization work better together? What help do the seven elements seem to provide to your problem?

2. Are you always talking about *the parts* or are you also talking about their interplay and the system-at-large? Do people see their slice of the big picture?

Outline to the Flake

IV. **Psychology: Mental Blind Spots, Target Fixation, and The Third Eye**

Although there are dozens of relevant psychological phenomena that affect strategic thinking, here are three key concepts that we should consider:

A. **Mental Blind Spots:** We all have them, and we do not know what we do not know. "How can you taste my tea if you do not empty your own cup first?"

   1. Examples in your own life? ("I had NO IDEA!")

   2. *Lesson: Are there biases or views you have that may be founded on your own perceptions rather than reality? How can you know what you do not know? How can you help others to see if you cannot see yourself?*

B. **Target Fixation:** As we fixate on a target, we veer toward it, sometimes to the exclusion of logic and everything else.

   1. When driving, have you ever noticed that if your eyes wander to the left or right for a prolonged period of time, the vehicle itself drifts correspondingly?

   2. "Remember three numbers and choose between cake or fruit."[57] In this experiment, participants in Group A are fed lunch followed by cake. Two hours later, they're asked to remember three numbers. As the numbers are being dispensed to each participant, a researcher innocuously enters the room and starts offering people cake or fruit as a snack. The vast majority of participants, remembering the cake from mid-day, choose fruit.

   3. "Remember seven numbers and choose between cake or fruit." Group B is asked to remember seven numbers. Time and again, these participants choose more cake than fruit, because the rational part of their brain is distracted, leaving decision-making to the limbic part of the brain.

---

[57] There's that darn limbic, getting in the way again.

4. *Lesson: Our mind goes where our eyes (or appetite) go. Be careful and en garde — do not let yourself, your leaders, your employees, or your organization become unknowingly distracted.*

C. **The Third Eye** (aka Magic Eye)[58]

1. Have you seen one of these pictures? The Magic Eye images look like some sort of colorful geometric mess — but as one stares with *lazy eyes,* a 3D image appears.

2. *Lessons: First, just because an individual doesn't see the image doesn't mean one doesn't exist. Second, just because another person can't see the image doesn't imply the strategist is wrong. So, assuming the image is there and the strategist is not wrong about its existence — he is obligated to make the picture clearer — to train others to see the image. Too often, we get frustrated when others don't see...or can't see what we see. Don't get frustrated and don't get angry. Get helpful. Get clever; think of new and fresh and more successful ways to help people see the vision, the strategy, or whatever it is you're trying to show them.*

Reflections

1. Do you surround yourself with people who help you know what you don't know?

2. Is your company or organization focused? What are you doing as a strategist to reduce distractions and maintain focus?

3. Do you ever get frustrated or angered by people *who just don't get it?* If so, look in the mirror: It's not their responsibility to get it — it's your responsibility to communicate effectively and make strategies clear.

---

[58] www.magiceye.com to order those great 3D images created using their patented stereogram algorithm.

Outline to the Flake

V. **Mathematics: Game Theory and Fractal Theory**

Undergirding the work of chaos theory and similar fields, mathematics plays a key role in many current pursuits and discoveries. Let's pause to consider just two areas of interest that help us think about strategic and systemic thought from a unique perspective.

A. **Game Theory**

1. A branch of mathematical analysis developed to study decision-making in conflict situations. Such situations exist when two or more decision makers who have different objectives act on the same system or share the same resources. There are two-person and multi-person games. Game theory provides a mathematical process for selecting an optimum strategy (specifically, an optimum decision or a sequence of decisions) in the face of an opponent who has a strategy of his own.

2. In game theory, one usually makes the following assumptions: Each decision maker (aka *player*) has available to him two or more well-specified choices or sequences of choices (*plays*).

    i. Every possible combination of plays available to the players leads to a well-defined end-state (win, loss, or draw) that terminates the game.

    ii. A specified payoff for each player is associated with each end-state (a *zero-sum game* means that the sum of payoffs to all players is zero in each end-state).

    iii. Each decision maker has perfect knowledge of the game and of his opposition; he knows in full detail the rules of the game as well as the payoffs for all other players.

    iv. All decision makers are rational; each player, given two alternatives, will select the one that yields him the greater payoff.

v. *These last two assumptions, iii. and iv.* in particular, restrict the application of game theory in real-world conflict situations.[59] Nonetheless, game theory has provided a means for analyzing many problems of interest in economics, management science, and other fields.

3. Two or more decision makers having different objectives and acting on the same system or sharing the same resources. [a common reality in strategies]

   i. *Lesson: Because of (iii. and iv.), we are reminded that strategies must account for — if not leverage — the emotional interests, aspirations, and aspects of human interaction in your enterprise. Simply put: Do not focus solely on the "cold, hard science" of strategizing to the exclusion of "the soft stuff." In practice: Involve people, recognize them, and link emotional payoffs to their contributions.*

B. **Fractals** — In the most generalized terms, a fractal demonstrates a limit. Fractals model complex physical processes and dynamic systems. The underlying principle of fractals is that a simple process that goes through many iterations becomes a very complex process. Fractals attempt to model the complex process by searching for the simple process underneath.

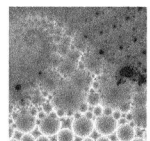

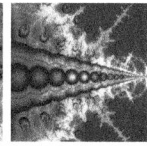

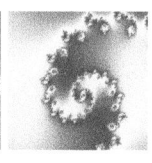

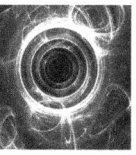

1. *Lesson: To what extent do we see leaders or employees overcomplicating the simple? Hello? Anyone? Is this not a most common reality? Come on — conduct a few man-on-the-street interviews (the sort you find on most late-night*

---

[59] For more on the *cooperative* aspects of game theory, see what is often referred to as "The Prisoners' Dilemma," Robert Axelrod's *The Evolution of Cooperation*, W. Poundstone's *Prisoners' Dilemma* or *The Arithmetics of Mutual Help* by Martin Nowak, Robert M. May, and Karl Sigmund.

talk shows) and tell me I'm wrong. It is the tendency of humankind to overcomplicate.

The best argument against democracy is conversation with the common man.
Winston Churchill

Reflections

1. What is your organization doing to account for the human side of the strategic equations it's developing? Deploying? How can you ensure that everyone wins something? What would be a triple-win (where the market, the organization, and employees benefit)?

2. Do you see fractals at work in your organization? If you were to interview the individual, would he understand, express, and be a representation at the granular level of what is desired at the organizational level? If not, your organization is not aligned. Each and every jot and tittle of the enterprise should contain the entire DNA strand. What can you do to ensure what's desired *at the top* is what's occurring *throughout?* Remember that old "telephone game" where the first person starts a rumor and passes it on down the line? This is a great analogy for any organization. What *rumor* or *truth* is being passed down the line where you work? The communication breakdown occurs at the intersections; what can you do to improve the exchanges between leaders and followers?

Outline to the Flake

VI. **Astronomy and More: Aristotle, Ptolemy, Copernicus, Tycho Brahe, Galileo, Johannes Kepler, Sir Isaac Newton**

Here, our particular interest is remembering that a common trajectory for early explorers, researchers, scientists, philosophers, creators and, in general, thinkers, is sometimes a progression from *unbridled curiosity* and *supposition* to *perceived heresy* to, ultimately, *acceptance* and *mainstreaming of a new reality*.

A. **Aristotle** (384-322 BCE)

   1. Greek philosopher and tutor to Alexander the Great. Aristotle was preceded by Plato who was preceded by Socrates. Aristotle is regarded as one of the most accomplished polymaths in human history. He wrote and taught extensively on subjects ranging from physics, metaphysics, poetry, theater, biology, and zoology to logic, rhetoric, politics, government, and ethics.

   2. To get the ball rolling, Aristotle believed in and described a *fixed, unchanging heavenly firmament* with a *prime mover* and endowed the universe with many philosophical abstractions rather than empirical observations.[60]

   3. Though brilliant and right about many things, Aristotle was wrong, of course, about the idea that the earth is "always at rest" and that the universe is "fixed," because the earth indeed moves and the universe is expanding and changing, but it's much easier to steer a moving ship — so at least with his contributions in astronomy we see the continuation of an important dialogue that echoes throughout the ages.

B. **Ptolemy** (approximately 87-150 CE)

   1. Greek Astronomer who spent much of his life in Alexandria, Egypt.

   2. Authored *Mathematike Syntaxis* (aka *Mathematical Composition*). This work was so admired that it became known as the *Almagest,* meaning "the greatest."

---

[60] *De Caelo* and *Metaphysics*.

3. In his work, Ptolemy rejected an existing idea that the earth moves. He pointed out that the earth is spherical and claimed that everything in the universe moves either toward or around the earth's center.

4. Yes, Ptolemy was wrong, too — the earth does move, as we all know, and it is not the center of our own solar system, much less the universe.

C. **Nicolaus Copernicus** (1473-1543)

1. Polish Astronomer, authored *On the Revolutions of the Celestial Spheres,* published in 1543.

2. Developed the theory that the earth is a moving planet. He is considered the founder of modern astronomy.

3. Copernicus espoused that every planet, including the earth, revolves around the sun. Also, that the earth spins around its axis once every day. He demonstrated how the earth's motion could be used to explain the movements of other heavenly bodies. Copernicus could not prove his theory, but his explanation of heavenly motion was mathematically strong and was less complicated than Ptolemy's theory.

4. Ah, now we're getting somewhere. This heliocentric view was extremely controversial so, while Copernicus was right — and later proven so by Galileo's telescope — many of Copernicus' contemporaries thought he was a loon.

D. **Tycho Brahe** (1546-1601)

1. "Tycho" (Tyge Ottesen Brahe) was a Danish nobleman and astronomer who authored *De Stella Nova* in 1573.

2. Tycho was the last major astronomer to work without the aid of the telescope. He worked to combine the geometric benefits of the Copernicum system with the philosophical benefits of the Ptolemaic system into his own model of the universe, the Tychonic system. At the end of his life, he was assisted by Johannes Kepler, who would later use Tycho's astronomical information to develop his own theories of astronomy.

3. Tycho is credited with the most accurate astronomical observations of his time, and the data were used by his assistant, Kepler, to derive the laws of planetary motion. No one before Tycho had attempted to make so many redundant observations, and the mathematical tools to take advantage of them had not yet been developed. He did what others before him were unable or unwilling to do — to catalogue the planets and stars with enough accuracy to determine whether the Ptolemaic or Copernican system was more valid in describing the heavens.

4. Tycho realized that progress in the science of astronomy could be achieved not by occasional haphazard observations, but only by systematic and rigorous observation, night after night, and by using instruments of the highest accuracy obtainable. He was able to improve and enlarge the existing instruments, and construct entirely new ones. Tycho's naked eye measurements of planetary parallax were accurate to the arcminute. His sister, Sophia, assisted him in

many of his measurements. These jealously guarded measurements became the possessions of Kepler following Tycho's death.

5. Tycho's death remains a mystery. Historians argue whether he died from a bladder infection, of a medicine containing mercuric chloride impurities, or by murder — poisoned by Kepler himself, who took possession of Tycho's data after his death, despite Tycho's desire that it be left to his family.

6. Now we're *really* getting somewhere. The use of *the scientific method,* the *integration of prior systems*, greater *accuracy* than ever before resulting from nightly attendance, and a murder plot followed by theft of intellectual property! I share so much about Tycho, because he is the lynchpin; much of what preceded him was conjecture and speculation, whereas much that followed him was predicated on more rigorous analyses. (By this time, we're starting to see what began as Aristotle's folly, Ptolemy's error, and Copernicus' suppositions giving way to Galileo's telescope and house arrest, culminating with his absolution at the hands of Kepler and Newton.)

E. **Galileo Galilei** (1564-1642)[61]

1. Italian astronomer and physicist; authored *Sidereus Nuncius (Starry Messenger)* in 1610, *Saggiatore (The Assayer)* in 1623, and *Dialogue Concerning the Two Chief World Systems* in 1630.

2. Galileo is considered the founder of modern experimental science. He made the first

---

[61] Though the internet is rife with information on individuals as prominent as Galileo, I find this one particularly thorough with respect to Galileo's relationship to the Church. www.newadvent.org/cathen/06342b.htm.

effective use of the refracting telescope to discover important new facts about astronomy. He also discovered the law of falling bodies as well as the law of the pendulum. Using his telescope, he became convinced of the truth of Copernicus' theory that all planets, including the earth, revolve around the sun.

3. Perhaps most famously, Galileo was placed under house arrest by the Catholic Church for his heretical scientific views. He was rehabilitated in 1741 (14 years after Newton's death) by Pope Benedict XIV, who authorized the publication of Galileo's complete scientific works.

4. Despite being right, Galileo's views and support of Copernicus' heliocentric observations so threatened the existing power structure of his time that he was silenced through house arrest for the remainder of his life. Don't cry for him, however — his remaining years were rather cushy; he was free to travel from friend's house to friend's house, and was received quite well by most. Ironically, Galileo went blind five years before his death.

F. **Johannes Kepler** (1571-1630)

1. German astronomer and mathematician.
2. Beating Galileo to the punch by just a few years, Kepler was actually the first astronomer to openly uphold Copernicus' theories.
3. Kepler articulated three laws of planetary motion:
    i. Every planet follows an oval-shaped path, or orbit, around the sun, called an *ellipse*.
    ii. An imaginary line from the center of the sun to the center of a planet sweeps out the same area in a given time. This means

that planets move faster when they are closer to the sun.

iii. The time taken by a planet to make one complete trip around the sun is its period. The squares of the periods of two planets are proportional to the cubes of their mean distances from the sun.

4. Benefiting from the work of Tycho and his collaboration with him, Kepler was able to extend the work of Copernicus and provide, with greater accuracy than ever before, a clear understanding of the heliocentric universe and planetary motion. By the end of Kepler's life, we're seeing firmer entrenchment and broader acceptance of ideas articulated 100 years prior by Copernicus.

G. **Sir Isaac Newton** (1642-1727)

1. English astronomer and mathematician; authored *Mathematical Principles of Natural Philosophy,* published in 1687. More commonly referred to as *Principia,* this work is considered one of the greatest single contributions in the history of science. It includes Newton's laws of motion and theory of gravitation. It was the first book to contain a unified system of scientific principles explaining what happens on Earth and in the heavens.

2. Amazingly, Newton invented calculus and identified gravity within an 18-month timeframe between 1665 and 1667.

3. Newton realized that "one and the same force" (gravity) pulls an object to Earth and keeps the moon in its orbit. He found that the force of universal gravitation makes every pair of bodies in the universe attract each other. The force depends on the amount of matter in the bodies

being attracted and the distance between the bodies. The force by which the earth attracts or pulls a large rock is greater than the pull on a small pebble, because the rock contains more matter. The earth's pull is called the *weight* of the body.

4. Using today's vernacular, *Newton was a rock star*. Calculus? Check. Gravity? Check. It would take the likes of Einstein to challenge Newton at his own game, and that would be more than 200 years hence. By the early 1700s, Newton had established astronomy, a new branch of mathematics, and combined findings that set the world ablaze for another two centuries.

Reflections

First and foremost, take comfort knowing that when people think you're a heretic or a dolt, you're in good company. Even luminaries are not always right. As Thomas Edison commented, *"We now know a thousand ways not to build a light bulb."*

But you gotta start somewhere. You gotta put a stake in the ground. *"A journey of a thousand miles begins with a single step."*[62]

It's important for strategists to be voracious learners, Shakespearean-level observers, and constantly curious about the world. Remember, conventional thinking won't yield quantum leaps. You gotta break some eggs to make an omelet. A recurring trajectory for those who challenge the status quo or who question convention is often:

1. Supposition ("I wonder...")
2. Perseverance ("I'll keep trying...")
3. Ridicule ("You crackpot!")
4. Heresy ("Burn him!")
5. Resistance ("Surely he's wrong...right?")
6. Reality, Acceptance, Mainstreaming ("Sorry, we were wrong.")

---

[62] Attributed to both Confucius and Lao Tzu.

Notice how these scientists worked. They built on prior efforts, integrated existing findings, experimented, made a few risky but educated guesses, challenged the status quo and faced the consequences, published their work, and invented software (like calculus) and hardware (like telescopes) to advance their inquiries. As a strategist, one is called upon at various times to do all these things. Remain a curious, open, committed leader, and one stands a fair chance of making one's own great discovery and contribution to humankind.

Outline to the Flake

VII. **Religion and the Importance of Immeasurability**

    A. How do we measure the following?

    Faith?[63]

    Hope?

    Love?

    Liberty?[64]

    Justice?

    Freedom?

    Happiness?

    Compassion?

    With great difficulty.

---

[63] 1 Corinthians 13: *[1]If I speak in the tongues of men and of angels, but have not love, I am only a resounding gong or a clanging cymbal. [2]If I have the gift of prophecy and can fathom all mysteries and all knowledge, and if I have a faith that can move mountains, but have not love, I am nothing. [3]If I give all I possess to the poor and surrender my body to the flames, but have not love, I gain nothing. [4]Love is patient, love is kind. It does not envy, it does not boast, it is not proud. [5]It is not rude, it is not self-seeking, it is not easily angered, it keeps no record of wrongs. [6]Love does not delight in evil, but rejoices with the truth. [7]It always protects, always trusts, always hopes, always perseveres. [8]Love never fails. But where there are prophecies, they will cease; where there are tongues, they will be stilled; where there is knowledge, it will pass away. [9]For we know in part and we prophesy in part, [10]but when perfection comes, the imperfect disappears. [11]When I was a child, I talked like a child, I thought like a child, I reasoned like a child. When I became a man, I put childish ways behind me. [12]Now we see but a poor reflection as in a mirror; then we shall see face to face. Now I know in part; then I shall know fully, even as I am fully known. [13]And now these three remain: faith, hope, and love. But the greatest of these is love.*

[64] Declaration of Independence: *We hold these truths to be self-evident, that all men are created equal, that they are endowed by their Creator with certain unalienable Rights, that among these are Life, Liberty, and the pursuit of Happiness.*

Reflections

1. Down with the notion: If we can't measure it, we don't value it.
2. The most worthwhile aspects of life are immeasurable. As a strategist, do not exclude them. Yes, whenever possible, one needs to include quantitative/measurable strategic objectives. But do not succumb to the pressure to exclude immeasureables, because it is generally these that create emotional imprints and get the heart pumping.
3. "S.M.A.R.T. goals?"[65] Half-hearted is more like it. These are neo-cortex goals, not limbic goals. And remember, employees may get out of bed for reasons of logic, but they work tirelessly and zealously for matters of the heart.

Summary from Kaleidoscope
(provided in the order in which they were presented)

1. Get beyond the cold, rational aspects of strategy toward *emotionality* and *passion.*
2. *Redirect* negative energy; *direct* positive energy.
3. Vigilantly *feed, nurture,* and *direct* your strategies; do not let them die. Cultivate to ensure the culture *embraces* strategies rather than kills them.
4. Make strategies *visible, palpable, tangible.*
5. Remember that strategies are nonlinear, systemic, complex, and noisy — and where possible, *leverage* these aspects rather than ignore or futilely fight.
6. Sure, consider the *parts*...but don't forget the *holistic/contextual/integrative* nature of strategies.
7. Try *new* approaches; *remove* the blinders; *question* what you know; welcome constructive *input* and enlightenment.

---

[65] Among other derivatives: *Specific, Measurable, Attainable, Results-oriented,* and *Time-bound.*

8. Don't fixate to the point of *myopia (don't lose sight of the forest for the trees)*.
9. *BELIEVE*; be open; learn to *visualize* and *see* the strategies.
10. Account for *others'* interests and aspirations in the *clinical* planning; involve.
11. Do not *overcomplicate;* find *the story* or *narrative* you want your strategies to convey.
12. Be *curious* and willing to *persevere,* despite the potential for *ridicule* or *resistance*.
13. Remember the *soft* stuff and that many of the best things in life are *immeasurable*.

Bonus reminder: HAVE FUN along the way.

Have you now twisted the kaleidoscope and found some new answers to the strategic question: "Is there anything here that *informs* me, helps me see *beyond my current worldview,* or serves as a *useful analogy?*"

V
Ideas and Tools

A man may die, nations may rise and fall, but an idea lives on.

John Fitzgerald Kennedy

Ideas shape the course of history.

John Maynard Keynes

Ideas are useless unless used.

Theodore Levitt

If you are possessed by an idea, you find it expressed everywhere; you even smell it.

Thomas Mann

We are apt to think that our ideas are the creation of our own wisdom, but the truth is that they are the result of the experience through outside contact.

Konosuke Matsushita

Ideas are the factors that lift civilization. They create revolutions. There is more dynamite in an idea than in many bombs.

John H. Vincent

Ideas are more powerful than guns. We would not let our enemies have guns, why should we let them have ideas?

Josef Stalin

Overview

Having twisted the kaleidoscope and, hopefully, introduced a few perspectives that allow the leader to see with new eyes, Part Five of *Cultivating the Strategic Mind* is designed to introduce specific *ideas* and *tools* for growing from leader to strategic leader.

There are 23 of them. Enjoy the ride.

1 The One I Feed

A Cherokee Elder Was Teaching His Grandson About Life[66]

"A fight is going on inside me," he said to the boy. "It is a terrible fight, and it is between two wolves.

One is evil — he is anger, envy, sorrow, regret, greed, arrogance, self-pity, guilt, resentment, inferiority, lies, false pride, superiority, and ego.

The other is good — he is joy, peace, love, hope, serenity, humility, kindness, benevolence, empathy, generosity, truth, compassion, and faith. This same fight is going on inside you — and inside every other person, too."

The grandson thought about this for a minute and then asked his grandfather which wolf would win.

The old Cherokee replied, "The one I feed."

Relevant Lessons

As you think about your Strategic Leadership, ask yourself, "What thoughts am I nourishing to become a great leader? A great strategist? What are the things I think upon?"

---

[66] Adapted from Vickie Smith's work, www.discoveret.org/etil/photos_smith.htm.

2 Two Principles of 1°

The Differences Between Leader and Strategic Leader are Subtle Yet Profound

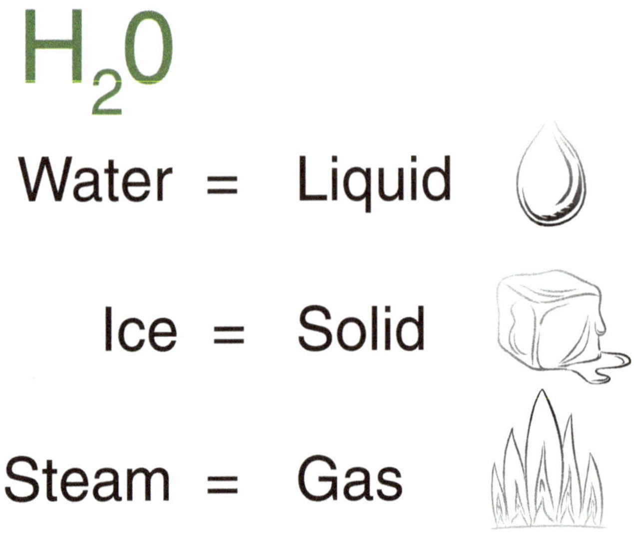

H_2O

Water = Liquid

Ice = Solid

Steam = Gas

Figure 9: *Two Principles of 1°*

In 1994, I was spending eight days a month working with a mining company. For various reasons, several mine sites had engaged our organization to help them with culture change and to create what they described as "a high-involvement work culture." I can honestly say, 23 years later, that miners are among my favorite people. They are salt-of-the-earth folk with a humbling work ethic and timeless values. I have many friends from those mines, even to this day, whom I met and worked with so many years ago. Some of our first meetings, however, were somewhat rocky. As outsiders, my colleagues and I were initially greeted with a degree of contempt, and our efforts to facilitate change were greatly resisted. In time, however, a tremendous amount of change occurred, and while we were only facilitators, I regard the mid-90s as one of my most intense growth periods.

It was during this three-year project of cultural transformation that *"Two Principles of 1°"* was born. I remember having lunch with several geologists and we were talking about change. Essentially, they believed in the aspiration to create a more participative workplace, but they didn't agree that dramatic change was possible, much less necessary. In my struggle to find an analogy or metaphor that would resonate with their scientific minds, H_2O came to mind.

"Maybe it's not a matter of buying in to the notion of needing *significant* change. Maybe *just one degree* is enough. Think of it like this. What's the difference between winning organizations and also-rans, and how broad is the chasm that separates them? Generally, isn't it much narrower than most leaders realize? Seriously, think about H_2O. How profound is the change between *just one degree* and another degree — especially, when it's *the right* degree?"

Based on this initial kernel of an idea, an observation unfolded that has served our organization well for many years now. *Two Principles of 1°* resurrects the childhood realization that H_2O can occupy three states — solid, liquid, or gas. No epiphanies here, but *the importance of 1°* and *leveraging the right 1°* cannot be overstated, because both have important applications in the world at large and certainly within every organization.

Focusing on the relevance of temperature (in this case, Fahrenheit) and tolerating no complex distractions from physicists regarding *pressure, triple point* or the like, H_2O occupies a different state at 32°F and 33°F and again at 211°F and 212°F. In the former, it transforms from a solid to a liquid, and in the latter, from a liquid to a gas. Clearly, the metaphor of 1° is a foundation for many extrapolations.

Consider the relevance of 1° in navigation. A journeying sailboat that is off course by just 1° will miss its destination by one mile for every 60 miles that it travels. An airplane leaving LAX bound for Seoul would land — not in South Korea, but, much to the passengers' chagrin — in an altogether different country.

One degree is a slight variance, but one that counts enormously. Yet this subtlety is overlooked by too many leaders and organizations.

For example, think about applying the 1° principle to Lance Armstrong's seven stripped victories in the *Tour de France*. Having raced precisely 15,133 cumulative miles between 1999 and 2005, Armstrong's seven 1st place wins separate him from the 2nd place finishers by a total of just 39 minutes and 40 seconds.[67] This is an

---

[67] Many thanks to Chad Truby, sports aficionado and all around great guy for helping me with these statistics.

astonishingly small margin of victory considering the 20 stages, three-week duration, and an average speed of 25-26 mph.

Or look at the sport of baseball.[68] Over the course of a 162 game season, a batter who hits .285 versus one who bats .300 makes approximately 80 fewer hits (assuming about 550 at bats for the season) or, stated another way, about one fewer hit for every 20 games played. Also, a .300 hitter will be a Hall of Famer, while a .285 player will not.

The same subtleties are true in golf. Tiger Woods' scoring average is 69 strokes per round.[69] At the time of this writing, the 125th ranked player (Bubba Dickerson) averages 71 strokes per round resulting in an earnings difference of $5 million for Tiger and $500,000 for Bubba.

How about motor sports (e.g., NASCAR, NHRA)? Typically, less than one second separates the winner from second place.

Whether it's cycling, baseball, golf, or race car driving, in each instance, it's the 1° that counts. This discovery reveals that winning (in sports and most organizations) is seldom about colossal failures. Instead, it is mostly a matter of degrees, and often just 1°.

Now envision a perplexed elementary student studying a beaker of H_2O and watching for changes as a blue flame warms the water to 62°F, then 63°F, and now 64°F. What happens? Nothing. *Absolutely nothing.* There is no drama, no breakthrough, no observable change within this temperature range. And so it is with many organizations that fail to identify the *right* or *relevant* degree upon which they should focus.

Take, for example, the airline industry. If an airline wanted to increase customer satisfaction, it should focus on the right aspects of customer expectations that will move the needle. What do passengers care about? Beyond comfort, three things matter most: *reliability* (e.g., safety and predictability), *timeliness* (e.g., departure, in-flight provisions, arrival), and *respect*. As a result, applying the 1° principle to improvements in these areas makes sense. For example, improving reliability through investments in equipment and technology, improving timeliness through efficient operations, ensuring on-time departures and arrivals, and improving respect

---

[68] I am indebted to Peter Lehrman for providing these facts.

[69] My, how times change. Tiger enjoyed 683 weeks as the No. 1 golfer in the world. By 2017, however, his scoring average ballooned to a whopping 73.29, and he is no longer ranked in the top 1,100 players on the tour.

Table 2: *Analysis of Armstrong's Seven (1°) Tour de France Victories*

Year	Distance (in miles)	Margin of Victory	Comments
1999	2,287	07 minutes, 37 seconds	Greatest margin of victory over 2nd place finisher, Alex Zuelle.
2000	2,050	06 minutes, 02 seconds	
2001	2,141	06 minutes, 44 seconds	
2002	2,035	07 minutes, 17 seconds	
2003	2,272	01 minute, 01 second	Smallest margin of victory over 2nd place finisher, Jan Ullrich. Armstrong won the 2003 race in the final of 20 stages during a rain-soaked time trial when Ullrich lost control of his bike and slipped on wet pavement and went down; the margin of victory would have been far less had this not happened.
2004	2,107	06 minutes, 19 seconds	
2005	2,241	04 minutes, 40 seconds	

by communicating empathy and being sensitive to the value of travelers' time are all proper applications of the 1° principle. Making investments in other areas might be appreciated, but new paint jobs, uniforms, and food packaging are less important than reliability, timeliness, and respect and — as a result — don't matter as much. They are not *the most relevant* degrees and, as one good ol' boy described it many years ago, "That'd just be polishin' the poo."[70]

---

[70] Which means, specifically, that you can *polish* and *shine* and *paint* all you want — but unless you change the essence, you're just creating an illusion of improvement.

Appreciating the 1°, the *right* degree, and the subtle differences between victory and loss is critical to extraordinary strategists pursuing a more *Strategic Mind*. Helping leaders, managers, and employees focus on 1° issues is sometimes the most important contribution one can make. Let's look at another example.

Consider *Two Principles of 1°* and the Dilbert-like words that are used daily in countless organizations. While I'm a believer in *vision, mission, purpose, BHAGs, values, capabilities, competencies,* and the like, I'm also jaded and all too aware of the eye-rolling and skepticism with which these terms are met. For years, I found myself in scores of vision/mission and strategic planning sessions. For the first few years, these were refreshing, exciting, valuable sessions. In time, however, as employees had engaged in a number of them, they became tiresome, repetitive, and often devolved into wordsmithing sessions where participants argued about grammar or word-count, and wound up creating homogeneous pictures and statements that could have applied to practically *any* for-profit business.

If I've seen the following statements once, I've seen 'em a hundred times: "Our mission is to maximize shareholder value and increase operational efficiency." "Our vision is to become the leader in our industry." Ugh. Kill me now. The final straw was when I completed two *mission sessions* for two separate organizations — one was a tire manufacturer and the other was a national laboratory — and ironically (with no input from me, only facilitation), they unwittingly created *identical* mission statements! Sure, when they're good, they're good; they help people make decisions, they provide direction, they increase engagement, and they align people toward the same purposes. But when they're milquetoast, vanilla, or neutered as a result of trying to be all things to all people, they wind up drivel. Good visions and missions provide clarity and focus. They are not supposed to be about motherhood and apple pie; they are, instead, supposed to unify, clarify, and provide direction.

How can the notion of 1° prove helpful here, in this liturgy on business terminology? When invited to help a group craft a vision or mission, for example, the first thing I ask the group to do is, "Get out a piece of paper. Define vision. Both the word itself, and the current vision for this organization. Do the same for mission." About five minutes later, I collect and read all the scraps of paper. Typically, it's a mess. The definitions and statements are all over the place. Had I not done this exercise and launched into a vision/mission session without exposing different interpretations of seemingly straightforward terms, no telling what sort of gumbo might have been created that day. After the group's laughter and heckling subsides, I then communicate the utility of vision, "When done right, here's what it is and what it can do." I explain the same for mission, values, and whatever other agenda items exist. I find that by defining them, then explaining their function, people are usually refreshed and more optimistic about the day and its value. Both the explanation, and now their common understanding of the terms is a 1° difference. There is more clarity, there is more commitment, and ironically, the day is usually *less* about the words, and more about the intent. Groups may not leave with a shiny, silver *vision statement of 22 words or less, per se,* but they always leave with a common, meaningful, in-the-bones/mind/heart understanding of what their collective direction is, where the organization is going, and why. I find this heuristic approach to be a nice antidote to the otherwise Dilbert-like, words-oriented grammar sessions that many of us have endured.

Relevant Lessons

As an individual and an organization, what are your differentiating factors? Rather than trying to be all things to all people, strive instead to identify the *one* and *right* degree upon which you should focus. Great strategists are very purposeful about this and work to help others do the same. I have introduced the notion of 1° now, because it is an important lens through which I encourage you to view the remaining ideas and tools. As you might have guessed, the differences between a strategist and a leader are not broad chasms; they are tiny increments — but yes, they are tiny increments that are consequential…as consequential as the differences between a solid, a liquid, and a gas.

3 The Philosopher King

The Spectra of Truth and Power[71]

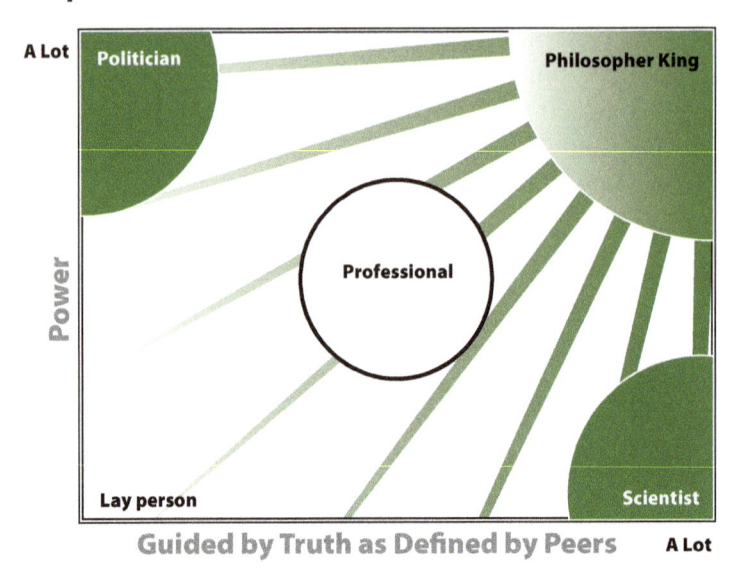

Figure 10: *Truth × Power = Philosopher King*

I don't wholly agree with the spectra as represented above, mostly because I think it's somewhat *elitist* (inferring that lay persons are neither powerful nor pursuers of truth) and *misleading* because it appears to discount politicians (many of whom *are* interested in truth), scientists (many of whom *are* quite powerful and influential), and professionals (many of whom are *both* powerful *and* guided by truth more than credited). That said, the model still has some metaphorical utility for us, so let's pan for gold.

First, I want to pin a particular reality to the corkboard. The reality is this: There are people in organizations who thirst for power more than truth, and there are those who pursue truth rather than power. Likewise, there are those who pursue neither, those who pursue both, and those who pursue varying degrees of each. Too often, we try to force-fit our perceptions of reality into little black and white boxes, and while that may be *convenient,* it isn't necessarily reflective of reality. As a strategist, we could do worse than striving toward what

---
[71] As defined by French, Raven, and Price, 1959 and 1965.

is described as a *Philosopher King.*[72] By maximizing one's influence with a quest for truth in all matters, one's character and integrity are beyond reproach and the capacity to effect change increases by leaps and bounds. I cannot understate the importance of character and integrity. To ensure I don't, let's parse them.[73]

Character & Integrity

- **Character:** the mental and moral qualities distinctive to an individual.
- ORIGIN Middle English, from Greek *kharakter* (a "stamping tool").

- **Integrity:** the quality of being honest and having strong moral principles; moral uprightness. The state of being *whole and undivided* in regard to one's beliefs and principles.
- ORIGIN late Middle English, from Latin *integritas*, meaning "intact."

- You make an impression on everyone you meet. You make a mark. What mark are you making?
- Remember, over time, your reputation will precede you.

What we build over a lifetime can be destroyed in an instant.

Relevant Lessons

Don't tolerate management malpractice. When you disagree with something, speak your mind. Sure, you need to be prudent, wise, circumspect, savvy, judicious...strategic, but don't acquiesce or sell your soul to toe the company line. Like you, I've learned that *the right thing is usually the difficult thing* and *doing what's easy doesn't come cheap.* Like the luminaries mentioned before, being right has as much to do with timing as it does with the content of one's message.

---

[72] A fantastic archetype from the West would be King Solomon. I Kings 4:29-34 *[29]God gave Solomon wisdom and very great insight, and a breadth of understanding as measureless as the sand on the seashore. [30]Solomon's wisdom was greater than the wisdom of all the men of the East, and greater than all the wisdom of Egypt. [31]He was wiser than any other man, including Ethan the Ezrahite—wiser than Heman, Calcol, and Darda, the sons of Mahol. And his fame spread to all the surrounding nations. [32]He spoke three thousand proverbs and his songs numbered a thousand and five. [33]He described plant life, from the cedar of Lebanon to the hyssop that grows out of walls. He also taught about animals and birds, reptiles, and fish. [34]Men of all nations came to listen to Solomon's wisdom, sent by all the kings of the world, who had heard of his wisdom.* Though not all kings, other, secular archetypes might include Amenhotep, Confucius, Miyamoto Musashi, and Sun Tzu, all of whom are attributed some combination of influence and wisdom of varying degrees.

[73] Etymology courtesy of *Oxford English Dictionary.*

Don't lose any sleep if you're perceived as being a radical. Chances are good that if you're not wrong, you're just early.

4 The Importance of Solitude

God speaks to me in the margins.

Unknown

Here's another truth about strategic leaders: They find time for themselves — to think. Sometimes they catch power-thoughts in the shower, in the car, on the airplane, or perhaps on a mountaintop... but often their greatest insights come in the silence of *real* solitude.

Our world is a busy one — busier each and every day.[74] For most people, the tyranny of the urgent precludes deep thought. The noise of the every day prevents us from diving deeply, introspectively, and really dialoguing with ourselves. One of my mentors, Dr. Steve Buchholz, writes, talks, and coaches extensively on the importance of "having a conversation with ourselves." He talks about an activity where he asks leaders to go away by themselves, for an entire day... eight hours, with nothing. "No cell phone, no notebook, nothing. Just themselves, and food for the day. After a couple hours, they finally have tuned out the noisy world around them, and get down to business in their mind. It's in this place of mental stillness and reflection that they finally, perhaps for the first time in years, have a meaningful conversation with themselves about things that truly matter in life."

Relevant Lessons

I don't know where you are right now. Are you on a plane? In bed? In a hotel? On a lawn chair on the beach? In the airport? In the back yard overlooking a lake? In a ski lodge overlooking the mountain? By a fireplace? In the tub? In your office? On the couch, multitasking with the remote control and telephone by your side?[75] Maybe you've

---

[74] Though written in 1993, Price Pritchett's little book, *New Work Habits for a Radically Changing World*, is packed with statistics and revelations about the rapid pace of change in contemporary society.

[75] For all I know, you're reading this while your child is reading Dr. Seuss.

got a half-dozen technological devices spread out on a table before you. You've got your cell phone, your tablet, your laptop, and a Starbucks coffee with your name on it.

Wherever you are, whatever you're doing, I have a request: *Make an appointment with yourself* for the near future. Open your calendar and *make* a day. Don't find a day; there isn't one. Not a single one. There is no day that is unaccounted for, I'm sure. If you're not at work you're running errands, and if you're not running errands you're with your family, and if you're not with your family you're heading somewhere… you see, there are no free days anymore. Not until retirement, and for many workaholics, not even then. So do it now: Make a day for *you*. Pen or type or thumb it in right now, and do some soul searching.

Go somewhere nice, somewhere peaceful. Tranquil. I'm not suggesting the usual places; I'm suggesting the unusual places, like the great outdoors. A forest, a grassland, a mountain, a secluded spot far, far away from the interstate and downtown. And don't engage in kayaking; this isn't about an activity. Activities are distractions. This isn't about jogging. That's exercise, another activity. And leave your technology in the car. If you take your devices, you'll just wind up making to-do lists and notes-to-self. Turn the phone off and detox — it's time to allow your mind, heart, and soul to slowly drift past the tyrannical urgency of every day and toward what's really important.

This is about stillness, about sitting on a rock, about standing alone and quietly just milling about, breathing deeply and seeing fresh sights. New and better thoughts will come to you if you allow them to, but you've got to give them some room. Some breathing space.

> *How can you taste my tea if you do not empty your own cup first?*
>
> ### Zen proverb

TAKE NOTE: If you don't do this for yourself, it'll never happen — and your followers are counting on a strategic, systems-thinking leader with deep, provocative, or simply overlooked ideas. And these are *not* the ideas that will come to you in the hurly-burly of every day. These are the ideas that only come to you in the margins.

> *I went to the wood, because I wished to live deliberately, to front only the essential facts of life, and see if I could not learn what it had to teach, and not, when I came to die, discover that I had not lived.*
>
> Henry David Thoreau

5 Solomonic Solutions

1 Kings 3:16-28 — A Wise Ruling

Now two prostitutes came to the king and stood before him. One of them said, "My lord, this woman and I live in the same house. I had a baby while she was there with me. The third day after my child was born, this woman also had a baby. We were alone; there was no one in the house but the two of us. During the night this woman's son died, because she lay on him. So she got up in the middle of the night and took my son from my side while I, your servant, was asleep. She put him by her breast and put her dead son by my breast. The next morning, I got up to nurse my son — and he was dead! But when I looked at him closely in the morning light, I saw that it wasn't the son I had borne."

The other woman said, "No! The living one is my son; the dead one is yours."

But the first one insisted, "No! The dead one is yours; the living one is mine."

And so they argued before the king. The king said, "This one says, 'My son is alive, and your son is dead,' while that one says, 'No! Your son is dead, and mine is alive.'" Then the king said, "Bring me a sword." So they brought a sword for the king. He then gave an order: "Cut the living child in two and give half to one and half to the other." The woman whose son was alive was filled with compassion for her son and said to the king, "Please, my lord, give her the living baby! Don't kill him!" But the other said, "Neither I nor you shall have him. Cut him in two!"

Then the king gave his ruling: "Give the living baby to the first woman. Do not kill him; she is his mother."

When all Israel heard the verdict the king had given, they held the king in awe, because they saw that he had wisdom from God to administer justice.

In this scripture we see an example of what I describe as a *Solomonic Solution*. Given the conundrum at hand, Solomon makes a seemingly unorthodox decision that (pardon another pun) cuts quickly to the truth. A Solomonic Solution has these features: *contrarian decisions that risk much, change the game, and challenge conventional wisdom yet leverage our true nature (e.g., one woman's selfishness, another's selflessness) and result in an unexpected, greater good.*

In one simple gesture, Solomon revealed truth. His actions initially seemed like those of a madman. Cut a baby in half? No! But in doing so, he exposed each woman for who she was, resulting in an indisputable conclusion. There's no haggling any longer over whose baby this is. The actions of the women have spoken for themselves.

The Greek word *akrasia* describes *a state of mind in which someone acts against his/her better judgment through weakness of will.* Literally, *without power.* A Solomonic Solution takes advantage of this, because its essence is all about one's will and true nature. In *Freakonomics,* author David Leavitt masterfully attributes the downfall of the Ku Klux Klan to the mockery that was children's incorporation of the group's secret rituals into play. The men's true nature (hate, inadequacy, fear, a sense of lost power and dominance resulting from an integrated world) was revealed through child's play, and the Klan's power — secrecy — became inert, because it became known. Or consider the GM spin-off, Saturn. For decades, the American public has held disdain for car salesmen. In a true reversal, Saturn advertised the final price of a car on the sticker and buyers came in droves. Remove the haggle and we're all in. The KKK and Saturn are diverse yet representative examples of the power of true nature and how a strategist can reshuffle the deck to change the game.

Relevant Lessons

You needn't be a shrink to understand human nature. You may be unique as a snowflake, but all snowflakes share common traits. Most people enjoy the hits played on WIIFM[76] radio. That's a great place to start. Tune in, listen, and you'll learn a lot.

---

[76] "What's in it for me." The extent to which you meet people where they are and provide them what they want for themselves often governs one's ability to influence.

What would a book be without the obligatory four-block matrix? So here's one:

1 Right

2 Control

3 Harmony

4 Recognition

Figure 11: *Typology: Interpersonal Inclinations*

There are scads of intra- and interpersonal typologies and taxonomies in the marketplace of ideas,[77] but here's a proven and constructive way to think about people. Most people gravitate predominantly toward one of these four cells.

1. **Right** — This person hungers for accuracy and thirsts to be correct. Their true nature is *Ready, aim, aim, aim, aim, aim...* ad infinitum. They tend to make few decisions, most of them correct. Know this and you'll create ways for them to win... to provide time for research and fact-checking, for accuracy, for sharing their work and quietly being acknowledged for it without making a spectacle. *Insider Note: This person has the greatest conflict with other people who like being correct, as well.*

2. **Control** — This person wants the steering wheel. Their true nature is *Fire! Fire! Fire! Did I hit something?* They tend to move swiftly, they like bullet points, they want the big picture, and if they ask questions...they often do so after the fact. To the extent you can, as their strategic leader, you should involve them, because they want some control (or lots) over people,

---

[77] For example, the *Myers-Briggs Type Inventory*®, Wilson Learning's *Building Relationship Versatility*™ (aka *Social Style*), or TRACOM's version of similar methodologies.

projects, schedules, resources, the works. *Insider Note: This person has the most conflict with others who prefer control, too.*

3. **Harmony** — These people want to know who's involved, because they want to anticipate the ripples or hurt feelings and how to quell them. Their true nature is *Ready, ready, ready... is everyone ready? Are we okay? Are we ready? Are you sure? Do you feel good about being ready? All right then, all together now... aim! Plink!* As strategist-leader, involve these folks and they'll be the glue that holds everything together, rather than the jam that gunks up the works. *Insider Note: These individuals experience as much conflict as others, but they internalize it, often to their own detriment. Whenever possible, help them out of their fetal position at the back of the cave and bring them into the light to deal with the frustrations they're feeling about others.*

4. **Recognition** — These party-going extroverts and performers want stage time. Mic time. They want to host and emcee the party; they'll bring the dip and beer. Their true nature is to seek acknowledgment, kudos, affirmation, affection, and recognition. In short, they wanna be heard! They wanna be seen! They *Fire, fire, fire! Did you see that? Did you see that? I shot the gun! I shot the gun! I might have even hit something! Did you see that?* Facilitate, coordinate, and direct their attention. Harness their energy. Allow them to diverge before requiring them to converge on a problem. Let them think aloud, then help them focus. They need their strategist-leader to help them manage their creativity, or it gets lost in the talk-bubbles over their heads. *Insider Note: Recognition-oriented people have conflict with others vying for attention and talk-time. Do not ignore the small stuff — even the tiniest acknowledgments and displays of appreciation go a long way. As Twain professed: "I can live for two months on a good compliment."*

6. Conscious Competence[78]

Strategic leaders are intentional and purposeful about developing employees. The following matrix and explanation may shed light on how one can work more effectively to help others reach their full potential.

1. Conscious Competence	2. Conscious Incompetence
3. Unconscious Competence	**4. Unconscious Incompetence**

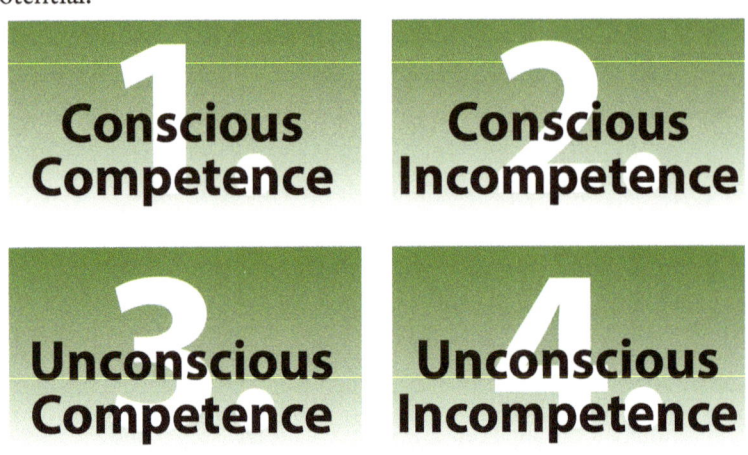

Figure 12: *Conscious Competence Matrix*

As a strategic leader, it pays to know your people. That's the real reason for another look at a behavioral typology. Generally, people can occupy varying degrees of each of these cells. Knowing where someone is will allow you to more effectively engage them in strategy, as well as manage your own and their expectations of performance, contribution, and substance.

1. **Conscious Competence** — At this level, an employee (or leader, manager, supervisor, athlete, teacher, fireman, whatever) *is good, and they know why*. This is dynamite, because the Consciously Competent individual is a high performer and a good cloner. In other words, because they're good and they know why, they're good teachers and self-replicators. If you were to ask them, "Can you go off and make some more of you?" they would say, "Sure. Be back in a sec."

2. **Conscious Incompetence** — At this level, a person

---

[78] To explore other research on the importance of consciousness itself, start with the contributions of Abraham Maslow.

sucks, and they know it. I'm sorry, but it's true. They just can't deliver. I've heard these folks described as "Ignorance on fire!" Here's the good news: Any multi-step program usually starts with *admission of the problem.* The saving grace of Conscious Incompetence is acknowledgment that "I suck." Now there's nowhere to go but up, and that's a good thing. Hey, at least I know I stink; now I can go work on it. What's *your* excuse, huh?

3. **Unconscious Competence** — Some argue this is the *highest* level of development. The *most advanced*, if you will. I get that. These folks are so good they perform in the zone without thinking. That's swell, but I still prefer Conscious Competence over Unconscious Competence, because the Unconsciously Competent individual is so far beyond being able to recall *how,* that he or she often fails as a teacher. The Unconsciously Competent individual is outstanding, but he or she either doesn't know why or can't remember how...they just *are*. It's very Zen, but here's the rub: If you ask an Unconsciously Competent person, "How can I be like you?" they'll say, "Uh, I dunno. Osmosis maybe? Why don't you ride around with me, and we'll see what rubs off on ya?" As a strategist and ultimately a developer of people, you've got to remember how you became competent — and learn to effectively communicate this to others in ways they can put into action. In such a scenario, Descartes' *reductionist* approach would be appropriate. Reverse-engineer your success, then break your competence into bite-size parts so others can emulate and apply. Along the way, be realistic, empathetic, and sensitive.

4. **Unconscious Incompetence** — Ouch. This one's gonna leave a mark. The Unconsciously Incompetent typify *ignorance is bliss,* because *their performance sucks, but they don't know it.* It's nice living in a bubble. Eventually, however, one gets popped or eaten, and that's a drag...but perhaps they'll pay attention and learn. Yes, this would be nice. As a strategic leader, you must protect these struggling,

low performers long enough for them to gain enough muscle mass and coordination to hold their heads steady, then crawl, then waddle, then run. They'll thank you in the long run and, heck — you owe it to them; after all, *I have seen the enemy and he is us*. We are ALL Unconsciously Incompetent at something, and I am a living testament to the ability to live a full and complete life without having ever understood calculus[79] or trigonometry.

Relevant Lessons

I trust that, by now, the relevant lessons are evident. If not, please refer to item "4" above.[80]

7 Visualization

I never hit a ball before I can taste the cup.

Arnold Palmer

I imagine myself jumping, swimming, my strokes, the walls, my turns, the water, clearing the surface, finishing strong, and ripping my cap off at the end.

Michael Phelps

[After winning a karate tournament] People always ask me, "How did you know he'd do that [specific kick, punch, etc.]?" I just tell 'em, "I had that fight yesterday. Today was just a repeat performance."

Chuck Norris

The Free Throws Study, University of Minnesota[81]

Baseline Data: A large, random sample of students is selected for the study. Each student shoots 25 free throws on the basketball court. Their shots become part of the "pre-" data.

---

[79] Though I praise Sir Newton, I curse him, too!

[80] Yes, I did write that. And yes, I'm talking about Unconscious Incompetence. You didn't know you could pay $20.00 to be harassed, did you? Me neither. This is fun.

[81] This study has been repeated elsewhere, including a similar, smaller demonstration at each *Strategic Mind* workshop.

Two Groups: The sample is divided in half, creating a group we can refer to as the "visualizers," and the other students we'll call the "shooters."

Over the course of the next 22 days:
- The "shooters" each shoot 25 free throws daily on the basketball court.
- The "visualizers" envision (i.e., "imagine") shooting *and making* 25 free throws daily in their minds.

Results? On the 23rd day, everyone is gathered together and shoots 25 free throws. How did each group progress? *Identically*. The improvement and accuracy of each group held constant.

The Piano Study, **Harvard Medical School**[82]

Neuroscientist Alvaro Pascual-Leone "instructed one group [of volunteers] to play as fluidly as they could, trying to keep with the metronome's 60 beats per minute. Every day for five days, the volunteers practiced for two hours. Then they took a test. At the end of each day's practice session, they sat beneath a coil of wire that sent a brief magnetic pulse into the motor cortex of their brain, located in a strip running from the crown of the head toward each ear. The so-called *transcranial-magnetic-stimulation* (TMS) test allows scientists to infer the function of neurons just beneath the coil. In the piano players, the TMS mapped how much of the motor cortex controlled the finger movements needed for the exercise. What the scientists found was that after a week of practice, the stretch of motor cortex devoted to these finger movements took over surrounding areas like dandelions on a suburban lawn.

The finding was in line with a growing number of discoveries at the time showing that greater use of a particular muscle causes the brain to devote more cortical real estate to it. But Pascual-Leone did not stop there. He extended the experiment by having another group of volunteers merely *think* about practicing the piano exercise. They played the simple piece of music in their head, holding their hands still while imaging how they would move their fingers. Then they, too, sat beneath the TMS coil.

---

[82] This lengthy explanation courtesy of A User's Guide to the Brain, *How the Brain Rewires Itself*, (pp 71-74) by Sharon Begley, TIME Magazine, January 29, 2007.

When the scientists compared the TMS data on the two groups — those who actually tickled the ivories and those who only imagined doing so — they glimpsed a revolutionary idea about the brain: the ability of mere thought to alter the physical structure of our gray matter. For what the TMS revealed was that the region of motor cortex that controls the piano-playing fingers also expanded in the brains of volunteers who imagined playing the music — just as it had in those who actually played it.

'Mental practice resulted in a similar reorganization' of the brain, Pascual-Leone later wrote. If his results hold for other forms of movement (and there is no reason to think they don't), then mentally practicing a golf swing or a forward pass or a swimming turn could lead to mastery with less physical practice. Even more profound, the discovery showed that mental training had the power to change the physical structure of the brain."

Relevant Lessons

It's been said that *where the mind goes, the heart goes also,* and Jesus Christ himself equated *lusting in one's heart with committing the sinful act itself.*[83] In his infinite wisdom, Solomon wrote presciently: "Where there is no vision, the people perish."[84] These words underscore the relationship between sight, the brain, and the figurative mind and heart. A disproportionately high percentage of the human brain is devoted to the faculty of sight, but new scientific evidence is in, and its implications are rich, fascinating, and overwhelmingly clear: The human brain has tremendous neuroplasticity — *our thoughts literally shape our brain, and our brain influences what we know to be our mind.*

The relevant lessons are many, but let's limit our focus to two. First, as a strategic leader, give great credence to the importance of visualization. Help people see.[85] Don't just *talk* about strategy, or vision, or the future — show them. *"Be the change you wish to see in the world."*[86]

---

[83] Matthew 5:27-28.

[84] Solomon, Proverbs 29:18.

[85] Because it is so different from the way many people have worked, the deployment of *lean manufacturing* literally incorporates a process entitled *Learning to See.*

[86] Mahatma Gandhi.

Second, be a sculptor of minds. Mold brains, starting with your own. Read, study, observe, interact, travel, inquire, *SEE*. Be a human sponge. If you refuse to be a learner, opting instead to be a passive couch potato, allowing the world's waste to just wash over you on a daily basis, how can you expect to be any sort of desirable, archetypal role model for others? Goodness, we're all fearfully and wonderfully made — Heaven forbid you ever forget that or squander your potential or allow others to squander theirs.

We are all worms. But I do believe that I am a glow worm.
                                                        Winston Churchill

Learning Lab: Idea(s) in Action

Chevreul's Pendulum

To experience the power of visualization — perform this exercise with your family, friends, or employees.

Set-up:

Tie a metal washer to the end of a 12" piece of colorful yarn.

Build a *target* — a bull's-eye of sorts, with concentric circles drawn on a piece of paper.

Chair and table.

Instructions:

Sitting at the table, drape the yarn over your thumb — holding it between the thumb and forefinger. Place your elbow firmly on the table. Dangle the washer — centered over the bull's-eye — about 1" above the piece of paper. Be sure the washer is still. Now, *envision the pendulum swinging forward and backward...forward and backward... forward and backward.* Don't move your hand — just imagine and concentrate upon the washer swinging forward and backward in your mind.

Summary:

Within 30 seconds, nearly all people who try this activity see the washer begin to swing forward and backward — first slowly and then quickly — moving about 3" to 4" in each direction. You can ask them to stop the swinging and again, using only their mind, to try moving the washer in a circle or sideways. Odds are, this will work, too. It's an absolutely mindblowing exercise. Even the most jaded skeptics experience movement, and it leaves most people incredulous. "Why does this happen?" they ask. Simply put, it happens, because where our mind goes, our movement follows. *Of course we are moving our hand to make this happen* even though we don't mean to, and that's the point: If our mind is set upon something, we can seldom stand in its way.

8 Transcending Politics

Figure 13: *Ideas Transcending Politics*

As a strategist, it is necessary to be the idea bigger than politics. Identify, create, sponsor, champion, and nurture ideas that transcend politics. Political correctness and politics-as-usual are strangling this country like milkweeds and crabgrass...choking out what would otherwise be a beautiful garden. The good intentions behind respect and support for diversity (and *diverse thinking* which, in my mind, is more important than race, ethnicity, age, gender, or sexual orientation) have somehow devolved. We must elevate our thinking, our dialogue, our love, and honor one another's uniquenesses. We were each born to serve a purpose and no one person's purpose (whether CEO or wastebasket emptier) trumps another's. Our society works like a beehive, with everyone contributing mightily. Without each and every effort, we all suffer — the chain is only as strong as its weakest link.

> *We trained very hard, but it seemed that every time we were beginning to form into teams we would be reorganized. I was to learn later in life that we tend to meet any new situation by reorganizing, and a wonderful method it can be for creating the illusion of progress, while producing confusion, inefficiency, and demoralization.*
>
> Gaius Petronius (66 CE),
Roman General, author of *Satyricon*,
forced by Nero to commit suicide

As a strategist within an organization, you will undoubtedly experience times of great frustration. Orchestrating change and leadership at the environmental and cultural levels is trying, tedious work. Gaius Petronius reminds us of fools' errands. We all run them from time to time. The opportunity, and your challenge, is to ensure that as many ideas as possible pass the sniff test. Are they legitimate, or are they illusions masquerading as progress? Find the pony in the pile — there usually is one (though sometimes not) — and see its essence. Craft *solutions* that are bigger than *answers*. Solutions that can revolutionize, transform, and in doing so lay waste to the political games of partisans, internal historians, turf defenders, and people still living in the past.

> *We want to revolutionize transportation at the turn of the century, but we've got to keep the horse.*
>
> Jimmy Rengel
Pillsbury

It's difficult abandoning (or even having to kill) the horse, and it's boorish to dump one's date at the dance. But these are just metaphors, and organizations must evolve. Sometimes, the biggest idea in the room requires moving on and chucking former, proven technologies or processes or structures that have outlived their purpose. As a Lockheed Martin engineer once commented to me, "Who wants to be the best buggy-whip maker in the world?" Indeed, with a few Pennsylvanian and old-world-traditionalists being exceptions, that market has seen its prime. Defining your company's future by its past can be as precarious as building a house on shifting sand. No quantity of nails or screws will hold it together. Take stock, be a realist, respect your core competencies, take a running start, and jump. Or, as a colleague once commented, "Set the house ablaze, so you're *forced* to move."

> *Diplomacy is the art of saying 'Nice doggie' until you can find a rock.*
>
> Will Rogers

There are times to be diplomatic as a change-agent, and there are times to grab a really big rock and just bash away. I've witnessed too many well-intentioned organizations run themselves into the ground. Leaders mean well; they want success, but they dance around the stinky mess in their midst, averting their eyes from reality and the need for change. It is noble and right to respect the past and to be courteous and kind when working with others, but ignoring the harsh realities of Organizational Darwinism only leads to extinction. We must all adapt if we are to survive, much less grow.

Relevant Lessons

Transcending politics requires a unique mixture of courage and delicacy, but here are three takeaways we can each apply immediately:

1. Be a realist and truth-teller in your organization. Be the mirror that reflects reality, or at least your take on it, for others. Filter ideas as they crop up, ensuring that whatever is pursued passes the sniff test and isn't just the flavor of the month or an executive's particular itch that needs scratching.

2. With great judiciousness, reverence, and care, be willing to abandon the horse. Is it really part of your future? How? Why? Why not? Maybe you need to consider a disruptive alternative. Maybe your current model is great, but its lifecycle is coming to an end.[87]

---

[87] BCG's infamous matrix might serve you well here. You know the one: *Cash Cow, Question Mark, Dog, Star.*

3. Help people transition from what was to what must be. Interestingly, many companies don't spend much time on transition. Intellectually, they go from old to new, ignoring the reality that our feelings take a little longer to catch up. You know, baggage. We like our binky,[88] and although we know the day comes to set it aside, understanding and doing are two entirely separate phases of maturation. Related, but distinct. As a strategic leader, you've got to be good with people, and helping them help themselves is key.

9 Principles of Hapkido

The Way of Coordinated Power

Let's start with an outline of the three primary principles underlying Hapkido.

I. **The Water Principle**
   A. Water flows easily downhill.   ⎫
   B. Water flows around obstacles. ⎬ *Path of least resistance*
   C. A single drop has no power or strength.   *Singularity*
   D. Water conforms to its vessel.   *Adaptation*
   E. When frozen, water is hard.   *Can be hard*
   F. When heated, water evaporates. *Can be soft*

Summary

Know the flow.
Build beyond singularity.
Know the shape, when to conform — when to avoid conformity.
When the opponent or challenge is *hard, be soft*. When it is *soft, be hard*.

II. **The Circular Principle**
   A. I bow, you bow. I respect, you respect. [*Mirroring*]

---
[88] Aka *talismanic blanket* or pacifier of some sort.

B. We reap what we sow. I bow as a student, you bow as my instructor. One day, my students will bow to me and I will bow to them in return. [*Reciprocity*]

C. Nature reflects circularity: Night yields to day, day yields to night. Season yields to season. [*Yielding*]

D. In Hapkido, force is never met with force; it is deflected and redirected. Use others' momentum rather than your own strength. [*Deflect, Redirect, Leverage*]

E. Accept nature without stress, achieve harmony where there is opposition, and never apply force against force. [*Harmonize*]

F. When you are attacked, you and the opponent are like two separate pieces. Using the Circular Principle, two pieces become one as you harmonize with your opponent. If you are confronted with anger and you return anger, there will be escalation; if you return anger with understanding, inquisitiveness, or calm, anger may dissipate or redirect toward something constructive. [*Calm the Storm*]

Summary

We are all *mirrors;* know the reflection(s). Understand the nature of *reciprocity* and its many implications (walk the talk, we reap what we sow, etc.).

Do not resist *insurmountable force;* know when and how to *yield*. *Deflect*, *redirect*, and *leverage* momenta around you.

Harmonize to your environment.

Be the *calm in the storm* that leads to something constructive.

III. **The Sum Principle**

A. The combination (sum) of the Water and Circular Principles.

B. Yin and Yang — Balance through opposite principles. Together, never-ending, and when together, there is harmony. They can remain independently; each is distinct. Yet together, there is completion and synergy.

C. Work and Rest. Men and Women. Together, there is balance and continuation.

Summary

The Sum Principle facilitates balance and harmony through combining the Water Principle and the Circular Principle.

When attacked, *deflect* and *redirect* the attack (Circular Principle), then *proceed around* and *through* your opponent's defenses to counterattack (Water Principle).

Concentrate on *where things come together* (mental, physical, social, spiritual, etc.), for this is where Potential and Synergy originate.

Relevant Lessons

The lessons are inherent in the name itself — Hapkido literally translates to *the way of coordinated power*. As a strategic leader, you know that energy exists. We all have momentum each and every morning when our feet hit the floor. Your challenge is to *direct* it.

I sat with a woman the other day who moderates focus groups for a living. She made an interesting comment as we were talking: "I am not a believer in *making things work*. Things are as they are, and I just try to direct them." Exactly. As Buckingham and Coffman pointed out in *First, Break all the Rules,* we are more apt to succeed when we help people develop what's already within them, rather than trying to work on…or *push things in* that are not already part of their personhood. This isn't a permission slip to abdicate one's developmental responsibilities. We all must continually work to improve ourselves, but as a Hapkidoist, the aim is to harness what is already there.

The utility of this philosophy has been applied to sales situations, negotiation, conflict resolution, marriage counseling — the works.[89] See the energy within your organization, community, synagogue, mosque, church, or Girl Scouts club for what it is, and just guide it. Berm it. Funnel it. Water it. Leverage it. Extend it. In short, rather than breaking hands and heads and hearts on concrete blocks, step aside and allow people to swing away — then guide their aim so it's constructive rather than harmful.

---

[89] See also, George J. Thompson's *Verbal Judo* and Hugh Young's *Aikido and the Art of Principled Negotiation.*

10 Outcomes vs. Incomes

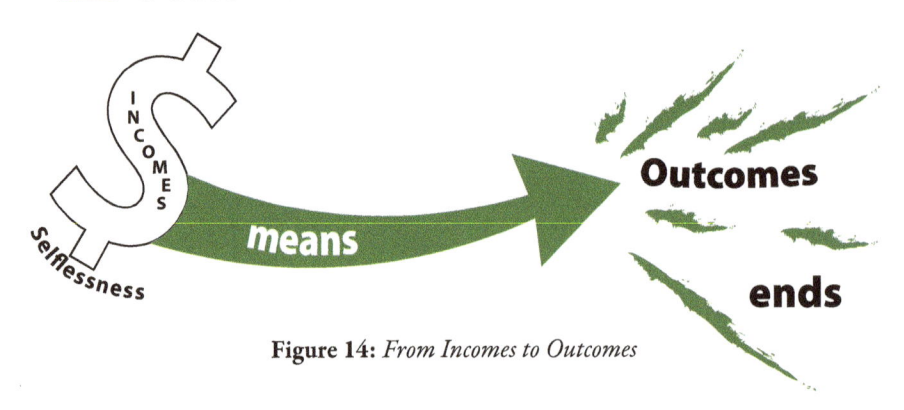

Figure 14: *From Incomes to Outcomes*

A person totally wrapped up in himself makes a small package.
Harry Emerson Fosdick

I acknowledge we're each a little (or a lot) selfish every now and then. We've got that radio blarin' WIIFM and we lose sight of all the other passengers' needs. Heck, we might even be threatening the safety of everyone else on the road, but as a strategist, we can lead more effectively when we help people think beyond themselves. I describe this process as "moving from incomes to outcomes."

I'm working with a company that is about to pay union employees only 60 percent of promised stock, while certain executives will receive full bonuses. It's unfortunate, because whatever goodwill has been garnered since prior contract-labor concessions will be frittered away in an instant. As Covey might say, "Tsk, tsk. Too many withdrawals and not enough deposits!"[90] Challengingly, because some leaders can grow accustomed to a certain degree of privilege, they may, in time, develop a fairly robust yet dysfunctional case of entitlement, too. What's good for the goose is good for the gander — if union members must concede, why shant I? *Can't we all just get along?*[91]

In recent years following the advent of the dot-com era (which, for many, was also the *dot-bomb* era), too many of us have seen overnight rags-to-riches transformations. We've watched people

---

[90] Read *Seven Habits of Highly Effective People* to learn more.
[91] Rodney King.

like Mark Cuban[92], Chad Hurley / Steve Chen / Jawed Karim,[93] Chris DeWolfe and Tom Anderson,[94] among many others become gazillionaires in a very short time with little more than a *1° different* idea. This meteoric wealth has propagated the delusion that such success is easy, or likely, or even worse — owed to us. I do wonder, quite frequently, what sort of world our children are being born into. Beyond Tom Brokaw's *Greatest Generation* and the Boomers, (who clearly grew up in a world of prosperity exceeding that of their parents) the Gen X and Gen Y and "M-Gen"[95] crowds are exposed to a multi-channel, multi-choice, *is this free* or *am I stealing it* sort of gray space. From Napster and its ultimate legitimization to iTunes and its ubiquity, intellectual property and work are not what they used to be.

As authors Joseph Pine and James Gilmore describe in their fantastic work, *The Experience Economy*, the U.S. has migrated through an *Agrarian Economy* (wherein 80 percent of the workforce was employed in agricultural work), to an *Industrial Economy*, to an *Information/Service Economy* (at which point, only 3 percent of the workforce held agricultural jobs, 17 percent held manufacturing jobs, and 80 percent held information/service jobs) to the *Experience Economy* (as exemplified by Starbucks, Niketown, Nordstrom, Bubba Gump Shrimp Co., Disney, or Rainforest Café). "An honest day's work for an honest day's pay" used to imply a few dollars for several hours of backbreaking manual labor in the scorching summer or freezing winter. Today, I see clearly that if we're not careful, it means an ever-widening divide between the haves and have-nots, continual outsourcing of jobs to all corners of the globe, and the belief that slackerdom eventually translates into an endorsement deal, fame, and untold millions.

This backdrop, though I've communicated it using American examples, is not confined to our shores alone. As I've written elsewhere,[96] what's happening here in the U.S. is representative of

---

[92] Current owner of the Dallas Mavericks who sold Broadcast.com for $6 billion.

[93] Co-founders who sold YouTube to Google for approximately $1.7 billion.

[94] Co-founders of MySpace, which Rupert Murdoch and NWS purchased (in addition to parent company Intermix Media) for $580 million.

[95] The "Millennium Generation," born in the year 2000 and since.

what's happening in every major industrialized entity with only three sizeable exceptions: the Middle East, Africa, and India. Living in a world defined increasingly by *me* and *where's my share?*, the strategist has her work cut out for her. She must be able to help employees and employers see beyond the black hole that is *personal financial gain,* and help people focus on the communal benefits of self-sacrifice, collaboration, and camaraderie. It is important, however, to maintain perspective, because my concerns that civilization is teetering on the brink of disaster because of a few glinty-eyed children is partially hyperbole. Has the world changed? Yes. Are children socialized in a different way than generations prior? Indeed, the evidence is there. They are exposed to much more, much faster, and at earlier ages. But is the sky falling? I do not think so.

> *The children now love luxury; they have bad manners, contempt for authority; they show disrespect for elders and love chatter in place of exercise. Children are now tyrants, not the servants of their households. They no longer rise when elders enter the room. They contradict their parents, chatter before company, gobble up dainties at the table, cross their legs, and tyrannize their teachers.*[97]
>
> Socrates (469–399 BCE)

Relevant Lessons

First and foremost, you will need to develop strategies that focus on the *means,* not just the *ends.* Don't allow people to get so focused on outcomes or objectives that they lose sight of the journey itself. Equally important to *moving from incomes to outcomes* is *moving beyond outcomes to means.* The Japanese have proven this to perfection, through contributions like Lean and other efforts that I presume would have brought W. Edwards Deming much joy had he lived long enough to see the fruits of his labor. Process improvement with an end in mind is pivotal.

---

[96] *The Triune for Attraction & Retention: Creating a Culture of Good Leaders, a Great Workplace, and Sustaining Employer of Choice Designation,* yours truly.

[97] Attributed to Socrates by Plato, according to William L. Patty and Louise S. Johnson, *Personality and Adjustment,* p. 277 (1953).

Give me a lever long enough and a fulcrum on which to place it, and I shall move the world.
                                                        Archimedes

Second, remember that amazing things can be accomplished if one doesn't care who gets the credit. This is sometimes described as the *reflected glory principle*. Rather than distracting yourself with the pursuit of praise, simply help everyone else around you. In the end, you'll accomplish oodles more.

If you help enough people get what they want, you'll get what you want.
                                                        Zig Ziglar

Third, remember that those who focus on themselves — on self-centric, self-preserving, myopic interests — will never achieve the greatest of goals. If you accomplish everything important to you in life, but fail those who matter most (or worse, step on them to get ahead), I would view that as utter failure.

No success can compensate for failure in the home.
                                                        David O. McKay

11 Microscoping and Telescoping:

Working For the Organization, In the Organization, and On the Organization

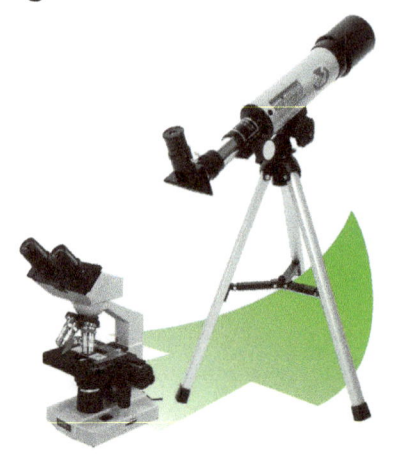

Figure 15: *Microscoping and Telescoping*

"May I take you to lunch?"

Susan Engebrecht (now Susan Thoma), a dear friend, client, and professional colleague, knew the last few months had been difficult. The CEO of our founding organization had passed away in September, and the holidays were especially difficult for all of us. It was January now, and I appreciated Susan's reaching out to lift me up.

We agreed she'd come by our office, pick me up, and treat me to a little Tex-Mex (one of my *major* weaknesses). We had a wonderful lunch, and she let me do all the talking. Ironically, I've determined — perhaps as you have — that sometimes when one does much of the talking and the other party does a lot of listening, inquiring, and encouraging, the conversation does seem to be quite pleasant![98] Talking about oneself can be, at the right time and when the mood strikes, quite cathartic. Although as a general rule I'd rather keep to myself, Susan really drew me out, and I found myself expressing feelings of loss

---

[98] I remember as a child telling my mom about a boy in the neighborhood whom I'd come to like. I carried on about how much he liked me, complimented me, inquired about me, and my mom commented matter of factly, "Oh, Honey, each of us likes those who like us. In fact, that's usually *why* we like them." This was one of many pearls of wisdom my mother dispensed. She was, and is, a true sage.

and concern that would have been overwhelming had she not been so capable and insightful. Once we had finished our enchiladas and the table was cleared, she made a comment that resonated so deeply it has come to define our business and the businesses of many clients. It rings particularly true with entrepreneurships, small businesses, and family-owned businesses that are trying to bifurcate, transition to the second generation, or aspire to grow beyond the circle of founders.

She crossed her delicate hands, placed her elbows on the table, leaned in like E.F. Hutton, and bored a hole into me with her soft, green eyes. "I know these past few months have been difficult for you, Blake. For your family...for everyone you work with, including your clients. Everyone just loved your business partner, and he's left a void that will never be filled. I know you're tempted to get heroic — to rush in, take control, and insert yourself in every client engagement, because only then can you be sure that you've done all you could. Yes, you could do this, and it would work for a while. It would work for the short-term. But I think you should take time to grieve, to empower those around you, and to trust in them. God has given you an opportunity to improve your business — the model itself, to find a new path for yourself, a path that allows more balance at the top. The former model is only duplicable if you're willing to live on the road and be involved in every aspect of every account. That's no way to live, Blake. Not for a young dad.[99] Listen to me. The day you stop working *for* the organization and *in* the organization and start working *on* the organization is the day you become an executive."

Wow. Bam. Zock. Shazaam. Kerplunk. Ding. Fireworks.

> THE DAY YOU STOP WORKING *FOR* AND *IN* THE ORGANIZATION AND START WORKING *ON* THE ORGANIZATION IS THE DAY YOU BECOME AN EXECUTIVE.

Figure 16: *Working ON the Organization*

Put that in neon lights, will ya? Carve it into stone. Tattoo it on the back of your hand. Emblazon it on a bumper sticker. Print it out

---

[99] My wife, Dawn, had just given birth to our daughter, Lauren, two years prior.

and tape it to your mirror. Scratch it on the surface of your bedside table with the car keys if you have to. Put it where you must to ensure the message is loud, clear, and front-and-center, because each letter in Susan's comment is worth a pound of platinum.

*Write it in your heart, in your mind, and most of all —
in your behaviors.*

Susan's wisdom brings us full circle to Maslow: "If not you, then who? If not now, when?" For the most part, *especially* in those smallish, tightly-knit companies and organizations out there, the people in charge...the people at the top...*define* the organization in many customers' minds. "Oh, you mean you're more than one or two people deep? I had no idea," they might say. For an organization to evolve and transcend its progenitors, it must grow larger than the inner circle and force open the tight fist of foundership.

The greatest of ideas, beliefs, faiths, and movements began with a charismatic leader, or a visionary, or a heretic, or a small band of bewildered zealots or followers — but if it has survived to this day or any day eons beyond — it did so because of its inherency, its stickiness, and ultimately, the willingness of those who nursed it to set it free...to allow it to spread its wings, fly away, and become what it must. Small-minded people clutch at barren ideas, but visionaries scatter seeds into the big, bad world...and as a result, see them grow, then multiply, then explode like tiny atomic dandelions in a crosswind.

Relevant Lessons

As a strategist, it is not your calling to protect your organization or hide its potential beneath the table. No, no, no. Your vocation[100] is birthmother. Champion. Advocate. Revolutionary. Liberator of ideas. Be a builder, hard at work to deconstruct and reconstruct your business from the foundation up if necessary. Maybe the plumbing's in place and you needn't start from scratch. Great. Bonus points. But as I described earlier, sometimes you have to put the horse down in order to drive forward.

There will be times, like so many days before, that you'll need to study your organization's inner workings like the watchmaker with a

---

[100] From the Latin *vocare*, which means "to be called."

jeweler's loop, like a researcher with the electron microscope studying the smallest particles known to man. There will also be times for stepping back and getting a fresh perspective from light-years away. Get out the Hubble. Unfortunately, many *strategists* are mostly *leaders,* and most leaders are really *managers,* and most managers are predominantly *working*-managers...which begs the question, *Who's minding the strategies?* Of course every role has equal value; I've said that before and say it all the time, because it's true. Knowing this is the case, and that individuals claiming they are strategists are really functioning like working-managers, then who the heck is strategizing in *your* organization?

Additionally, just as you should not be frequently lured into the trenches to do others' jobs, don't be seduced by the allure of heroism like Zorro. Power, inclusion, and solving problems, *being needed* can be aphrodisiacal. The *reflected glory principle,* remember? Don't insert yourself in the center of everything. Don't become the sun. Set your sights on your tiny universe itself, tinker with the rules of planetary motion, attend to the planetary bodies, and define new means and methods. Again — nature (like traffic) abhors a vacuum. The seat you vacate at the table of tactical contribution will be filled before your chair rocks back into place. And don't be a bonehead and just move to the head of the table. You're not thinking big enough. Get thee into the mind of the marketplace, that defines the demand, that creates the customer, who buys from the retailer, who purchases from the wholesaler, who purchases from the manufacturer, who sub-contracts with the woodshop, that collaborates with the design group, that envisioned your table and chairs in the first place. Once you're *there* in your strategist-mind, *and able to think of it all at the same time, seeing it as a river of tides and eddies and needs,* you have become an executive strategist of the highest order. You are, for all intents and purposes, now a grand poo-bah of strategy with ten stripes on that thick, *so-sweaty-and-old-and-worn-that-now-it's-not-white-anymore-it's-black* belt around your waist.

Yippee ki-yay, birthmother. The world is waiting: Go get it.

12 From Reconnaissance toward Renaissance

Proceeding from Scouting & Investigating toward Rebirth & New Starts

Figure 17: *Reconnaissance to Renaissance*

Just as it's important to oscillate between microscoping (less often now, I hope) and telescoping (more often now, I hope), a good strategist employs one part *reconnaissance* and two parts *renaissance* to achieve his or her ends. In my years working with thousands of leaders, I've seen two major camps: the soldiers and the philosophers. The soldiers are constantly in the field, hauling their packs and weapons on the front line. The philosophers are encased within mahogany, within ivory, in the tallest spire, of the tallest tower, on the tallest mountain. Obviously, both extremes have their drawbacks. The soldier, who's engaged daily with the men and the enemy, lives minute to minute in harm's way but has a pulse on reality and is privy to accurate, first-person reconnaissance. By contrast, the philosopher, who is otherwise engaged with the machinations of the galaxy, immersed in abstractions and theoretical wonderment.

It's no wonder that the Renaissance period began just a couple hundred years following Gutenberg's inventing the press.[101] And it's no coincidence that information is doubling, then tripling,

---

[101] Gutenberg unleashed his press on the world in 1455, and the Renaissance began circa 1650.

every half-dozen years since the expansion of the internet. There is an intense correlation between knowledge (and the absence of ignorance or naïveté) and progress or transformation. Just ask Michael, the subsequent Rice graduate, or the thirty-something who finally arrives at the epiphany *I am not the center of the universe.* With the broadening wisdom that life affords us as we outgrow the narrowness of being too close to a reality to see it from another perspective, we ultimately see with wide eyes.

Relevant Lessons

Your success as a strategist will hinge, to some extent, upon the quality of information at your disposal. Garbage in, garbage out. While away your days as a philosopher, and you forego the shot to see your strategies played out on the stage of real life. Crawl on your belly for too long engaged in the fog of battle, and you'll never have a sense of the larger theater of war. Find a logical medium, from this day to that, and purposefully invest yourself where you can hone your craft and the practice of strategy. Perhaps surprisingly (or perhaps not), the best strategists have at some point in their careers been tacticians, and the best tacticians have a little strategist in them. Alert your organization constantly of the need for reliable truths from the field, and be ever-diligent about the importance of asking *what if* questions that make the world go 'round, and I'm confident you'll occupy a niche that few leaders ever discover: master of war games, able to metamorphose at the drop of a hat. Always be you, always be true, yet always adapt as necessary.

13 The Archer's Aim: An Outside-In Approach

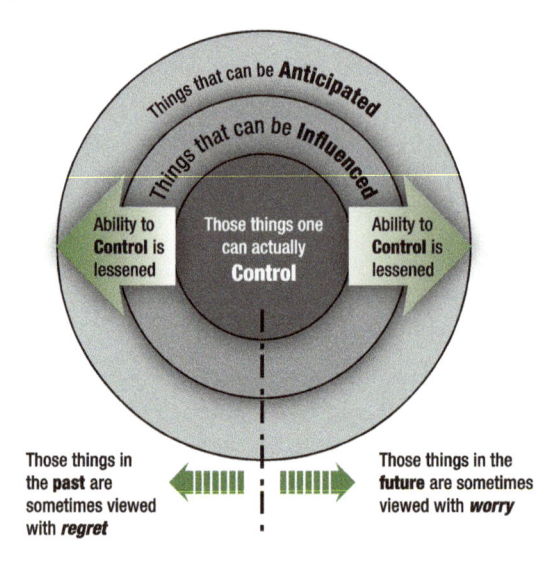

Figure 18: *Archer's Aim (aka Worry Wheel)*

"What are the things you *control* in life?" I ask. Hands shoot up.
"I can control how I behave," a man says.
"What I eat!" shouts another.
"My attitude!" hollers the stocky fellow in the back of the room.
"Great," I say, "and what do all these things have in common?"
"Me," they note.
"Yes, exactly. The only thing we can really control in life is us. How we behave, how we conduct ourselves when interacting with others in the world in which we live."

Of interest, perhaps, is that sometimes people argue with this logic — and their arguments have merit. "But I can't *fully* control me! Sometimes people make me angry, and I don't want to feel angry. Sometimes people betray me, and I don't want to feel betrayal. Sometimes people lie to me, and I don't want to feel deceived. Sometimes people hurt me, and I don't want to feel hurt. Or sometimes, I think things I don't want to think." Indeed. Points taken. But these reinforce the point: *If the most I can control is me, how futile it is to try and control things beyond me.*

"Okay, next question," I say. "Beyond what you can control, what can you *influence* in life?" More hands.

"I can influence my company," the tall woman on the front row says.

"I can influence my family," the man beside her adds.

"And other people," the woman to my right comments.

"Very good," I say, "and what do all *these* things have in common?"

"They're outside of me, and start with other people," the keen gal in the snazzy suit summarizes for us.

"Precisely. While I *can* control myself, I cannot control others. At best, I influence them. For example, if I don't want others to act like jerks toward me, I should not act like a jerk toward them."

People chuckle; time to move on.

"Third question. If I can't control something, and I can't influence something, what should I do?"

Silence. Eventually, a few guesses percolate to the top, which is the most anyone can hope for, given my feeble and abstruse framing of the question.

"Here's what I'm trying to get at," I say. "If I can't *control* something, and I can't *influence* something, then I should *anticipate* something. For example, let me share a personal story. When I first entered this field…change leadership, human development, whatever…I was failing every day. I was living out of a suitcase, my wife was a thousand miles away, eating alone night after night, and I was banging my head against the wall, racked with failure. There I was, sharing *truths* with organizations, and they weren't having any of it. I was constantly reduced to a sales mode, always trying to convince them of ideas that had long ago been established and proven by leaders in the human sciences, and each organization just stared at my third eye. It was surreal; I was baffled. Day after day I plodded along, perpetually hoping against hope that *tomorrow* I'll be adequate enough to communicate more effectively. Tomorrow, they'll realize what I'm saying is truthful, and here they've been wallowing in old illusions served up by antiquated thinkers like Henry Ford who lamented, "Why — when I only want to hire a pair of hands — do I get a whole person?"[102] Well, that tomorrow never came. And it never came. And it never came.

---

[102] See *Managing for Excellence* by David L. Bradford, senior lecturer in organizational behavior at Stanford University Graduate School of Business.

So I made a decision. *I can either persevere to change others, or I can change me.* I chose to change me.

> *Two roads diverged in a wood, and I — I took the one less traveled by, and that has made all the difference.*
>
> Robert Frost

From that day forward, I entered each engagement anticipating the organization would stare at my third eye. I was seldom disappointed, but fortunately this new perspective emboldened me. *I needn't worry any longer about whether the individual or organization believe what I'm saying.* In time, I'll improve my skills and find receptive ears…and then we'll be cookin' with propane. At long last, my new worldview was rewarded. By not pushing, by allowing truths to fall where they may, I found my niche. I needn't agree with everyone, and they needn't agree with me. Remember, as Twain wrote, "If we both agree, one of us is unnecessary." As experience reveals, deep and sustainable change usually originates with just a handful of eager, receptive leaders anyway — leaders well-versed in the past, but thirsty for a better future. Like a single match in a million acres of forest, their tiny spark scorches entrenched ideas and gives rise to reclamation through new growth.

> *Never doubt that a small group of thoughtful, committed citizens can change the world. Indeed, it's the only thing that ever has.*
>
> Margaret Mead

Returning to our target again, you'll notice that to the right are those people who live in the future, particularly a future denoted not by vision but, rather, by worry. To the left, you'll notice individuals who remain mired in the past…covered in the residue of regret.

Worry

Here's a mental picture for ya. Friday, 5:00 p.m. "Hey Charlie, listen. I need to give you some feedback. Oh, hey. Will you look at that…huh…it's five o'clock. I hadn't realized; that last hour just slipped right past me. Hey, let's do this. Why don't you come by my office on Monday, first thing, and we'll have that chat."

Wow, what a weekend. You know the one; you've had it too. All weekend long, you're amped up, loaded for bear. You're playing out scenarios, imagining the worst, and trying to recall what foibles you've made in recent weeks that have led to your imminent firing. Come Sunday, your spouse says, "Hey Sweetie, let's blow this ice cream stand. You need to get off that couch and get out of here. Let's go see a show or something, eh?"

"No. I'm gonna sit right here, Hon. I've got some more worrying to do!"

Well come Monday, guess what? About eight of ten times, the issue is a non-starter or, even better (or worse, because while you were building moats in the sky, *el jefe* was apparently golfing), the boss means to compliment you. "Yeah, I was thinking," he begins, "you've been doing a dynamite job, Charlie, and I just wanted to be sure you knew that it hasn't gone unnoticed. Keep up the good work, will ya? Thanks."

Hmm. So bittersweet. Mostly sweet, 'cause wow, what a relief. But man, *I sure did waste my weekend.* Criminy, *we shoulda gone to the show!*

> *Worry is like interest paid in advance on a debt that never exists.*
>
> **The Spanish Prisoner,** film by David Mamet
> from a story by Arthur Train

Regret

Now imagine the opposite scenario. The one at your twentieth high school reunion where you run into Heather, your class' Sweetheart, Homecoming Queen, and all around most popular girl. What's she up to now? Commiseration, that's what. She's let herself go, she's frayed around the edges, and she ain't nowhere near as shiny as the silver dollar you knew her to be way back when.

"I *knew* I shouldn't have run off with Josh. I just *knew* it! I should have gone to school, hiked Europe, gotten a good job. Heck, by now...who knows, I could have had my own business. *I coulda been somebody!*" she laments. There is much ruing as Heather *coulda-woulda*-and-*shouldas* all over the place. There are no rose-colored glasses to be found, only grimy dime store-cheapies that transpose anything bright into something dark.

Each extreme is a foretold tragedy. The individual who lives in an unalterable future of worry is equally miserable as the dolt banging her head against the rent-a-bar in the corner of the linoleum cafeteria that serves as tonight's Shangri-La for the class o' '87.

> *The chains of habit are too light to be felt, until they are too heavy to be broken.*
>
> Warren Buffet

Back to the Bull's-Eye: Ten Trust-Builders

Returning to the bull's-eye, let's review one of the most valuable forms of currency any individual can possess in order to broaden her circle of control: *Trust*. Trust is like money: Possess it, and you have choices. Lack it, and you possess fewer choices and are bankrupt in your relationships with others. The extent to which we perceive trustworthiness in others is shaped by the following ten trust-builders. We'll begin at the bottom of the coin stack and work our way upward.

Figure 19: *Trust Coins*

- **Approachability** — We can control many of the behaviors that exude *approachability* in the eyes of others. Are you kind? Are you warm? Are you receptive? If you purport an *open door policy*, do you demonstrate it? Be approachable, and you're more likely to be trusted. In the absence of approachability, people fill the white space with junk. They wonder, "Does this person think she is more important than me? Does she think her time is more valuable than mine — and that I am a waste of time? Does this person not like me?" Such ruminations and interpretations destroy relationships, and they certainly erode trust.

- **Audience** — Know your audience. Whether you're interacting with one person or a thousand people, know who your audience is and what they need from you to perceive trust. Are they faster-paced? Introverted? Scientific? Anecdotal? Big picture? Detailed? Knowing this, and being able to meet another where he or she is, will dramatically improve the likelihood of your being trusted.

- **Character/Integrity** — As differentiated earlier when introducing the notion of *The Philosopher King,* character derives from the Greek word *kharakter,* which means *stamping tool.* In ancient times, smiths of all kinds, from silversmiths and coppersmiths to leathersmiths, emblazoned their creations with their logo — their kharakter — and the quality of one's work became his reputation. Our reputations (and therefore our character) precede us. What impression are *you* making on others? What reputation precedes you? The word integrity derives from the Latin *integritas,* which means *undivided.* Using contemporary language, we would describe someone with integrity as *walking the talk.* Specifically, integrity means that someone's beliefs, feelings, thoughts, words, and behaviors are congruent — regardless of circumstance, time, and audience. *What you see is who they are, and what you see is what you get.*

- **Competence** — Be good. Be a capable individual who performs, who meets or exceeds expectations and can be counted on. I boarded a flight one time and the pilot — who was greeting passengers as we boarded — made the comment, "I'm excited about this flight. It's my first!"

We all laughed...nervously. He was joking, but it crossed my mind: *Even if he's nice, even if he's funny, even if he's smart — it doesn't matter a lick if he's not competent.* This is generally true in most realms, so be good.

- **Commonality** — This plays off the social phenomenon known as *centrism*. From sociocentrism to ethnocentrism, we see that the more we have in common with others — *the more we see ourselves in them* — the more likely we are to value them and trust them. Unfortunately, the converse is often true as well, and this (along with ignorance and life experience) is a cause behind racism, bigotry, and altogether small-mindedness. To increase trust in relationships with others, start with common interests, beliefs, aspirations, values, etc. For example, "We both value our lives." Or land, or religious freedom, or economic independence, or whatever.

- **Credibility** — Be believable. Be a person of your word. Be a promise-keeper, not a promise-maker-and-breaker.

- **Empathy** — Understand others' feelings. You needn't weep with them; that's sympathy. But realize that we all feel the same range of emotions, and your own emotions don't trump others'. The day will come (and often) that you'll want others to be empathetic with you, so prepare the soil today for that eventual reckoning by being empathetic with all others in their multitude of circumstances.

- **Intent** — Demonstrate triple-win intent: good for them, good for you, good for the organization(s) involved. Do this, and you'll develop a great reputation for thinking larger than yourself.

- **Propriety** — Demonstrate *appropriate professional behavior.* From keeping confidences to dressing appropriately, be professional in your language, demeanor, and behavior, and more people will trust you. Don't allow *background noise* to drown-out your message. For example, showing up in a blue-collar environment wearing a three-piece suit and wingtip loafers is a great way to create excess background noise and drown-out whatever intentions you might have. People will wonder, "Who is this dandy from NYC? Is this fella here to acquire our company?" I know these may sound like small things — but they're not. They're part of a larger constellation of concerns that people have, and you don't want to be your own worst enemy and orchestrate them against you by making tiny, stupid decisions that undermine your intentions.

- **Pattern of Behavior** — This is the one instance where *flatlining* is good. You don't want your pattern to be up-and-down...erratic. You want your pattern of behavior to be consistent — to be flat. Typically, we judge people by their pattern of behavior and their last win or sin against us. Unstable people with unstable patterns are trusted *about as far as we can throw them*. The most trusted people in our universe are those upon whom we can rely...those with stable track records...the Steady Eddies of the world.

Work to control these ten trust-builders, and your inner circle will expand. You'll become more trusted and that will, in turn, make you more influential as well in your interactions with others.

Relevant Lessons

Where do trained professionals aim? At the bull's-eye or, given the distance and some wind, maybe a little higher. As a strategic leader, one finds himself surrounded by all manner of humankind, from the pessimist to the realist to the optimist to Pollyanna herself.

> *If the only tool you have is a hammer, you will see every problem as a nail.*
>
> Abraham Maslow

Meet people where they are. Be a graceful merger. Don't require others to meet you in the middle or entirely on your side of the fence; for many people, this is simply more than they can deliver. See Charlie and Heather for who they are: world-weary travelers burdened and lost on the dusty side roads of life, desperate for anyone empathetic and interested enough to saddle up beside 'em or willing to help carry a portion of the load. We all need encouragers, and some more than others. Go on, exemplify the Golden Rule. You'll be glad you did, and I know those who only shoot the air around the target will, too.

I cannot change another without first changing myself.
Me

14 Self-Management and Burnout

Please don your own oxygen mask before assisting others around you.
U.S. Department of Transportation Federal Aviation Administration Passenger Safety Information Briefing

The course of life instills in most of us a sense of obligation to care for those who are young and old. As children, we often observe this two-fold as our parents care for us and perhaps, in time, we see them care for *their* parents. This socialization process, along with consistent messaging *(e.g., honor thy father and mother, respect your elders, pick on someone your own size,* or *stop teasing him, he's only a child)* attune us to society's general hierarchy of care and imbue us with norms about the roles of children and elders. While this is all quite fitting, healthy, and, I would submit, *as it should be,* there is a subtle, latent effect of this tendency that can jeopardize one's long-term ability to lead and sustain continuous improvement. A detrimental consequence of caring for others at the expense of oneself is *burnout*.

Burnout is *the exertion of more energy than can be recovered.* There is an enormous population of burnout victims in our world, and their mark is quite noticeable. They are the people who:

- Constantly volunteer (or are nominated) to lead organizational efforts, projects, teams, review committees.
- Start as optimists with a gleam in their eyes.

- Are initially eager to champion change.
- Have swung hard and made contact nearly every time at bat.

But sadly, having become the go-to gals and guys and having carried the bulk of the organization's weight for weeks, months, or even years on end, these eager beavers ultimately succumb to the laws of nature and, having consistently expended more energy than they recover, peter out. With shaky legs, hunched backs, and calloused hands, they look at you with their now vacant, hollow eyes and plead, "Please, Boss, may I sit a spell?"

> On a beautiful, sunny summer day in 1996, I was standing before a group of perhaps 25 frontline supervisors in a manufacturing facility. We had been talking about change, and they had just given a summary of the plethora of "change initiatives and projects" underway. I kid you not, they had over 50 initiatives at this tiny plant. I was shocked. *That is way too many*. It slays me that in this age of enlightenment, leaders can be deluded enough to believe that any organization can successfully focus on so many initiatives. As a rule, most human beings can consistently manage, focus upon, and perform to approximately three to five core expectations. Expand to seven, and we see dilution, distraction, competing priorities, and an overall decline in contribution. Many of these supervisors were members of more than 12 "project teams" in addition to the usual duties they possessed such as supervising direct reports, conducting performance appraisals, dancing with the union, and so forth. While nothing much flabbergasts me anymore, I stood slack-jawed at the workload before these men. "How do you do it?" I asked.
>
> "Poorly," Frank said.
>
> The most senior supervisor, Dennis, shifted in his seat and began to speak. "Do you think this is too much, Blake?"
>
> "Absolutely," I replied. "Just as the notion of multi-tasking is an exaggeration, so is the belief that people can contribute at a high-performing level across an array of activities over an extended period of time. Simply put, Dennis, it zaps energy. It's vampiric."
>
> "Come again?"

"Vampirism, you know? You're a blood bank, and the company is sucking you dry. You're the walking dead, are you not?"

Had a pin dropped, its tinny bounce would have sounded like a 20-pound steel pipe.

"You tell me," I said. "Am I wrong, or am I just saying what you've all been thinking and feeling for so many months now? If I'm wrong, tell me. But if I'm just being politically incorrect, so be it. The truth of the matter is, sometimes organizations' appetites exceed their ability to ingest. It's the python that tries to eat a cow. A pig, sure. A man, yes. But a cow? Wow, that's too much. The gluttony will be what kills you."

And just like that, Dennis sat back in his chair, opened his arms wide as if being crucified, and started to tremble and cry as he spoke. "Guys, that's it. That's exactly it. I think we all agree that what we're doing is important. Each and every initiative has merit, and we believe in everything we're doing...I don't know about the rest of you, but I am *wiped out*. Just wiped out. I love this place, but I can't keep this up. I'm thinking about work on the drive home, I'm thinking about it when I fall into bed, and it's on my mind every hour of every day that I'm not here. I just don't think I can keep going like I've been going."

This is burnout. Just change the names involved, and I'm confident it could be your organization at one point in time or another. Trying to be lean, progressive, financially conservative, responsive, and inclusive, organizations unknowingly grind their people into powder. Over the course of the next two days, Dennis, Frank, and their peer group engaged with leadership to combine seemingly redundant initiatives, prioritize them, and in many cases, expel or delay commitments. Each individual was then asked to participate in just one project, knowing these were in addition to their "day job," as it was described. Within four years, due to these efforts and others that followed across the sales force and leadership, the company's revenues had nearly doubled, employee satisfaction increased, and I'm happy to say, Dennis retired contentedly at age

65, and Frank succeeded him. The current culture remains healthy, and the supervisors are a vibrant bunch.

What happened here? Was it simply a matter of learning to say no? At its essence, this was a situation that required awareness, acknowledgment, conscious competence, courage to call a spade a spade, and affirmation that we can indeed achieve *more traction* by doing *less*. Like a broken record, I find myself constantly repeating, "If you try to be everything to everyone, you'll be nothin' to nobody." In our pursuits to appease the many, we disappoint the few who matter most. While there are occasions for shotgun approaches, sniper-work has its advantages.

Following the expenses incurred by the U.S. military in WWII, snipers were introduced in larger numbers during the Korean, Vietnam, and Gulf wars. The contrasts are staggering. In the Vietnam war alone, an average of 50,000 M16 rounds were fired per U.S. infantryman to yield one Vietcong death compared to just 1.3 rounds fired per kill by U.S. snipers using the M40 sniper rifle.[103] Additionally, the military discovered an invaluable *combat multiplier: Two-man sniper teams can optimally dominate terrain, force an enemy to alter its plans, and swiftly demoralize enemy combatants and their will to fight* — often more effectively than an entire company of infantry. There are times that call for cavalry-like infantry tactics and times that call for the tactics of a two-man sniper team.[104]

This holds true for many organizations. Rather than exhaust your people by expending excess energy on insatiable initiatives, find ways to ensure *one shot, one kill,* and to deploy groups and teams efficiently, enabling them to provide a *business multiplier*. If you don't, you'll become your own worst enemy, and your appetite will be what kills you.

The antonym of burnout is *rustout,* which is *the death of ambition.* This is an equally pervasive problem, exhibited by employees whom many describe as "R.O.A.D. warriors. *Retired on Active Duty.*" In other words, chair-holder-downers. They exist, they collect their paychecks, and they expend "N.G.F. energy. *Just enough energy to Not Get Fired.*" Or, as one employee described them many years ago, "Paycheck Players, 'cause they're only in it for the P-A-Y."

---

[103] *Weaponology, Episode One: Sniper Rifles,* The History Channel, January 15, 2007.

[104] Many thanks to David Allen Scholl for his expertise and contributions in this area.

In working with a federal agency and having spent the previous hour presenting the importance of leadership, involvement, and change, we heard a voice shout from the rear of the ballroom: "Why should I change? I've only got seven years left 'til retirement." Uh, okay, if you wanna be an outright idiot, I'll bite.

"Okay, Sir, I suppose you could adopt that mindset. Just be an office-oxygen-thief and parasitically thrive off the hard work of others. Yeah, that sounds like a grand plan. I bet you're really popular at work. You continue doing your worst, so that as a taxpayer, I feel really stellar about the ROI on my tax dollars. Continue breeding apathy among your peers, along with cancer among those who actually want to contribute to society."

That shut him up, but he was steamed. Fine — be steamed; I've got no use for bottom-feeders who blame their laziness on the absence of meritocracy. If everyone were to lie down because the world didn't reward him for his efforts, there wouldn't be enough pillows to go around. Shame on him for demanding his employer or peers or customers owe him or single-handedly own the responsibility to motivate. Yes, in an ideal world we would all work for a mutually reinforcing, fulfilling employer — but this isn't utopia, this is Earth, and that's just not how things always work.

There are other people, people who simply view change as — *this too shall pass* — who exhibit rustout because they withhold their energy, anticipating yet another, and another, and another change coming 'round the bend. Either way, whether malevolent like the ballroom guy or innocuous like the employee who has never been led, rustout can (and *has* and *does*) cripple an organization even worse than burnout. Why? Because at least in burnout, people's energy is already being exhibited within the organization, and all one must do is redirect it in more healthy, manageable ways. Relatively speaking, that's much easier than trying to *restart* or *recapture* energy, energy that long ago was diverted away from work and into other life pursuits. Energy *is,* and our job as strategic leaders is to harness and direct it. But when it's not even channeled into the workplace, one is confronted with the challenge of competing for energy that was long ago pointed toward the bowling league or book club or part-time work on the side. In these cases, we're vying for energy the employee has already volitionally redirected to areas in his life where he anticipates a greater return on his investment; getting it back can be a Herculean task for any employer. This should motivate all of us to prevent a workplace that allows employees to become rusted out in the first place.

Recall Seth Godin's article (*Learn to Be a Better Liar,* mentioned in *The Omniscience Octagon*) and the phenomenon wherein people come to believe things, and any efforts we make to change their mind essentially require them to abandon what they've come to believe is true. Displacing their belief with our belief is challenging, to say the least. *This is the hurdle we face when confronting victims of rustout.* They don't believe our lie that work can be as fun as bowling, as intellectual as their book club, or as profitable as their business-on-the-side. Those succumbing to burnout, on the other hand, have believed for so long that they were willing to die on the battlefield for the cause.

Relevant Lessons

Lesson #1: Avoid, at all costs, becoming a rustout employer in the first place. If you already have, improve leadership and improve culture by working with employees to reestablish the social contract. "What must we change to become an employer of choice and, moreover, a significant, meaningful, fun aspect of your life?" This initial dialogue will lead to some potentially painful answers, but it's far better than delusion and whiling away too many tomorrows, always wondering, "Why does it require so many employees to accomplish so little?" In this reality, you are experiencing what one financial advisor describes as "leakage." There's no evident hole in the boat; there's no $1 million loss that is hemorrhaging. Rather, it's the miniscule, unnoticeable, daily losses of psychological energy and commitment that in the particulate are unnoticeable, and in the aggregate become staggering.

Lesson #2: The remedy for burnout requires a three-pronged approach.
1. Be realistic about the environment. If the market or industry has always been and will always be frenetic, hire leaders and employees with the complementary mentality and temperament required to *thrive* in such an environment, then do whatever you must on a consistent basis to help these people maintain their sanity and sense of balance through frequent breaks and respites.

2. Refine the work. If there are too many initiatives, projects, or efforts underway, cluster the redundant ones, prioritize the urgent ones, and pay credence to the important ones in an appropriate timeframe. Quarantine the unhealthy, infectious efforts until you can quash or kill them altogether. Partition the meritorious yet cannibalizing initiatives or, like black holes, they will suck all nearby energy into themselves, growing beyond control.
3. On the personal, individual level:
   a. Give people time to rest.
   b. Give people time to disconnect from the stressors of the everyday.
   c. Give people a change of setting (e.g., meet in unusual places, at unusual times, with unusual but powerful agendas).
   d. Help people re-enter with fresh, new focal points.
   e. Improve the nature of one's work.
   f. Distribute the workload properly and fairly; don't ride the good mules to death, as we're all too prone to do, because *they deliver*.
   g. Assign partners responsible for ensuring one's buddy doesn't drown.

15 Honoring the Fundamentals

VMV and Teleological Pursuits

We are all teleological beings.

Aristotle

As Aristotle noted, we are indeed goal oriented and, having already defined some important terms in *The Omniscience Octagon*, let's briefly re-cap and proceed to describing their utility for the strategist.

Vision — A realistic (doable), worthwhile (perceived as adding value), desired (impassioned) future state that is better in significant ways than what exists today.

Mission — Our unique purpose for existence, beyond making money.

Values — Core ideals that exemplify what we believe and how we commit to treat one another.

Relevant Lessons

For the strategist, there are few arrows in one's quiver that have as much utility as the notions of *Vision, Mission,* and *Values* or, "VMV." Here are some ways to engage them for your own endeavors:

1. Whether you call it *Vision* or something as featureless as "direction," just do it. Engage people to identify where they're going, and they'll thank you for it in the long run.

2. What's our core purpose and sole reason for existence each and every day, beyond money? That's *Mission*, and without it we constantly see organizations struggling with resource distribution, prioritization, and attention drift. Keep it simple, specific, and differentiating, and it can serve as a powerful surrogate for inaccessible or poor management. In the absence of someone who can tell me what to do when I run into trouble, *Mission* transcends a statement and becomes a robust tool for decision-making.

3. The relational rules of engagement we adopt when working with each other are important. I've seen organizations take two approaches, *Deductive* and *Inductive*. In the *Deductive* approach, leaders craft value statements that reflect what is clearly operating already. In other words, "We do such and such all the time with each other...what shall we call this? How shall we describe it?" In the *Inductive* approach, leaders craft *Values*, then work to ensure they operationalize these. "Okay, we've all agreed that we value Honesty, so how will we demonstrate this? How do we expect it to manifest or play out among us?" There are pros and cons to each method, but let's not nit-pick. Just capture *Values*, communicate what they are and how you expect to see

them play out, and link them to your performance appraisal system, and you'll be right as rain.

16 Turning *Vision* into *Action*

In the kaleidoscope, we explored the Cartesian perspective of reductionism and contrasted it against the Eastern view of holism. The following model illustrates the key components of many great organizations and how they interact to form a whole.

Figure 20: *The Vision to Action Puzzle*

Here's the inventory and the order in which I typically describe it. Follow along as I move clockwise, starting with Endgame:

Component	Reminders	Commentary
1. Endgame	Endgame is *the likely, significant reality looming in the contextual distance within which vision occurs.*	
2. Vision	*A realistic (doable), worthwhile (adds value), desired (wanted) future state that is better in significant ways than what exists today.*	
3. Mission	*Our everyday reason for existence, beyond profit.* Good missions define uniqueness, constituents, and deliverables.	Like the black and white keys on a piano, Mission, Strategies, Goals, Tasks, and Employee Behaviors must be in the right placement and sequence to be aligned. Alignment assures an organization that everyone is rowing in the same direction.
4. Strategies	Simply, *the means to the end.* More fully, *a systemic means to achieve the desired endgame that leverages philosophical and polymathic pragmatism with holistic thinking and inclusive ownership.* Strategies run the gamut, but often address topics like Employee Development, Marketing, Advertising, Growth, Technology, Structure, and other similarly broad issues that shape the focus of all enterprises.	
5. Goals	*Quantitative and qualitative targets, aims, outcomes, objectives.* Goals possess evidence that help organizations answer the question: Are we there yet? Remember, the best goals aren't just S.M.A.R.T.; they are emotional and meaningful, too. Limbic.	
6. Tasks	*The value-added and necessary occurrences that comprise goals.*	

Component	Reminders	Commentary
7. Behaviors	*The human movements that comprise tasks.*	
8. Actions	*The doings that employees execute* — and that need connecting to the Vision itself. People need to know, "How does what I do from 8 a.m. to 5 p.m. help us accomplish the Vision?"	
9. People	*The most important of all God's creations.* All those folks running around your organization expecting clarity, direction, recognition, compensation, satisfaction, meaningfulness, growth, challenge, and so much more.	Just like pianos, organizations need tuning. Once all the components are in the right place and sequenced, invest in People, build Teams, shape Culture using the seven levers, and be realistic about the Ecosystem in which you exist. Do this, and Attunement is yours.
10. Groups/ Teams	Created when individuals come together to collaborate.	
11. Culture	*What we cultivate (grow) based on our Beliefs, Language, Behaviors (and Processes), Tools, Social Structure, and Environment.*	
12. Environment	*The ecosystem within which we work (and live).*	

Component	Reminders	Commentary
13. Values	*Relational and operational beliefs to which an organization ascribes great importance.*	What sheet of music are we playing? Values answer this. Bach, Mozart, Beethoven? Great, each one of them. But simultaneously? A cacophony. Cultivate values to build an aligned, attuned, and harmonious culture.
14. Competencies	Competencies are generally individual in scope. *The skill to do something effectively and efficiently.* They are more narrow, immediate skills seen in current employee performance.	
15. Capabilities	Capabilities are generally *organizational* in scope. *The extent of our power or ability to do something.* They are broad, often long-term abilities required for an organization to succeed, compete, and thrive. (Note: If your strategies leverage your capabilities, and your capabilities are not easily replicated, then your competitive advantage in the ENDGAME is *dramatically* strengthened.)	

Relevant Lessons

The *Turning Vision into Action* illustration is quite popular. Please consider using it in an upcoming strategy session. Start with *Endgame* and *Vision*, then *Mission,* then *Values,* then work clockwise — populating each cell as you go. You'll be glad you used it, as will your employees. It may be the first time that *all these things* come together in people's minds in a very clear, concise way.

Learning Lab: Idea(s) in Action

Snowflake Factory

To experience the power of *Endgame* and *Vision* — perform this exercise with your family, friends, or employees.

Set-up:

An 8.5"x11" piece of paper.
A blindfold.

Instructions:

For this activity to work, you need multiple people. Each person is blindfolded and receives a sheet of paper. Then, proceed by giving these instructions: *We're here to create identical snowflakes. Please don't ask me any questions. First, fold your paper in half and tear off the top left corner of the paper.* Allow time. *Next, fold the paper in half again and tear off the top right corner of the paper.* Allow time. *Next, fold the paper again and tear off a small piece along the top — a tiny crescent moon. Now, remove your blindfold, and let's compare snowflakes.*

Summary:

You can imagine where this is headed. Disparity. Dissimilarity. With just three folds and three tears, participants usually create different snowflakes. *And this was a simple vision...a simple endgame.* The application is straightforward: *Given the complex nature of an organization, the various goals, the various resources...how much more important is a clear, well-understood vision?* Communication is key — and most organizations create very dissimilar snowflakes on a daily basis, ranging from inconsistent customer service to misaligned goals across departments.

17 Bluetooth Strategies

Figure 21: *From Bluetooth Devices to Bluetooth Strategies*

Technically speaking, Bluetooth is the name for a short-range radio frequency (RF) technology that operates at 2.4 GHz and is capable of transmitting voice and data. The effective range of Bluetooth devices is 32 feet (10 meters). Bluetooth transfers data at the rate of 1 Mbps, which is from three to eight times the average speed of parallel and serial ports, respectively.

Why is the technology called Bluetooth?

Bluetooth technology is named after Harald Blatand (Harold Bluetooth), who united the warring factions of Denmark, Sweden, and Norway in the 10th Century. In the beginning of the Bluetooth wireless technology era, Bluetooth was aimed at unifying the telecom and computing industries.

How is Bluetooth used?

Bluetooth can be used to wirelessly synchronize and transfer data among devices. At the most basic level, Bluetooth can be thought of as a cable replacement technology. Typical uses include automatically synchronizing contact and calendar information among desktop, notebook, and palmtop computers without connecting cables. Bluetooth can also be used to access a network or the Internet with a notebook computer by connecting wirelessly to a cellular phone.

What is the future direction of the Bluetooth standard?

Developers anticipate the Bluetooth SIG to evolve technology to provide greater bandwidth and distances, thus increasing the potential platforms and applications used in the emerging personal area networking marketplace.

Summary

A vision for Bluetooth involves unification, data transfer, synchronization, and platform integration.

Bluetooth strategies, therefore, are similar to the Hapkido Sum Principle — they are the combination of much that we've been exploring together.

By using Bluetooth as an analogy, we might unify Systemic Thinking and Strategic Intentions to transfer, synchronize, and integrate our efforts to achieve desired results.

Systemic Thinking considers the nature and effects of interrelated parts.

Strategic Intent describes our coordinated means to exploit opportunities, positions, and interests.

Bluetooth Strategies then, by definition, are *those coordinated means to exploit opportunities, positions, and interests through consideration of the nature and effects of all interrelated parts.*

Relevant Lessons

As introduced in Part One, I don't believe it's optimal to consider strategies in isolation. Instead, they should be thought of contextually and, as much as possible, systemically. Here's the simple fieldwork assignment — as a strategist, do this:

1. Build strategies to pursue green fields, white spaces, or blue oceans. In other words, uncharted territories or waters where the timid explorer doesn't dare enter, fearing the warning, "Here be dragons."

2. Like the criminal profiler, do what you must to mentally embody your competition, thereby understanding their world view and positional interests. *To destroy thy enemy, know him.*

3. Then, telescope out. See the nature, placement, and effects of the many parts at play. Even an engineer may come to regret rushing through the construction of a doll house on Christmas Eve when, nearing completion, he discovers seven leftover screws, an important-looking piece of plastic, and three moving parts that seem to have no home.[105]

18 Unlearning & Learning:

Mental Habituation and Ruts

Examples for *Unlearning*:
1. Q: **How many letters are in the alphabet?**[106]
2. Q: **What state is surrounded by the most water?**[107]
3. Q: **A woman has seven children; half of them are boys. How is this possible?**[108]

I hope you didn't cheat, because these sorts of questions are designed — not to boost your ego — but to make a point:

1. In question one, "26" immediately comes to mind for everyone, but then we pause — knowing the question must be a trick — and think harder, more creatively. Fine. Me, too. But sometimes, thinking harder and more creatively doesn't yield any new insights, and dontcha just hate it when that happens?

---

[105] The experience of a grandfather (lacking one iota of engineering prowess) yields more wisdom in such efforts than the *overzealous MIT graduate/first-time father* embarking on his inaugural Christmas Eve construction project.

[106] Did you say 26? There are 11 letters in "t-h-e a-l-p-h-a-b-e-t."

[107] Hawaii. All of it is surrounded by water. *Most* people miss this one. They often guess Maine, Florida, Alaska, California, and yes, even Michigan.

[108] ALL the children are boys, so half are boys, and so is the other half.

2. In question two, Hawaii seldom occurs to us. This is because, among other reasons, we're microscoping instead of telescoping. The contiguous United States come(s) to mind, and Hawaii falls too far west beyond our peripheral vision to even enter the radar.

3. Question three is trickier, because even after knowing the answer, one is left wondering, "3.5 children? How is that possible?" It's possible mathematically, and physically, but that doesn't make it any more attractive to envision or easier to arrive at the answer in hindsight. But so be it; these are trick questions, and this third one serves its purpose.

All three of these questions are reminiscent of the story that goes as follows:

A boy and his father were driving at night when their car slid and crashed. The father died immediately, but the boy was still alive. He was rushed to the hospital in critical condition. The paramedics told the doctor that the boy needed an operation ASAP. The doctor replied, "I can't operate on this boy; he's my son."

Q: **The doctor is who?**[109]

What do *all* these questions and this story have in common?[110] They highlight the blazing speed of the brain's *shorthand* tendencies, specifically, the formation of rapid first impressions. The thoughtful strategist in each of us must pause, reflect, then respond — and be willing to replace immediate, perhaps habitual reactions with critical thinking and higher-order answers. What appears obvious is sometimes wrong, and this is an important lesson for a strategist.

Relevant Lessons

First and foremost, strategists must not succumb to the momentum present in all organizations. It's all too easy to do the bidding of superiors or to simply update prior years' strategies with new dates. But as I've said before, I'll say with a new inference: Doing what's easy

---

[109] The doctor is the boy's mother.

[110] For more riddles, visit www.etni.org.il/farside/riddleanswers.htm.

is seldom right. *Right* and *Easy* are not mutually exclusive, but they contrast so often, they might as well be.

A key function of strategists is to help hoist vehicles out of bogs, ruts, and roadside ditches.

> *If some is good, more must be better.*
>
> Reynolds' Supposition
Richard "Dick" Reynolds

Dick's spot-on, because with the momentum of last year carrying a company into next year, it's incredibly difficult to teach the singer new lyrics, much less deconstruct the entire song as she knows it. But this is what great strategists do all the time. Like the self-destructing addict who drinks, drugs, gambles, or philanders himself into oblivion, there comes a point at which an organization becomes so conditioned…so numbed to the effects of its own vices and habits that it can no longer see with the acuity required to thrive. The strategist, in many ways, is an intervener, often acting with the patient's best interests in mind, but cast in a role that is quite unpopular. Remember, whether one believes he or she were radical or progressive (e.g., Galileo Galilei, Alfred Kinsey,[111] Susan B. Anthony, Charles Darwin), mythical (e.g., Prometheus), prophetic, a zealot, or even God incarnate, history is clear about one thing: Anyone who challenges the status quo, particularly with respect to the issues that matter most, is regularly viewed with great contempt in his own time by the powers that be.

> *To be nobody but yourself, in a world which is doing its best, night and day, to make you like everybody else, means to fight the hardest battle which any human being can fight, and never stop fighting.*
>
> e.e. cummings

---

[111] American biologist and professor of entomology and zoology who founded the (now) Kinsey Institute for Research in Sex, Gender, and Reproduction at Indiana University in 1947.

Learning Lab: Idea(s) in Action

Arms Crossed

To experience the power of unlearning — perform this exercise with your family, friends, or employees.

Set-up:

Nothing.

Instructions:

This one is a piece of cake. Simply cross your arms. Now — *cross them the opposite way.*

Summary:

For most folks, there's a slight delay of one to two seconds during which one has to ponder. What fascinates me about this simple exercise is just that: It's simple. And yet it often requires brief deliberation, then action. *Imagine, therefore, how much harder it is to unlearn more complex behavior — from personal habits (like diet or time management) to social habits (like pace when speaking with others, or body language, or touching, etc.).* If *crossing my arms differently* requires some effort, imagine how much harder it is to steer a battleship...to steer one's organization. Think of the countless behaviors that must change across many people. It's really quite astounding to imagine the ramifications — and it's surprising that we can accomplish the magnitude of change that we do!

19 Luddism

Figure 22: *One Example of a Luddite Panic-Inducer*

Luddite[112]

a member of any of the bands of English workers who destroyed machinery, especially in cotton and woolen mills, which they believed was threatening their jobs (1811-1816).

a person opposed to increased industrialization or new technology: *a small-minded Luddite resisting progress.*

Derivatives

Luddism (noun)
ORIGIN perhaps named after Ned Lud, a participant in the destruction of machinery.

Anecdote

Luddism was referred to during the Microsoft Antitrust case by attorney John Warden when he commented, "This is not really an antitrust case, but a return of the Luddites."

Relevant Lessons

Similar to the troglodytes who bury their heads in the sand, there will always be those who resist new ideas, new directions, new approaches, new tools. There are always those who are suspect

---

[112] Definition courtesy of the *Oxford English Dictionary*.

of others who challenge the status quo. By definition, change is about *becoming different,* and progress is about *advancing forward.* There are many employees who are vested tremendously in the past; leading them into some new, amorphous future is dicey at best. Just as the Luddites opposed technological progress specifically, so, too, are many employees inclined to defend the plentiful anachronisms in any given workplace. It never ceases to amaze me how attached we all get to those blankets that comforted us in our formative years. But as a strategist, one must represent growth, evolution, and bifurcation from *prior* to *following.*

- **Old Paradigm:** *If you do what you've always done, you'll get what you've always gotten.*

- **Presupposition:** *We live in a static ecosystem, and the world is not changing.*

- **Contemporary Paradigm:** *If you do what you've always done, you're likely to get run over, left behind, gobbled up.*

- **Presupposition:** *We live in a dynamic ecosystem, and the world is changing. Those who fail to adapt may become extinct.*

Every great strategist possesses, as Andrew Groves noted,[113] a little paranoia. Possess too much, or, more to the point — *show* too much — and you run the risk of panicking everyone around you. Better to be the duck: smooth as silk above the surface while paddling fervently *beneath* the water.

As a dear friend of mine always jokes, "It's a dog-eat-dog world out there, and I'm wearing milkbone undershorts!" True indeed, Mark, but as you know all too well — *Never let 'em see you sweat.*

Better to lead proactive change than become the over-reactionary, panic-inducing, prepubescent boy who cries wolf.

---

[113] *Only the Paranoid Survive,* published in 1996 by Currency.

20 Behind the Curtain of Oz

Figure 23: *The Curtain*

It's practically a law in this country that everyone must see *The Wizard of Oz*. I've never met anyone over 12 who hasn't. And most of us...five times or more, right? In our earliest years, the flying monkeys gave us nightmares, and in our later years, the characters become iconographic representations of weaknesses we see in ourselves and those around us, with little Dorothy leading us through her dream parading as reality.

A pivotal scene comes near the end when we collectively realize *there is no Wizard*. He is, in fact, all hat and no cattle.[114] In and of itself, this epiphany is devastating enough, but there's more to it than meets the eye — there is a deeper metaphor for which I'm fishing — one that is provocative for each strategist. This metaphor is not about the lack of a wizard; it is, in fact, about *the curtain*. Specifically, the idea that there are curtains in life and forces behind them. Seeing the curtains and the forces at play can be extremely determinant for any individual.

Those who live life at the visceral level, going whichever ways their appetites or emotions beckon, live *on this side of the*

---

[114] This colloquialism refers to the cowboy who looks the part, but has nothing to show for it...no homestead, no ranch, no cattle; just the ten-gallon hat, the big silver belt buckle, and unbroken-in blue jeans and fancy boots. Think "John Travolta" in *Urban Cowboy*.

curtain. Those who want for much, but never grasp how to achieve more, live *on this side of the curtain*. Consumers who waste all their grocery money on the end-of-aisle displays before getting the items on their list are living *on this side of the curtain*. The impulse buyer who sees the car commercial (produced by the contrived *poor-inventory-managing* and *exasperated* owner hocking, "We're overstocked and won't be undersold! You must come this Friday and Saturday. Everything must go! This is a once-in-a-lifetime event![115] Blah, blah, blah!") and runs out and buys the car that weekend is living *on this side of the curtain*. The broken, destructive black widow[116] who functions as a highly efficient relationship-killing machine, yet continually blames "those losers" for her own misery, is living (and dying) *on this side of the curtain*. The unfortunate child born tragically into a flowing stream of abuse who vows never to *be like that* only to become a striker of his own children — thus repeating the cycle of abuse — is living *on this side of the curtain*. The organization that churns through employees, always succumbing to the misguided notion that *it's rare to find the right caliber talent* and never looking in the mirror to determine the root causes of employee failure and turnover is living *on this side of the curtain*.

As a strategic leader, part of your job description is to see beyond the curtain to the other side. Why do impulsive buyers spend themselves into bankruptcy? Because they cannot say no, lack discipline, or were never taught the skills of money management. Why is it that many people live lives of quiet (or *not so quiet*) desperation, through means like destroying relationships, beating their children, addicting themselves into homelessness, or squandering whatever gifts God gave them? For a sea of reasons, ranging from the crucible of their development, the tapes they play in their head, the reinforcement provided by their environment, and the temperament bestowed upon them at birth. In short, due to some confluence of nature and nurture.

It is not one's job as strategist to become therapist, but given one's raw materials are people, becoming a student of the human condition

---

[115] A once-in-a-lifetime event that, shockingly, happens like clockwork every weekend.

[116] Yes, I'm talking about a specific kind of woman who suffers from a known psychological pathology: a sexual predator who destroys everyone she hopes to love.

is in one's best interest. Perhaps in the same way traditional Cajun meals cannot be prepared without a few onions, bell peppers, and garlic, a French meal without cream, a Korean dish without proper kimchi, an Italian plate without olive oil or pasta, or a Japanese sit-down without requisite rice or fish, so, too, may the strategist struggle if she cannot learn to include people in her own unique recipe for success.

Relevant Lessons

In all things, do what you can as strategist to help the organization see for itself what is really happening externally and internally *on the **other** side of the curtain*. It is vitally important to see who/what is pulling the levers in one's world, market, and industry. There are indeed many patterns in life and, as Occam[117] assures us, they are often quite simple. It is your obligation, as the guide, to lead the organization on this expedition. Upon settlement, you may then become a titan of industry or mogul if you must; just help the company construct what it needs in order to compete. Along the journey, will you find yourself in the role of listener, counselor, encourager? Absolutely. But should you wander off course, and find yourself in the role of shrink or therapist, I encourage you to extricate yourself from that slippery slope, and call in the experts. Better to know one's calling and stick to it than jeopardize one's credibility and reputation by tackling problems for which one may be ill-equipped.

> A scorpion and a frog meet on the bank of a stream and the scorpion asks the frog to carry him across on its back. The frog asks, "How do I know you won't sting me?"
>
> The scorpion says, "Because if I do, I will die, too." The frog is satisfied and they set out but, midstream, the scorpion stings the frog. The frog — now paralyzed — starts to sink and gasps, "Why?"
>
> The scorpion replies, "It's my nature."[118]

---

[117] See Occam's Razor or *parsimony*.

[118] *The Frog and the Scorpion* is essentially a derivative of Aesop's *The Frog and the Mouse*.

We each have our nature; our responsibility is to identify it so that we might know our calling and fulfill our destiny in life. If you remain at all puzzled by this, seek out someone you trust and respect and ask him this simple question: "What do you perceive as my talents, and how can I improve upon these to more adequately lead and serve others?"

21 Four Types of Thinking

There are four types of thinking, all of which have tremendous situational utility and, ideally, all of which can be demonstrated to some degree by the competent strategist. To the extent one finds oneself lacking (as any mortal shall) in any of the four, one should surround oneself with peers and trusted advisors who complement one's weaknesses. (The same is true for friendships, marriages, and other important unions, but that's another discourse altogether.) I have had numerous strategic leaders tell me, after hearing my explanation of these four types of thinking, that *great teams are comprised of all four*. I agree, and this underscores the need to surround oneself with complementary (not "complimentary") thinkers. As one ascends the hierarchy of any organization, truth-tellers become rarer. Be sure to not readily believe the hype; surrounding yourself with a well-rounded group of thinkers will help you remain grounded in reality.

Let's review the thinking.

First up, *conceptual thinking*. At its heart, this is about thinking abstractly and is exemplified by fields such as mathematics and philosophy. As a strategic leader, you will not be supplied with the ark of the covenant, or the map to find it, so it's immensely helpful if you can organize the colorful and seemingly random shards of glass in order to create the stained glass window through which you see your destination.

Critical thinking is the province of the accountant, researcher, and general fact-checker. In the role of strategist, having a good BS detector helps, as does being able to judge the veracity of data and its consequences.

Table 3: *Four Types of Thinking*

Conceptual	Critical	Creative	Intuitive
• Grasp abstract ideas • Make connections from pieces • See interconnectedness	• Analyze • Evaluate • Pros/Cons • Implications	• Generate options • Visualize possibilities • Formulate new approaches 1. Envisioning: New futures (TIME) 2. Experimenting: New uses (APPLICATIONS) 3. Exploring: New areas (ARENAS) 4. Modifying: New twists (REVISIONS)	• Hunches • Gut • Reactions • Empathic • Immediate

Thinking *creatively* comes in four sub-flavors:[119]

1. *Envisioning* is about time, abductive reasoning and, specifically, embracing what might be. Great "envisioners" are futurists, soothsayers, and designers. Some examples include: Martin Luther King Jr., the Aeron chair, Walt Disney, Pixar.

2. *Experimenting* is about applications, fast learning and, specifically, rapid prototyping of concepts, implements, environs, etc. Some examples include: children, the Apollo 13 Mission, IDEO.

3. *Exploring* is about arenas and scenarios and, specifically, seeing new areas and potential outcomes in which an organization, product, or service can play, compete, add

---

[119] Many thanks to Jeff Pollard for refining my thinking with regard to these four sub-flavors and providing examples.

value, or dominate. Some examples include: Southwest Airlines, Starbucks, *Art of the Long View* by Peter Schwartz (The Long Now Foundation).[120]

4. *Modifying* is about revisions and, specifically, seeing new twists to existing products or services. Some early examples include: 3M Post-it notes, Target, iPod, Wiki, www.makezine.com.

When I think of *intuitive thinking*, I always conjure up the image of Deanna Troi on *Star Trek: The Next Generation*.[121] This character — an *empath*[122] — enters a room and readily assesses most everyone's mood or emotional state (with the exception of Data, of course, because he's an android and has no emotions[123]). I don't know about you, but *I know a few empaths*. My mother would be a great example, and not just in regard to her easy ability to size *me* up. No, more than this, she can determine with eerie accuracy the mood or temperament of most everyone who enters her force field. The capacity for a strategist to quickly assess the emotional states of others is a facet of situational awareness in general, and serves as a rudder that helps him navigate the choppy waters of the human element of strategy.

Relevant Lessons

I do know people, strategists among them, who demonstrate an uncanny proficiency in all four types of thinking. And yes, in very rare cases, these individuals are at the top of their respective fields or professions. But I emphasize: One needn't be eligible for membership in Mensa[124] or more prestigious societies like Mega,[125]

---

[120] www.longnow.org.

[121] The cat is officially out of the bag. While not a Trekker (aka "Trekkie" — *sorry for the less-preferred reference*), I have been known to catch a show every now and then.

[122] Aka *clairsentient*.

[123] I just can't control myself.

[124] To learn more about sundry high IQ societies like *PARS, The Ultranet, Vertex, CIVIQ*, and so many more — visit http://en.wikipedia.org/wiki/High_IQ_society.

[125] *The Mega Society* is a high IQ society open to people who have scored at the one-in-a-million level on a test of general intelligence credibly claimed to be able to discriminate at that level.

the Triple Nine Society,[126] or Prometheus[127] — indeed, **we mortals need not despair.** The point is not *thanks for coming*, it is: *Surround yourself with people who improve you.*

Know thyself.

Pausanias

Here lies a man who knew how to enlist the service of better men than himself.

Andrew Carnegie's tombstone

Where possible, improve yourself. Exercise, eat right, grow, and stretch your muscles. Read, listen to people, inquire. Spend time with good people — interesting, disparate people. And where you fail or are deficient, as we all sometimes embarrassingly and painfully are, seek others who can...complete you.[128]

My wife is a bit like Oscar, and I'm Felix.[129] She's creative, quick-paced, social, fun, altogether liberated, and very enterprising. I, on the other hand, re-tighten the bed sheets for about five minutes before I crawl under the covers. I hide at parties and busy myself with mundane tasks, making them as equivalent to *launching a man into space* as humanly possible. When one of our weaknesses is radiated, I joke, "Together, Dawn, WE MAKE A WHOLE PERSON!"

Remember, the first step of any 12-step process (the step right after *unconscious incompetence*) is *admission that one has a problem.* Despite our desire to be complete in and of ourselves, realizing that we need others to fulfill ourselves is a sign of maturity and wisdom. Nature means for us to be together, to complement one another. Yes, sometimes it is a problem, but at least it's one of the few worth laughing about.

---

[126] Members of the *Triple Nine Society* must test at or above the 99.9th percentile on at least one of several standardized adult intelligence tests. www.triplenine.org.

[127] *The Prometheus Society* is open to anyone who has received a score on an accepted IQ test that is equal to or greater than that received by the highest 130,000th of the general population. www.prometheussociety.org.

[128] Yes, I saw *Jerry Maguire*, as did many people — since it grossed an amazing $274M in 1996.

[129] For anyone born after 1975, this is a reference to Neil Simon's 1965 stage play, *The Odd Couple*, made into a film in 1968 and then a hit ABC TV show in 1970 starring Jack Klugman and Tony Randall.

22 MindTaffy: Methods for Transcending the Proverbial Box

Figure 24: *MindTaffy*

It is *so* easy to get trapped in routine and so difficult to think beyond its confines. It's no wonder that we don't all exhibit some degree of learned helplessness more frequently.[130] One of the greatest currencies in which the outsider trades is a fresh perspective. Just stepping off an airplane and into an organization for the first time has inherent value if, for no other reason, to ask the naïve and stupid questions that employees long ago became conditioned to stop asking. It is hard to be a prophet in one's own land and, despite our profession and legion of resources, we are not immune, and we fight daily to see the forest for the trees and vice versa. Here we are, dispensing inoculations for myopia, and we, too, fall prey to it. This becomes so clear when we onboard a new employee and they ask a blindingly simple question to which we have no handy answer.

As part of our own repertoire in combating ignorance, malaise, and stifled creativity, I suggest what can best be described as *MindTaffy*, because its sole purpose is to stretch the gray matter when addressing a particular problem that an organization must overcome. Any book on creativity will serve up a longer, deeper list than the four items I'm about to share, but I don't want to deviate too far beyond my chosen course. Creativity is just one of many facets of a *Strategic Mind*, so we mustn't be distracted by any more shiny objects on our quest than we already are.

To truly generate creative, unanticipated, and random ideas often requires counterintuitive feats of detachment that are infrequently

---

[130] Read Martin Seligman's brilliant work *The Hope of Optimism* to learn more.

achieved in the course of everyday life. To overcome this fact, I suggest these exercises be performed after a period of quieting the mind. It is necessary to clearly identify the problem you wish to solve, and to have pen and paper ready during these exercises. As thoughts enter your mind, you may only have a fleeting chance to record them before they are gone. Better to capture them all than try to remember the few gemstones later. Together, let's consider a *nimble number, doodling, word association,* and *dreamthinking*.[131]

Nimble Number

For this MindTaffy, use a tool such as Whack Pack,[132] a deck of cards, dice, page #s of a book, etc., to randomly generate a number — any number. Then, think upon the number. How does that number appear to you? What does the number tell you when related to your problem? How can that number change your current situation? In what ways does that number modify your problem? Imagine the number as an object…turn it on its side, upside down, rotate it, spin it, hold it in one hand, both hands, lay it down carefully, throw it (watch it in slow motion as it flies away). What ideas related to your problem come to mind as you perform the actions on the number? *It is important to write your ideas as you think.* If possible, ask someone to assist with writing as you free-think the number, its associations, and the paths you travel to reach any new ideas.

Doodling

The aim of doodling is to express your subconscious mind on paper. Take a blank sheet of paper. Grasp a pencil in your non-dominant hand and close your eyes. Doodle. Take another blank sheet of paper. Repeat the same exercise with your dominant hand. Doodle. Observe the doodles. What objects, shapes, or thoughts come to mind as you observe? Write them down. What solutions can be gained from the doodles? Are these more ideal than what currently exists? If not, are there any usable aspects of the ideas that might be applied to the problem at hand?

---

[131] Great thanks to Seth Jantzen for his contributions to this section. A lifelong learner and practitioner of Lean (most often, lean *manufacturing,* though the tools benefit corporate white collar work as well), Six Sigma, and TRIZ, Seth is a wonderful resource for many organizations fortunate enough to use him.

[132] www.creativewhack.com.

Word Association

Think of your problem for a short while. When you feel you have thought enough, write it down on a blank piece of paper, crumple the paper, and throw it away from you as far as you can. Go to a dictionary, close your eyes, and open it to a random page. Pick the ninth word on the right-hand page and the third word on the left-hand page. Combine the two words...what ideas come to mind? Write them down. Now go back to your crumpled piece of paper, open it, and relate the new ideas with your old problem. What solutions come to mind? Are they applicable in whole or in part to the problem?

Dreamthinking

Set your alarm for 30 minutes and take a nap. As you are falling asleep, tell your mind about your problem as if you were explaining it to someone else. As soon as your alarm goes off, get up immediately and write down the thoughts that come to mind — they may have been the first inklings of dreams or simply thoughts that sprang as you were awakened. It is critical that you do this immediately upon waking; otherwise, you will lose those thoughts. Most people lose their dreams within a few minutes of waking. Observe your writings. What ideas come to mind? How do they relate to your problem? Can any of them be used to resolve your problem? Convert the text to numbers. Analyze numerically. Draw the numerical results graphically and analyze. Add color. Analyze the combined results. State the analysis verbally. Write down the analysis results. What solutions to your problem come to mind? Is the solution an improvement on what you have already?

Relevant Lessons

Most of us develop a keen ability in a limited number of fields, but too few take the time to explore other options outside their field of expertise as potential sources of solutions for problems. The importance of interdisciplinarity cannot be overstated as it applies to systems and strategic thinking. The purpose of doing these exercises is to take advantage of neuroplasticity and create new channels of communication within your mind. It is entirely possible that the solution to your problem has already been discovered, documented, and catalogued. It is also possible that you know absolutely nothing about that discovery and will never come across it in any of your research. Therefore, by de-emphasizing your knowledge and problem and emphasizing the establishment of a new perspective, it is possible to introduce new ideas that may help resolve your particular problem with the resources at your disposal. Doing these exercises will facilitate the centrifuging of creativity and the breaking away from routine and psychological habituation that plague problem solving all too often.

Learning Lab: Idea(s) in Action

Toothpicks

To experience the power of thinking outside the box — perform this exercise with your family, friends, or employees.

Set-up:

Lay six toothpicks down on the floor or on a table.

Instructions:

Using these six toothpicks, create four equal-sided triangles.

Summary:

Eventually, participants find a way to accomplish the goal, but the most creative solution requires 3D thinking. In other words, *build a pyramid.* Too often, we struggle to create a solution, because we are using (or altogether blinded by) a pre-determined paradigm. Thinking outside the box, literally, yields a highly creative solution to a simple problem that often confounds most people. Organizationally, it's helpful for the strategist to remind her followers that old paradigms — constructs for viewing the world — often inhibit us and our ability to evolve beyond what we know today. Just imagine what *music players* would be like had we not evolved beyond *the plastic record, the tape,* or *the CD.* Being chained to old or obvious ways of thinking about the world ensures stagnation and extinction.

23 Three Types of Winning

The Competition Typology

Figure 25: *The Competition Typology*

To Defeat the Competition:

First, attack their strategy
Second, attack their alliances
Last, attack them
*...and **never** attack their customers.*

adapted from Sun Tzu[133]

I presume it's quite obvious that no organization should ever attack customers, but equally obvious yet often exhibited is the tendency to attack *oneself*. Yes, sometimes, organizations get cancer... the equivalent of rogue tissues that turn on the body. Or maybe we could describe a flesh-eating virus like necrotizing fasciitis[134] that becomes a worst nightmare. Or the 20-feet-long tapeworm which began life no larger than a pinhead and silently and stealthily bathes in one's bowels and raids our internal fridge like Kramer in so many *Seinfeld* episodes. By the time we realize we're in trouble, the cancer is

---

[133] *The Art of War.*

[134] www.nnff.org.

Stage IV, our arm is half gone, or we've dropped to a fighting weight of 80 pounds.

Competition can be good. It can be quite healthy and a vigorous means to improvement. An inherent advantage to true capitalism is competition itself and the struggle for limited resources in a cluttered world and market. As iron sharpens iron, so one man sharpens another.[135] Having observed the drawbacks of communism, capitalism ain't a bad way to go. As a blueprint, socialism has its advantages, particularly with regard to generalized quality-of-life issues like healthcare and education, but when it comes to the delivery of products and services hinging on the profit motive, the capitalistic realties found most congruently within democracies are self-evident, particularly in the long haul. By way of example, the United States still comprises 38 percent more Fortune 500 firms than China itself, despite the former's industrial lethargy circa 2008-2013 and the latter's tremendous emphasis on growth in a coordinated yet rigged economy, one that is particularly advantageous to Party or otherwise connected entrepreneurs in a system hardly bothered by world standards for process, safety, employees' quality-of-life, and transparent, systematic regulation.[136] Though China's recent growth has clipped along at rates virtually unprecedented since the advent of the Industrial Age in Britain, it has done so primarily because it still remains, in key ways, unfettered and unchecked, except by its partial government (and rarely, if ever, by industry bodies or peers). Unfavorable optics — arguably coming to a head during the widely visible 2008 Beijing Olympics, and continuing with 14 employee suicides at Apple's Foxconn facility — have created a sense of urgency among Party leaders to bow rather publicly to international pressure for deeper regulatory stances on key issues like reproduction, air quality, and employee work conditions. If I am able to believe most analysts, once China's economy matures beyond the wild west and is required to abide by then-comparable 21st century rules for the road, there should be more industrial "speeding tickets," and therefore fewer tragedies. Such is the sobering yet eventually sustainable comeuppance for

---

[135] Proverbs 27:17.

[136] www.grindgis.com/blog/global-fortune-500-list-companies.

systems of checks and balances. To the extent more regulations are imposed, accepted, and enforced, we shall see clearer whether China's version of capitalism — uniquely advantaged by comprising 1.4 billion citizens loosely bermed by one Party — incorporates democratically participative principles to their innovative gain, or subverts them in the short-term and, in effect, limits their potential for the long-term.[137] It's as if people forget they're working on the same team. With colleagues like these, who needs enemies? Heaven forbid we should evolve beyond the cave and see one another for what we really are: the internal partner that is one's lifeline. Yes, yes, I'm simplifying and generalizing, I know, but gosh darn if this stuff doesn't chap my hide.[138]

In all instances, *we don't know what we don't know* and, perhaps a portion of that is the problem here. I'm being optimistic, but nonetheless I do believe that a large part of the problem is naming it and, once diagnosed, we can indeed proceed to prescribing and remedying; this is why I believe differentiating the three major permutations of competition is helpful. As we unpack each, ask yourself this question: "Does this describe any aspects of our organization?"

Upward Competition

I do not try to dance better than anyone else. I simply try to dance better than myself.

Mikhail Baryshnikov

Forget your opponents; always play against par.

Sam Snead

Upward competition is *when an organization or individual aspires to set a new standard, competes against an existing standard, or simply strives to be better than oneself or one's track record of performance.* Mr. Baryshnikov chose to dance against himself, and perhaps for good

---

[137] To explore this further, devour *Understanding China: There is a Reason for the Difference* by my bud, Gary Moreau, who lives there and describes it firsthand.

[138] Sorry, another case of *I just can't help myself.*

reason, given he was among the best. Mr. Snead chose to play against par, knowing this party standard and some requisite strokes below it often lead to victory. If one's employer engages in upward competition, the strategist will have succeeded at creating standards and metrics of excellence, along with the added incentive of compelling employees to be the best they can at whatever endeavor merits their attention.

Collaborative Competition

Collaborative competition is being hailed as the most powerful form of competition the free economy has ever known.

Saeed Mohasseb

Collaborative competition is when internal groups ally to face the competition *out there*. Too often, companies are their own worst enemies, as internal groups vie for shared resources and fight against one another — destroying the organization from the inside-out. Collaborative competition is often deficient where the strategist finds groups with seemingly contradictory agendas. For example, maintenance groups are about *preservation,* while manufacturing groups are about *creation*. Rather than seeing these pursuits as complementary, like yin/yang, employees sometimes view them as mutually exclusive, counter-productive, or just downright inconvenient and at odds with one another. When working with such an organization, I have always required the groups to come together and create expectations and aspirations that transcend functionally myopic goals. Only through empathy and collaboration can perceptions become personal; then, former "competitors" begin to see the interconnectedness involved in success. *Your success is my success, and vice versa.*

Zero-Sum Competition

Winning isn't everything; it's the only thing.

Vince Lombardi

Lombardi was the consummate victor, and in all reality, he had a right-minded head on his shoulders. "God, family, and the Green Bay

Packers" was among his many mantras, so it's misleading of me to infer that the man himself symbolized zero-sum competition. Nonetheless, the *winning* quote stands on its own and certainly reflects a shadow of what zero-sum competition is all about: *my winning at your expense.* As described in *The Omniscience Octagon,* zero-sum competition is akin to a growing number of party guests fighting over the remaining slices of pizza. It's easy to see why co-workers might engage in zero-sum competition: With finite budgets, leaders, team members, equipment, tools, meeting time, space, and overall real estate for any given ideas or commitments, we're sometimes reduced to snarling dogs with our paws entrenched, teeth bared, and neck muscles stretched taut as we tug and gnash at the last available clump of gristle.

Relevant Lessons

Start with an appreciation for the type of work one's organization does. The nature of work attracts and shapes the types of persons attracted, and this pool of talent responds uniquely to varying notions of competition. This said, I would have to exert myself quite extensively to imagine an organization that would not benefit from both upward and collaborative competition. Any time an entity strives to be better than its past performance, better than accepted standards indicative of excellence, and more unified in its objectives, the likelihood of success and improvement increases. Similarly, while zero-sum competition is an ever-present reality and breeds a *survival of the fittest* mentality, it correspondingly fosters a *we/they* mindset and predictably and tenuously pits co-workers against one another, twisting friends into foes.

Involve people in creating higher-order, exterior atmospheric layers of aspiration. To elaborate, when one microscopes into the earth's atmosphere, he sees the comings and goings and daily grind of our everyday reality. But once he rises high enough to penetrate the earth's atmosphere where gravity has lost some sway and one is no longer earthbound...*do you hear that? Silence. Stillness. Peace. Tranquility. We're out of the fray now.*

It's within this philosophical state that one can facilitate the creation of overarching, transcendent purposes and goals that can then bring constituents of all shapes and sizes closer together and more perfectly aligned. If under certain circumstances prisoners can develop an affinity for their captors as the result of proximity, interaction, and predictability,[139] surely the employees from different functions can work together to elate customers, increase margins, and reap the rewards.

Finally, and perhaps obviously, the strategist must ascertain the origin of whatever invisible rules of engagement or belief systems drive the current reality. As described prior, one cannot see gravity, but we readily see its effects. Similarly, competition itself is invisible, but the way it manifests is quite clear. Does your organization suffer from destructive competition that tears at people, or does it support constructive competition that tears at the walls *between* people? Get your lab coat and latex gloves on. It's time for you to get tactical and isolate the organism 'neath the microscope that's killing everything it touches. Once you know this, you can infect the organization with your own strain of antibodies and counterattack. Sometimes one solution will work, and other times call for a broad-spectrum approach over a long period of time. Either way, whether you're Polk or Pasteur, you'll have made a silent contribution that may very well reverberate through the ages within your organization.

Learning Lab: Idea(s) in Action

Thumb Wrestling

To experience the power of collaborative and upward competition — perform this exercise with your family, friends, or employees.

Set-up:

Two participants.

Instructions:

Most Americans know what *thumb wrestling* is. A YouTube search will reveal what it is. Pair-up participants with a partner, and instruct them to *get as many pins as you can in 60 seconds.*

---

[139] *The Stockholm Effect,* or *Stockholm Syndrome,* as coined by Nils Bejerot.

Summary:

Nine times out of ten, participants engage in zero-sum thumb wrestling. They wriggle and gyrate, lean in, and sweat it out. The typical scores will be in the teens or lower. But every now and then, participants realize that the most effective way *to get as many pins as possible* requires collaboration. You let me pin your thumb down, and I let you pin my thumb down. *Repeat as quickly as possible.* Or, just let me pin you repeatedly. Or vice versa. In any of these approaches, the scores are in the 60s, 70s, 80s, or 90s. *We achieve the most by collaborating and working together.* At work, employees, teams, departments, functions, locations, divisions, regions, or business units often compete in a zero-sum way...thereby ensuring sub-optimization and a squandering of resources, time, and people. Teach people to work together, and they'll accomplish much more.

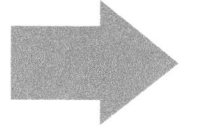

VI Tomorrow

Conclusion

From Simplicity to Complexity & Difficulty to Ease

Everything in strategy is very simple, but that does not mean everything is easy.

Carl von Clausewitz

Let's revisit our initial aspirations for *Cultivating the Strategic Mind*. We began with this:

The gamut I hoped to address started with *definition* and ran as far right as *new skills and a more formidable, integrated approach to strategic and systemic thinking*.

The three primary research questions we hoped to answer included:

1. What is strategy, and why aren't more leaders better strategists?

2. While strategy is as foundational as DNA within the most exemplary companies, why are so many organizations missing it altogether?

3. Across the myriad existing approaches to thinking and behaving strategically, what are the most prescient common denominators and best practices, and how can I apply these in pragmatic ways within my organization?

As a result of demonstrating a more *Strategic Mind,* we envisioned two specific payoffs:

1. For perhaps the first time in many organizations, individuals will utilize a common language regarding systemic strategies, the result of which is an aligned, integrated approach to thinking about one's world and succeeding within it.

2. Adopters will demonstrate an organizational capability that is quite difficult to replicate, resulting in competitive differentiation and advantage.

The degree to which we have been successful is much larger than *Do you feel more capable as a strategist?* It's much larger than *Do you know more about being a strategist and strategic leader than before?* It's even larger than *Having applied many of the tips and tricks in this book, are you succeeding as a systemic and strategic leader?* Were the first, second, or third question(s) answered in the affirmative, I would be ecstatic. But alas, these are inadequate. Real success, true satisfaction, and deep fulfillment will manifest more if the answer to the *following* question is answered in the affirmative:

Are families, employers, communities, or societies improving in the aggregate because of the ideas espoused here?

Let's be real. I want to sink into the pillow tonight knowing that people are benefiting in intrapersonal, interpersonal, and societal ways that are transforming their being. Gosh, this is audacious... presumptuous...and high-minded. So be it. Better to strive and fail than never roll out of bed. Again, those words of Robert Browning: "Man's reach should exceed his grasp, or what's a heaven for?"

Perhaps I should aim lower. *No, Pygmalion.* Perhaps I should aim broader. *No, shotgun.* Perhaps I shouldn't aim at all...*No, Regret & Worry.* Perhaps I'll make nary a difference other than having chopped down my unfair share of trees in the process of writing the 1,800th book this year on the glutted topic of leadership. *No, Edison and his thousand ways to not make a lightbulb.* You see, just as the frog and the scorpion are possessed by their nature, so, too, am I. I'm *the biggest fan* of all these guys and gals, from Frankl, Maslow, Follett, Fayol, Taylor, and Mayo to Roethlisberger, Barnard, Likert, Drucker, McGregor, Herzberg, McClelland, Wheatley, Gladwell, Grant, and the brothers Heath — all of whom have contributed to this reverberating discourse on leadership, management, and the efforts of enterprise. I buy their books 50 at a time and ship them all over the continent.

The *Biggest* Fan.

And in my humility and stupidity and reverence, like the excited puppy who cannot control his bladder when tickled, I cannot restrain myself from striving to, in the words of Steve Jobs, "make a dent in the universe." Only time will tell whether the least or the most of my goals has been achieved, but I look at it this way: Whether *Cultivating the Strategic Mind* helps you become a more confident strategist, or *The Strategic Triune* or the *Four Pillars* or the *Kaleidoscope* or *The Two Principles of 1°* or *telescoping* or *MindTaffy* or *zero-sum competition* or any of the tools in between help you to become the consummate strategist…I believe this:

The journey itself is worth the effort.

In the end, being a strategist is the highest level of leadership, and true leadership — timeless leadership — is about service. I do hope *Cultivating the Strategic Mind* serves you.

> *You don't have to have a college degree to serve. You don't have to make your subject and your verb agree to serve. You only need a heart full of grace, a soul generated by love.*[140]
>
> Martin Luther King Jr.

The aim is dying unto oneself in the ambition of serving others. Arriving, at the end of life, all used up. Along the way, should you accept the mantle of strategist, you'll have persevered to accomplish noble, honorable, egalitarian pursuits. Will you stub your toe and bump your head? Of course; it takes a while for the pupils to adjust, but in my book, doing nothing is worse than doing something, even if you fail to hit the bull's-eye nine out of ten shots. Because, along the way, maybe leadership will improve, maybe culture will improve, maybe trust will improve, and morale and energy and passion. And if only one of these improves, or one of the dozens of other side-effects of the ride, *wouldn't it have been worth the price of a meal and a half-day of your time?*

For the pragmatist in you, I offer one final swig from the canteen before we say our farewells. Being the last drop, it's no different than the first, varying only slightly due to an appreciation that it is the last. It comes not from my canteen, but from a canteen shared with me many years past by a dear colleague. Perhaps fittingly, I conclude with a matrix.

---

[140] In his *The Drum Major Instinct* sermon given in February 1968 at Atlanta's Ebenezer Baptist Church.

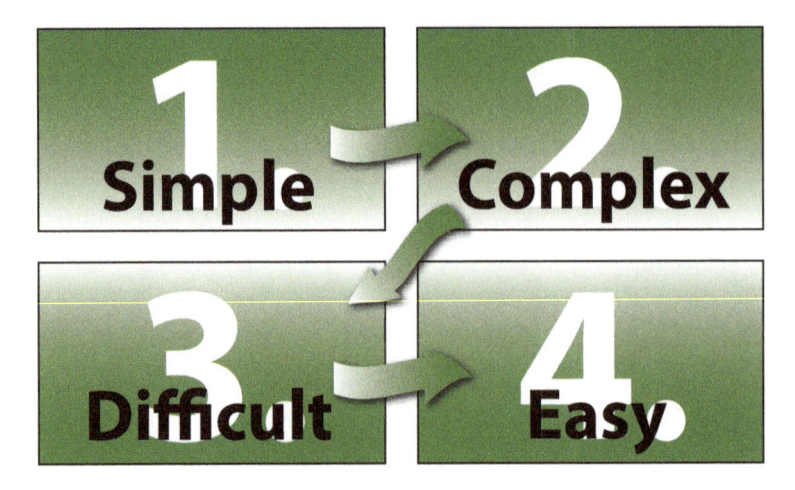

Figure 26: *From Simple to Easy*

1. **Simple** — As you may recall from Bruce Lee's observations about the punch, many ideas or skills appear quite simple upon first blush.

    I felt this way about most sports when I was four or five. I busied myself with a soccer ball on an open field, kicking it into the opponents' goal with the unknowing aura of self-satisfaction permeating my every pore.

2. **Complex** — Somewhere along the way, you might have become overwhelmed with the many nuances and permutations of the many philosophies and tools wielded by the strategist.

    I felt this way about most sports when I was six or seven and people began explaining them to me in great detail. An indirect free kick *is what again? The* yellow card *means what?*

3. **Difficult** — Here, the *mental* segues to the *physical*, and we see the first inklings of *attempt*, typically followed by frustration and failure.

    While I never learned to read music or play an instrument, I watched dozens of friends who did. The chasm each crossed between hearing it in one's head *and* emitting that tune from said instrument *was a broad, deep, formidable one.*

4. **Easy** — In time, repetition leads to muscle memory, muscle memory leads to habituation, and habituation moves beyond conscious competence to unconscious competence and in-the-zone, nearly-effortless high performance.[141]

> *Finally, we cross the threshold, and what became complex and difficult is now relatively simple and easy. For you, it may be mathematics or music or leading people. To your list, I hope you can also include Strategy and know that others would concur.*

Tonight and Tomorrow

For tonight, I ask only that you quiet your mind and get a good night's sleep. I know for many, that in itself is a feat. For tomorrow, I encourage you to do the following:

1. Somewhere in your day, schedule that appointment with yourself.
2. Flip back through the book and transfer some gentle reminders about any ideas, tools, or suggestions that you deem worthy of your time and instructive for your purposes.
3. Prioritize. I always encourage people to consider *Impact* and *Readiness*. Among the content, what elements would have the greatest impact in your life, your family, your organization, your community, or society at large that you can affect? Among those elements, which ones are you the most prepared for...most ready for? Identify the intersections between impact and readiness and work the list.
4. Huddle with someone who can hold you accountable for your commitments. Tony Robbins' podcasts are great in the car, but once you get to work, the environment crushes his talk. *Cultivating the Strategic Mind* is no different. Bring the ideas and tools to life by getting the book out of your bag, out of your bedroom, and

---

[141] See *Flow: The Psychology of Optimal Experience* by Mihály Csíkszentmihályi, published in 1990 by Harper Row.

into the fabric and board room of your organization. Make the *Strategic Mind* part of the language of your organization and any relevant social groups of which you are a member, and you'll begin shaping culture, just as we explored earlier.

5. Open your calendar and set a date — maybe three months hence — to recalibrate. Write the words *Strategic Mind Check-up*. When the reminder pops up 90 days out, catch yourself and pause. *What am I doing? What's different? The same? What has improved? What remains unpursued? What's next?* Reflect on these questions across all the groups in which you participate, but starting with yourself as an individual.

Write me about your failures and successes in equal measure; they each matter, and I'm certain we learn more from misfires than we do achievements. While you can reach me at coordinates easily found herein, the more important coordinate is where *you're* heading. You can reach most any goal you set your mind to, so set 'em high and demand that others around you do the same. Set 'em *really* high. There's a deficit of visionaries with the horsepower to lead others, and it's only through the collective dreams of many that a better tomorrow can become a reality for the rest of us.

Should you agree, strive to be a quixotic mixture of the following, and we'll revel in your example: Be humble, be great; be less, be more; be optimistic, be realistic; be kind, be courageous; be faithful, be rigorous; be a friend to someone, and always be yourself. And above all, never, ever be contained.

Our deepest fear is not that we are inadequate. Our deepest fear is that we are powerful beyond measure. It is our light, not our darkness, that most frightens us. We ask ourselves, who am I to be brilliant, gorgeous, talented, and fabulous? Actually, who are you not to be? You are a child of God. Your playing small doesn't serve the world. There's nothing enlightened about shrinking so that other people won't feel insecure around you. We are all meant to shine, as children do. We are born to make manifest the glory of God that is within us. It's not just in some of us, it's in everyone. And as we let our own light shine, we unconsciously give other people permission to do the same. As we are liberated from our own fear, our presence automatically liberates others.[142]

Marianne Williamson

---

[142] These words were also delivered in a speech by Nelson Mandela following 27 years of imprisonment for his anti-apartheid efforts in South Africa. Mandela received more than 100 humanitarian awards over four decades, the Nobel Peace Prize among them.

VII
Appendix

Strategist Matrix[143]

Who	Leader	Strategic Leader	Neither	Why
Jeffrey Skilling			✓	Notoriously poor with people + creative accounting techniques = hard time.
Sergey Brin, Larry Page		✓		Made Google a household name, a verb, and in the process — transformed information.
Dr. Dieter Zetsche	✓			Ultimately sold out, but kept Chrysler on life-support through surprisingly hip Dr. Z ad campaign.
John Scully	✓			Despite marketing savvy and vision, he never *personally* succeeded at positioning Apple as a powerhouse alternative to PCs.
Howard Schultz		✓		Ubiquity, popularity, long lines, great health care plans for employees, hip culture, music outlet…the hits at Starbucks just keep on comin'.
Fred Smith		✓		FedEx founder did for *mail* what the automobile did for the *pony express*.
Alexander Kummant			✓	Any Amtrak CEO will struggle in this quasi-government corporation. What will always amount to a slightly increasing share of a relatively stagnant market is generally bad news.
eBay, Amazon		✓		As revolutionary to retail sales as FedEx was to localized trade and barter economies; made the storefront virtual and local at the same time. With Jeff Bezos' acquisition of the Washington Post, his pursuits through Blue Origin, and Amazon's ingestion of Whole Foods, it's not difficult to see where this is going, and it's staggering.

---

[143] At the risk of a Tom Peters' *In Search of Excellence* debacle (in which many of his exemplars ultimately took nosedives), I present this list. I provide this caveat: There are seasons and cycles in most organizations, markets, and industries, and being today's exemplar is no protection against tomorrow.

Who	Leader	Strategic Leader	Neither	Why
Herb Kelleher (SWA), Dave Neeleman (JetBlue)		✓		The former succeeded at differentiation within a commoditized market (and profited in the process, for more years than any other company in the Fortune 500), and the latter extended this with a few additional bells and whistles.
Too many other airline CEOs			✓	Flown anywhere lately? Poor quality, late departures, bad customer service, disgruntled employees and customers...what a circus. With few exceptions, too many airline CEOs are often managers — and seldom leaders.
Ringling Bros. and Barnum & Bailey	✓			Contrasted against Cirque du Soleil or Cavalia, elephants and clowns couldn't cut it. Kaput.
Atari, Sears, JCPenney, Kmart			✓	Did you know Atari went out of business recently? Wow, I thought that was 20 years ago. Need I say more? Okay, I will: If the remaining brands can't leap into the future swiftly, they (along with shopping malls and countless big-box retailers) will go the way of Blockbuster. Here's hoping they can create a second act, perhaps like successful record stores. Fortunately, what's old is new again, so in the case of vinyl — and record stores — the sky's the limit.
The Land of Nod, Pottery Barn, L.L.Bean, Gap, J. Crew, Banana Republic, Nordstrom, Target		✓		Sure, they're not perfect — but they chug along (with the exception of Gap, which is declining), and their presence and influence cannot be denied. I shall be very curious to see what comes of Chip and Joanna Gaines, and their next foray into retail which, at the time of this writing, was a store within a store, the first of its kind at Target. I suspect, if successful, it could herald a retail resurgence that might be mimicked at stores in the same way farm-to-table was in restaurants and supply chains, becoming a social movement.

Who	Leader	Strategic Leader	Neither	Why
All but a teensy, weensy handful of politicians			✓	Small-mindedly confined by tradition and party lines, too few fresh faces "get it" and are able to multiply *followers* × *brilliant strategy* to achieve *revolution*. When I observe most politicians, I perceive tired mouthpieces in suits bobbing in a sea of compromise and mediocrity, or altogether thrashed by waves of dissension and division.
Dee Hock		✓		Inventor of Visa, he transformed our understanding of "currency" and, in the process, exemplified servant leadership and began Chaordism (chaos + order + control), a philosophy typified by the internet, which thrives on collective organization.
John Roberts		✓		During his hearings and confirmation, Chief Justice John Roberts delivered a tour de force performance and promises to be a strong leader and unparalleled strategist on many fronts.
Steve Jobs				Macintosh? Pixar? iPod? Mac OS X? iTunes? [Retail] Apple Stores? iPhone? [Virtual] App Store? iPad? Apple Watch? At the time of this writing, a whopping $842.19 billion Apple Inc. market cap? 'Nuff said, other than: Regarding your adoption, you liked to say, "I prefer to think I was *chosen*, not *abandoned*." Talk about wish-fulfillment and poetic justice: Your legacy lives on — in products, in processes, in people, in groundbreaking and breathtaking Apple Park — but primarily in culture...corporate, popular, and societal. In death, *you have been embraced universally*...in our collective consciousness, in business ethos writ large and, perhaps most rewardingly, in the *inventive design* firmament, your name frequently invoked when brainstorming recent examples [e.g., Jeff Bezos, Elon Musk] of luminaries like Leonardo or Edison. You seemingly *willed* yourself into being, into the cosmos, into the establishment, then proceeded to upend it as a disruptor, shattered the status quo like panes of glass, and imposed new paradigms on everyone in the ecosystem, from Microsoft to China to strangle-holding record companies and labels. Heck, if creating a world in which Dr. Dre and Jimmy Iovine must work for Apple Inc. to survive, thrive, and remain relevant and impactful isn't proof-positive that you succeeded, I don't know what would be. But I believe, in a phrase, that *entrepreneurial spirit and grit* will perhaps be your most enduring legacy. With that behind you, may you now — *finally and forevermore* — be at peace and rest in it.

Who	Leader	Strategic Leader	Neither	Why
Jack Welch, Jeff Immelt		✓		Who can argue? A passionate commitment to excellence, investment in employee development, and cutting edge strategies made this toaster maker *so much more*. Though Jeff's tenure was rocky (culminating in a seemingly abrupt departure), GE's innovations and influence during his reign are indisputable.
Benjamin Franklin, Thomas Jefferson, and other founding fathers		✓		Each had his quirk, but give 'em a break. So many contributions...from bifocals and stoves to fire departments and libraries to...a Nation.
3M, Microsoft, Sony, Dell, IBM, P&G, Virgin, Samsung, Walmart, Toyota, Intel, IDEO, BMW		✓		Innovation, power, form-factor, internet marketing models, brand breadth, diversification, inventory management, quality...for so many countless reasons, these organizations often come out on top.
RadioShack			✓	CEO churn, failure to innovate, a choice to "not pursue" bio-products, general shortsightedness, and a name no sexier or more contemporary than Kmart. So what if 94 percent of Americans live within three miles of a store? If they don't keep going, it won't matter.
Mother Theresa, Nelson Mandela, Rosa Parks, Margaret Thatcher, Bono, et al.		✓		In their own ways, at their own time, each of these persons catalyzed a particular constituency and elevated discourse in lasting, often significant ways.

Appendix

Interested to learn how you stack-up?

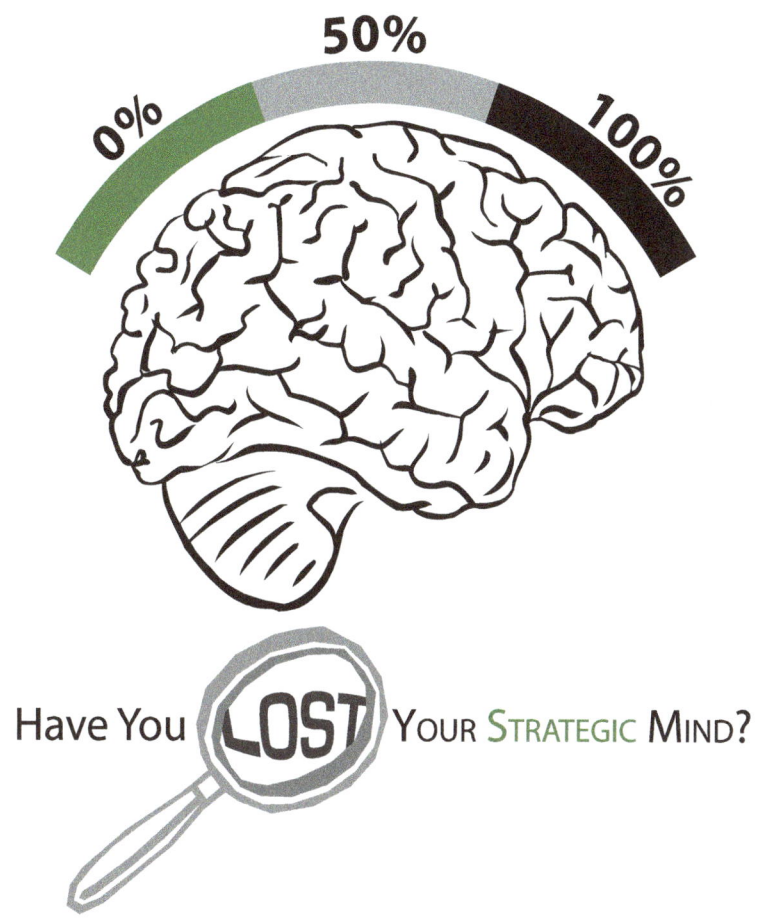

Have You **LOST** Your Strategic Mind?

visit **https://assessment.thestrategicmind.com/**
to find it and gain the tools to cultivate it.

Figure 27: *The Strategist Self-Assessment*

Sources and Resources

Books
(Alphabetized by Author)

Altshuller, Genrich. Translated by Lev Shulyak. 1996. *And Suddenly the Inventor Appeared: Triz, The Theory of Inventive Problem Solving.* Worcester, MA: Technical Innovation Center, Inc.

Argenti, Paul, and C.M. Barnes. 2009. *Digital Strategies for Powerful Corporate Communications.* New York: McGraw-Hill.

Argenti, Paul. 2009. *Strategic Corporate Communication.* New York: McGraw-Hill.

Argyris, C., and Schon, D. 1978. *Organizational Learning: A Theory of Action Perspective.* Reading, MA: Addison-Wesley Publishing.

Besanko, David, David Dranove, Mark Shanley, Scott Schaefer. 2000. *Economics of Strategy.* Hoboken, NJ: John Wiley & Sons, Inc.

Bossidy, Larry, and Ram Charan, with Charles Burck. 2002. *Execution: The Discipline of Getting Things Done.* New York: Crown Publishing.

Bossidy, Larry, and Ram Charan. 2004. *Confronting Reality: Doing What Matters to Get Things Right.* New York: Crown Publishing.

Campbell, Andrew, J. Whitehead, and S. Finkelstein. 2009. *Think Again: Why Good Leaders Make Bad Decisions and How to Keep It From Happening to You.* Boston: Harvard Business School Press.

Christensen, Clayton. 2000. *The Innovator's Dilemma.* New York: HarperCollins Press.

Christensen, Clayton. 2003. *The Innovator's Solution: Creating and Sustaining Successful Growth.* Boston: Harvard Business School Press.

Colley, John L. Jr., D.B.A., Jacqueline L. Doyle, Ph.D., and Robert D. Hardie, Ph.D. 2002. *Corporate Strategy.* New York: McGraw-Hill Professional.

Collins, James C. and Jerry I. Porras. 1994. *Built to Last.* New York: HarperCollins Press.

Collins, Jim. 2006. *Good to Great.* New York: Random House Business Books.

Collis, David J. and Cynthia. A. Montgomery. 1997. *Corporate Strategy: A Research-Based Approach.* New York: McGraw-Hill Professional.

De Kluyver, Cornelius. 2000. *Strategic Thinking: An Executive Perspective.* Upper Saddle River, NJ: Prentice-Hall.

Dixit, Avinash, and Susan Skeath. 2004. *Games of Strategy.* New York: Norton & Company.

Douglas, John, and Mark Olshaker. 1995. *Mindhunter: Inside the FBI's Elite Serial Crime Unit.* New York: Simon & Schuster.

Douglas, John, and Mark Olshaker. 2000. *Anatomy of Motive.* New York: Simon & Schuster.

Finkelstein, Sydney, C. Helfat, W. Mitchell, M. Peteraf, H. Singh, D. Teece, and S. Winter. 2007. *Dynamic Capabilities: Understanding Strategic Change in Organizations.* Hoboken, NJ: Wiley-Blackwell Publishing.

Finkelstein, Sydney, D.C. Hambrick, and A. Cannella. 2008. *Strategic Leadership: Theory and Research on Executives, Top Management Teams, and Boards*. Oxford: Oxford University Press.

Finkelstein, Sydney. 2003. *Why Smart Executives Fail: And What You Can Learn From Their Mistakes*. Charlotte, NC: Portfolio.

Gardner, Howard. 1982. *Art, Mind & Brain: A Cognitive Approach to Creativity*. New York: Basic Books.

Gardner, Howard. 1997. *Frames of Mind: The Theory of Multiple Intelligences*. New York: Basic Books.

Geisel, Theodor Seuss. 1961. *The Sneetches*. New York: Random House.

Ghemawat, Pankaj, Ed. 2000. *Strategy and the Business Landscape*. David J. Collis, Pankaj Ghemawat, Gary P. Pisano, Jan W. Rivkin. Upper Saddle River, NJ: Prentice-Hall.

Gibson, Rowan, Ed. 1997. *Rethinking the Future*. G. Hamel. *Leadership, Markets and the World*. London: Nicholas Brealey Publishing.

Gibson, Rowan, Ed. 1997. *Rethinking the Future*. Peter Senge. *Through the Eye of the Needle*. London: Nicholas Brealey Publishing.

Gomes-Casseres, Benjamin. 2003. James Bamford and Michael Robinson. *Mastering Alliance Strategy: A Comprehensive Guide to Design, Management and Organization*. San Francisco: Wiley/Jossey-Bass.

Grant, Robert M. 2002. *Contemporary Strategy Analysis: Concepts, Techniques, Applications*. Maiden, MA: Blackwell Publishing.

Gray, Colin S. 1996. *Explorations in Strategy*. Westport, CT: Praeger/Greenwood.

Gray, Colin S. 1996. *Modern Strategy. Only the Paranoid Survive*. Groves, Andrew. New York: Currency, Doubleday.

Haines, Stephen G. 2000. *The Complete Guide to Systems Thinking & Learning*. Amherst, MA: HRD Press.

Hamel, Gary, and C.K. Prahalad. 1994. *Competing for the Future*. Boston: Harvard Business School Press.

Hamel, Gary. 2002. *Leading the Revolution*. New York: Plume.

Handel, Michael I. 2001. *Masters of War: Classical Strategic Thought*. London: Routledge.

Jomini, Baron Antoine Henri. 1992. *Art of War*. London: Greenhill Books.

Kaplan, Robert and David Norton. 1996. *The Balanced Scorecard: Translating Strategy into Action*. Boston: Harvard Business Press.

Kaplan, Robert S. and David P. Norton. 2004. *Strategy Maps: Converting Intangible Assets into Tangible Outcomes*. Boston: HBS Publishing.

Kaplan, S. 1996. *An Introduction to TRIZ: The Russian Theory of Inventive Problem Solving*. Southfield, MI: Ideation International, Inc.

Kim, W. Chan and Renee A. Mauborgne. 2005. *Blue Ocean Strategy: How to Create Uncontested Market Space and Make Competition Irrelevant*. Boston: Harvard Business School Press.

Liker, Jeffrey K. 2004. *The Toyota Way: 14 Management Principles from the World's Greatest Manufacturer.* New York: McGraw-Hill Professional.

Mintzberg, Henry. 1994. *The Rise and Fall of Strategic Planning.* Upper Saddle River, NJ: Prentice-Hall.

Morey, David, and Scott Miller. 2004. *The Underdog Advantage: Using the Power of Insurgent Strategy to Put Your Business on Top.* New York: McGraw-Hill Professional.

Murray, Williamson, MacGregor Knox, and Alvin Bernstein. 1996. *The Making of Strategy: Rulers, States and War.* Cambridge, MA: Cambridge University Press.

Neustadt, Richard E., and Ernest R. May. 1986. *Thinking in Time: The Uses of History for Decision-Makers.* New York: Collier Macmillan.

Ohmae, Kenichi. 1982. *The Mind of the Strategist: The Art of Japanese Business.* New York: McGraw-Hill Professional.

Paret, Peter. 1986. *Makers of Modern Strategy: From Machiavelli to the Nuclear Age.* Gordon A. Craig and Felix Gilbert. Oxford: Oxford University Press.

Peters, Tom, and R. H. Waterman. 1982. *In Search of Excellence.* New York: Harper & Row.

Porter, Michael. 1980. *Competitive Strategy: Techniques for Analyzing Industries and Competitors.* New York: Simon & Schuster.

Prahalad, C.K., Coimbatore Krishna, and Ramaswamy Venkatram. 2004. *The Future of Competition: Co-Creating Unique Value with Customers.* Boston: Harvard Business School Press.

Quinn, James Brian. 1992. *Intelligent Enterprise.* New York: Free Press.

Ramsey, Phil, and Robin Mazo. 1997. *Billibonk & The Big Itch.* Wendell, MA: Pegasus Communications.

Sanders, T. Irene. 1998. *Strategic Thinking and the New Science.* New York: Simon & Schuster.

Senge, Peter. 1994. *The Fifth Discipline Fieldbook.* New York: Bantam Dell Publishing Group, Random House.

Senge, Peter. 1990. *The Fifth Discipline: The Art and Practice of the Learning Organization.* New York: Currency, Doubleday.

Spar, Debora L. 2001. *Ruling the Waves: Cycles of Discovery, Chaos, and Wealth from the Compass to the Internet.* New York: Harcourt Trade Publishers.

Stacy, R. 1992. *Managing the Unknowable.* San Francisco: Jossey-Bass.

Stowell, Stephen, and S. Mead. 2016. *The Art of Strategic Leadership: How Leaders at All Levels Prepare Themselves, Their Teams, and Organizations for the Future.* Hoboken, NJ: John Wiley & Sons, Inc.

Sweeney, Linda B. 2001. *When a Butterfly Sneezes.* Wendell, MA: Pegasus Communications.

von Clausewitz, Carl, and Frederic Natusch Maude. 1908. *On War.* Ed. James John Graham. London: Kegan Paul, Trench, Trubner & Co.

Wilson Learning. 2004. *The Social Styles Handbook: Find Your Comfort Zone and Make People Feel Comfortable with You.* Australia: Wilson Learning Library.

Articles, Blogs, Journals, and Websites
(Alphabetized by Author)

Adner, Ron, and D. Snow. 2010. "Old Technology Responses to New Technology Threats: Demand Heterogeneity and Technology Retreats." *Industrial and Corporate Change.* 19(5):1655-1675.

Adner, Ron, and R. Kapoor. 2010. "Value Creation in Innovation Ecosystems: How the Structure of Technological Interdependence Affects Firm Performance in New Technology Generations." *Strategic Management Journal.* 31(3):306-333.

Adner, Ron, and R. Kapoor. 2016. "Innovation Ecosystems and the Pace of Substitution: Reexamining Technology S-curves." *Strategic Management Journal.* 37(4):625-648.

Adner, Ron, J. Oxley, and B. Silverman. 2013. "Collaboration and Competition in Business Ecosystems." *Advances in Strategic Management.* 31:9-18.

Adner, Ron. 2016. "Navigating the Leadership Challenges of Innovation Ecosystems." *Sloan Management Review.* 58(1):141-146.

Adner, Ron. 2017. "Ecosystem as Structure: An Actionable Construct for Strategy." *Journal of Management.* 43(1):39-58.

Argenti, Paul, R. Howell, and K. Beck. 2005. "The Strategic Communication Imperative." *MIT Sloan Management Review.* 46(3).

Argenti, Paul. 2017. "Strategic Communication in the C-Suite." *International Journal of Business Communication.* 54(2).

Audia, Pino, and J. Kurkoski. 2012. "An Ecological Analysis of Competition Among U.S. Communities." *Industrial and Corporate Change.* 21:187-215.

Begley, Sharon. 2007. A User's Guide to the Brain, How the Brain Rewires Itself. *TIME.* January 29.

Day, G. 1994. The Capabilities of Market-Driven Organizations. *Journal of Marketing.* October, pp. 37-52.

Elliott, Jane. 1970. *Eye of the Storm.* Documentary film.

Fahey, L., and L. Prusak. 1998. The Eleven Deadliest Sins of Knowledge Management. *California Management Review.* 40, (3).

Faucheux, Ron. 1997. Strategies That Win: Political Campaigning. *Campaigns & Elections.* December.

Finkelstein, Sydney, and J. Kim. 2009. "The Effects of Strategic and Locational Complementarity on Acquisition Performance: Evidence from the U.S. Commercial Banking Industry, 1989-2001." *Strategic Management Journal.* 30.

Godin, Seth. 2005. Small Business. *Fortune.* May.

Hamel, G. 1996. Strategy as Revolution. *Harvard Business Review.* July-August, pp. 69-82.

Hamel, G., and C.K. Prahalad. 1989. Strategy Intent. *Harvard Business Review.* May-June, pp. 63-76.

Headden, Susan, Andrew Curry, Peter Cary, David LaGesse, Lisa Moore, Will Sullivan, Eduardo Cue, Paul J. Lim, Beth Brophy, Angie C. Marek, Kim Palmer,

Diana Cole, Adam Voiland, Thomas K. Grose, Elizabeth Weiss Green, Dean Clark, Linda Creighton, Alison Go, Todd Georgelas, Bret Schulte, and David E. Kaplan. 2007. 30 Valuable Lessons that America Can Learn from the Rest of the World. *U.S. News & World Report*, March 26.

Heracleous, L. 1998. Strategic Thinking or Strategic Planning. *Long Range Planning*, 31, (3), pp. 481-487.

Leath, Blake. 2007. *The Triune for Attraction & Retention: Creating a Culture of Good Leaders, a Great Workplace, and Sustaining Employer of Choice Designation*. Southlake, TX: Allagi Learning.

Liedtka, J. 1998. Linking Strategic Thinking with Strategic Planning. *Strategy and Leadership*, October, (1), pp. 120-129.

Liedtka, J. 1998. Strategic Thinking: Can it be Taught? *Long Range Planning*, 31, (1), pp. 120-129.

Mintzberg, Henry. 1999. Bees, Flies, and CEOs; Do We Have Too Many Bees Making Strategy and Not Enough Flies? *Across The Board,* January.

Moore, James. 1993. Predators and Prey: A New Ecology of Competition. *Harvard Business Review,* May/June, p. 76.

Raimond, P. 1996. Two Styles of Foresight. *Long Range Planning,* April, pp. 208-214.

Senge, P. 1992. Mental Models, *Planning Review, Vol. 44.* March-April, pp. 4-10.

Wallis, Claudia, Sonja Steptoe. 2006. How to Bring Our Schools out of the 20th Century. *TIME,* December 18.

Wilson, Ian. 1994. Strategic Planning Isn't Dead — It Changed. *Long Range Planning,* 27 (4).

www.creativewhack.com Creative Whack Company, Stamford, CT.

www.discoveret.org/etil/photos_smith.htm Vickie Smith.

www.goabroad.com Jacksonville, FL.

www.icgg.org/corruption.cpi_2006.html Transparency International.

www.tui.edu Union Institute & University.

www.whitehouse.gov/nsc/nss.pdf National Security Strategy of the United States of America.

Moving Pictures: Films, Shows, and Streams

A Beautiful Mind
A Few Good Men
Awakenings
Braveheart
Breaking Bad
CSI
Dangerous Minds
Dead Poets Society
Game of Thrones
House
Jerry Maguire
Lean on Me
Limitless
Lorenzo's Oil
Manhunter
Mind Games
Mindhunter
Mindwalk
Minority Report
Mr. Holland's Opus
Numbers
Solomon
Stand & Deliver
Stranger Things
The Alienist
The Emperor's Club
The Game
The Godfather
The Natural
The Paper Chase
The Princess Bride
The Secret Life of the Brain
The Spanish Prisoner
The Wizard of Oz
To Sir, with Love
Tora! Tora! Tora!
Walk the Line
We Were Soldiers
Without a Trace

About the Author

About the Author

Dr. Blake Leath is the founder of **Leath Group, LLC** — a dynamic curriculum development and intellectual property greenhouse that grows leaders and shapes cultures. He is the author of more than 90 copyrighted organizational science solutions implemented for clients around the world.

Blake has worked with clients as diverse as Adidas, AT&T, Bausch + Lomb, BHP Billiton, BNSF Railway, Capital One, Citigroup, Daimler, Ericsson, GE, Kodak, Libbey, Lockheed Martin, Los Alamos National Laboratory, Momentous Institute, Northwestern Mutual, Pfizer, Sony, and the U.S. Departments of Agriculture, Defense, and Interior. Blake and Leath Group colleagues provide consulting & communication services and tools that transform leaders, cultures, and processes to achieve dramatic breakthroughs in strategy and performance. Since 1992, he has worked with practitioners in over 300 companies and numerous federal, state, and local agencies/departments/bureaus, as well as with individual researchers from leading universities to understand and maximize employee involvement, success, longevity, and passion.

In 25 years as an organizational sociologist and strategist, Blake has instructed in excess of 14,000 participants across 41 states, and his content has been used by leaders in 27 countries. Leath Group has worked with more than 200,000 individuals, and well over 2,000,000 imprints have been made of the Group's combined intellectual property. Blake's primary interests include strategy, culture, leadership, change, communication, effects of a multi-generation workforce, systems thinking, M&A integration, trust & influence, and the process of acculturation.

In 2007, Blake published the first edition of *Cultivating the Strategic Mind*. The modest and very personal text consistently received high praise from professional strategists embracing its approach to reinforce more systemic strategic thinking. This commemorative 10th anniversary second edition is a response to the first's reception, and the result of desiring to add a few new thoughts.

Today, Blake and his colleagues continue to research, write, design, deliver, facilitate, train, present, and film extensively, and most often in conjunction with long-term internal/external communication efforts designed to define and shape client cultures.

Gleanings from the Group's contributions to knowledge and best practices (plus hobbyhorses *Blake's Blog, Language Hound,* and *Movie Reviews*) can be found at www.leathgroup.com. Lifelong learners are encouraged to visit the site to experience Leath Group's work, download freebies, and to participate in and contribute to an organic community of dialogue. Follow @blakeleath on Twitter (or Instagram) to engage in lighthearted musings, riffs, personal photos, and puff-piece observations.

Blake earned his bachelor's degree in *Management & Marketing,* his master's degree in *Organizational Management,* and his doctorate of philosophy in *Organizational Sociology*. Postdoctoral studies exploring the integration of strategy, leadership, and corporate communication in postmodern management have proven quite inspiring in recent years, and are sure to be published in a new, forthcoming book. Blake remains an Adjunct Faculty member at the Tandy Center for Executive Leadership in TCU's Neeley School of Business.

Blake, his beloved wife, Dawn, and their precious daughter, Lauren (along with their microscopic Cavalier King Charles Spaniel, Daisy) make their home wherever they find themselves. For play, the Leaths enjoy traveling, exploring, reading, moviegoing, attending concerts, plays, and musicals — and embarking on fun design projects of virtually any nature that get their creative juices flowing.

Index

Angelou, Maya 19, 95

Archer's Aim 184

Archimedes 177

Aristotle 24, 123, 134, 135, 138, 198

Astronomy, as part of the Kaleidoscope 9, 134, 135, 136, 137, 139, 141

Bailey, Mark 24

Baryshnikov, Mikhail 2, 226

Biology, as part of the Kaleidoscope 9, 118, 120, 124, 135

Blatand, Harald 205

Bluetooth 9, 205, 206

Brahe, Tyge Ottesen "Tycho" 134, 137, 138, 140

Buffet, Warren 188

Burnout 66, 192, 194, 195, 196, 197

Carnegie, Andrew 219

Churchill, Winston 134, 167

Collins, Jim 9, 31, 32, 51, 57, 58, 74

Competence, Conscious 117, 162, 163, 195, 237

Competence, Unconscious 162, 163, 237

Competition, Collaborative 227, 228

Competition, Upward 226, 227, 229

Competition, Zero-sum 224, 227, 228, 235

Complexity 47, 49, 121, 124, 125, 233

Conceptual, as part of the Four Types of Thinking 216, 217

Confucius 141, 155

Copernicus, Nicolaus 134, 136, 138, 139, 140

Covey, Stephen 9, 57, 174

Creative, as part of the Four Types of Thinking 217

Critical, as part of the Four Types of Thinking 208, 216, 217

Culture, as part of the Four Pillars 69, 85, 86, 101, 102, 112, 200

cummings, e.e. 209

Curtain of Oz 213, 214, 215

DePree, Max 100

Diogenes 100

Drucker, Peter 9, 68, 234

Edison, Thomas 141, 234

Einstein, Albert 52, 55, 123, 141

Emerson, Ralph Waldo 100

Epictetus 101

Fosdick, Harry Emerson 174

Four Pillars (of Strategic Organizations) 8, 18, 85, 90, 111, 112, 113, 235

Franklin, Benjamin 7, 85, 119, 246

Frost, Robert 186

Galilei, Galileo 123, 134, 136, 138, 139, 209

Gibson-Meier, Elizabeth 101

Hapkido 9, 74, 109, 171, 172, 173, 206

Holmes, Oliver Wendell 115

Hydrick, James 60

Inclusive Ownership 48, 63, 79, 82, 112, 113, 201

Incomes vs. Outcomes 174, 176

Incompetence, Conscious 162, 163

Incompetence, Unconscious 162, 163, 164, 219

Intuitive, as part of the Four Types of Thinking 217, 218

Jolson, Al 112

Kaleidoscope 115, 143, 144, 147, 200, 235

Kasparov, Garry 62, 97

Kennedy, John Fitzgerald 24, 50, 145

Kepler, Johannes 134, 137, 138, 139, 140

Keynes, John Maynard 145

King Jr., Martin Luther 217, 235

Lao Tzu 141

Leadership, as part of the Four Pillars 85, 90, 91, 105, 107, 112, 147

Learning and Unlearning 82, 207, 210

Lee, Bruce 46, 236

Levitt, Theodore 145

Lombardi, Vince 227

Luddism, Luddite 9, 211, 212

Mann, Thomas 146

Maslow, Abraham 54, 83, 115, 117, 162, 180, 191, 234

Mathematics, as part of the Kaleidoscope 9, 62, 124, 132, 216, 237

Matrix, Competence 162

Matrix, From Simple to Easy 235, 236

Matrix, Interpersonal Inclination Typology 160

Matrix, Strategist 243, 244, 245, 246

Matsushita, Konosuke 146

McClelland, David 95, 234

McKay, David O. 177

Mead, Margaret 186

Microscoping 178, 182, 208

Mind Map 18, 34, 65, 112, 113

MindTaffy 9, 220, 221, 235

Mind-Talk 44, 80, 88

Mission, as part of Vision, Mission, Values 152, 153, 199, 200, 201, 204

Mohasseb, Saeed 227

Muoio, Anna 100

Newton, Sir Isaac 123, 124, 134, 138, 139, 140, 141, 164

Norris, Chuck 164

Omniscience Octagon 18, 34, 66, 67, 78, 79, 104, 112, 113, 197, 198, 228

One I Feed 147

Organizational Darwinism 8, 170

Outcomes vs. Incomes 174, 176

Oz, Curtain of 213, 214, 215

Palmer, Arnold 164

Pausanias 219

Peters, Tom 9, 30, 57, 74, 243

Petronius, Gaius 169

Phelps, Michael 164

Philosopher King 154, 155, 189

Physics, as part of the Kaleidoscope 9, 62, 121, 123, 124, 135

Picasso, Pablo 111

Pillars, Four (of Strategic Organizations) 8, 18, 85, 89, 90, 101, 102, 105, 107, 111, 112, 113, 235

Politics 9, 16, 18, 30, 31, 36, 64, 135, 168, 170

Potential Envelope 90, 95, 96, 97

Potts, Paul 2

Principles of 1° 148, 149, 152, 235

Processes and Performance, as part of the Four Pillars 18, 85, 86, 105, 107, 112

Proust, Marcel 55

Psychology, as part of the Kaleidoscope 9, 80, 130

Ptolemy 134, 135, 136, 138

Pygmalion Effect 90, 93, 94, 234

Reconnaissance 61, 182

Reflected Glory Principle 112, 177, 181

Religion, as part of the Kaleidoscope 9, 53, 142

Renaissance 9, 21, 182

Rengel, Jimmy 169

Reynolds, Richard 209

Rogers, Will 28, 170

Ryan, Alan 100

Sales and Service, as part of the Four Pillars 85, 87, 107, 112

Self-management and Burnout 66, 89, 92, 192, 194, 195, 196, 197

Seven Questions Every Life Must Answer 90, 97, 99

Shakespeare, William 61, 141

Simplicity 50, 233

Snead, Sam 226, 227

Sociology, as part of the Kaleidoscope 9, 128

Socrates 1, 3, 28, 135, 176

Solitude, Importance of 156

Solomon, Solomonic Solutions 155, 158, 159, 166

Stalin, Josef 146

Strategic Management 35

Strategic Planning 29, 35, 52, 53, 57, 73, 152

Strategic Thinking 9, 34, 35, 36, 38, 52, 53, 62, 73, 97, 130, 222

Strategic Triune 18, 34, 57, 59, 61, 65, 101, 111, 112, 113, 235

Strategist Matrix 243, 244, 245, 246

Strategy, definition 28, 29, 30, 48, 57, 111, 120, 132, 233

Sun Tzu 30, 155, 224

Systemic Thinking 8, 35, 128, 206, 233

Table 1: Sample Findings, Literature Review of Dominant Strategy Theories 30-33

Table 2: Analysis of Armstrong's Seven (1°) Tour de France Victories 151

Table 3: Four Types of Thinking 217

Telescoping 178, 182, 208, 235

Thinking, Four Types of 216, 217, 218

Thoreau, Henry David 100, 158

Twain, Mark 6, 74, 100, 161, 186

Two Principles of 1° 148, 149, 152, 235

Unlearning and Learning 82, 207, 210

Values, as part of Vision, Mission, Values 67, 70, 71, 152, 153, 199, 200, 203, 204

Vincent, John H. 146

Vision 22, 33, 34, 35, 50, 51, 58, 69, 70, 79, 82, 85, 89, 111, 131, 152, 153, 166, 186, 198, 199, 200, 201, 202, 204, 206

Visualization 164, 166, 167

VMV 198, 199

von Clausewitz, Carl 30, 233

Whitehead, Alfred North 101

Williamson, Marianne 239

Winning, Three Types of 224, 225, 226, 227, 228

Woods, Tiger 150

Ziglar, Zig 177

Zuboff, Shoshana 101

For such a common word, **strategy** is often misunderstood, misinterpreted, and misapplied. Given the complex challenges facing organizations — and entire societies — we must grow more and better strategists.

Tackling three simple yet sweeping questions, *Cultivating the Strategic Mind* delivers the goods:

1. What is strategy, and why aren't more leaders better strategists?
2. While strategy is as foundational as DNA within the most exemplary companies, why are so many organizations missing it altogether?
3. How can I apply strategy in palpable, pragmatic ways to the benefit of those around me?

As a result of demonstrating a more *Strategic Mind*, leaders will employ a robust language and methodology for crafting, communicating, and implementing strategic aspirations and commitments.

Contemporary business is screaming for equally *creative* and *critical thinkers* capable of leading teams and entire organizations. Blake Leath's breezy writing style, intuitive models, research-based solutions, and sticky storytelling make *Cultivating the Strategic Mind* a stimulating, fun, and immensely credible approach toward developing strategists for our evolving world of work.

If you believe in the fundamental importance of *thinking* as a differentiating competency for exemplary leaders, it's time you treat yourself to the book you'll want to share with your colleagues — the one written with you in mind and designed to guide leaders on the journey to visionary, creator, and architect of strategy.

leathgroup.com